Español Santillana

Become an online "fan" and part of the adventure through Español Santillana's

fansdelespañol.com

We've created a website just for you! Log on and travel with us. Find out more about the fascinating places that Andy, Tess, Tim, and Diana visit.

Who will win the cultural challenges they take on in Spain, the United States, Argentina, and Chile? You decide!

¡Nosotros somos unos fans del español! ¿Y tú?

- View photos, watch cool videos, and read about the adventures that Andy, Tess, Tim, and Diana share through their website.

- Place your vote for the team you think best meets the various cultural challenges.

- Take on your own challenge and demonstrate your knowledge of Spanish through fun online projects.

fans del Español

Log on to **fansdelespañol**.com and have fun practicing Spanish!

The letter ñ, a very special letter

Spanish has a letter that does not appear in other languages: ñ. The letter ñ is used in words like *español* (Spanish), *España* (Spain), *niño* (boy), *pequeño* (small), *año* (year), *mañana* (morning, tomorrow), *otoño* (autumn), and many others. The letter ñ is also used in our webpage: www.***fansdelespañol***.com

How can you write the letter ñ on your computer?
That depends on the system you have:

MAC COMPUTERS

Press **Alt** [option] + **N** and then N or n.

COMPUTERS WITH MICROSOFT WINDOWS

Press **Alt** + **1 End** **6 →** **4 ←**, with **Num Lock** activated.

COMPUTERS WITH LINUX/BSD

Press **Shift** + **Ctrl** + **U** and then the code **F1** followed by the **Enter ⏎** key.

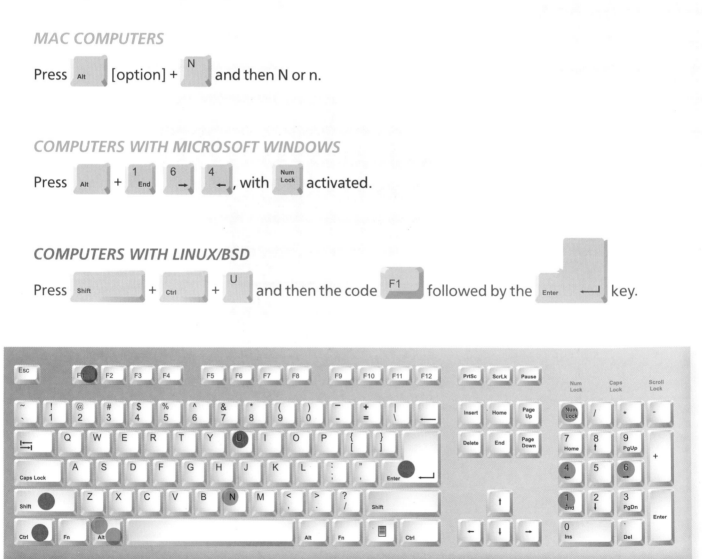

Middle School 1B

Español
Santillana

fans
del
Español

SANTILLANA USA

Español Santillana is a collaborative effort by two teams specializing in the design of Spanish-language educational materials. One team is located in the United States and the other in Spain.

© 2010 by Santillana USA Publishing Company, Inc.

Published in the United States of America.

Español Santillana
Student Book Level 1B
ISBN-13: 978-1-61605-084-9
ISBN-10: 1-61605-084-5

Illustrators: **Bartolomé Seguí, Jorge Arranz**
Picture Coordinator: **Carlos Aguilera**

Cartographer: **Tania López**
Cartographic Coordinator: **Ana Isabel Calvo**

Production Manager: **Ángel García Encinar**

Production Coordinator: **Jesús A. Muela**

Design and Layout: **Marisa Valbuena, Javier Pulido, Alfonso García, Fernando Calonge**

Proofreaders: **Gerardo Z. García, Jennifer Farrington, Marta López, Lawrence Lipson**

Photo Researchers: **Mercedes Barcenilla, Amparo Rodríguez**

Santillana USA Publishing Company, Inc.
2023 NW 84th Avenue, Doral, FL 33122

Printed in China

7 8 9 10   APO   15 14 13

Editorial Staff in United States
Anne Smieszny
Ana Isabel Antón
Andrea Roberson

Editorial Staff in Spain
Susana Gómez
Cristina Núñez
Belén Saiz

Linguistic and Cultural Advisers in Latin America and in the United States

Antonio Moreno
Editorial Director, Santillana México

Mayra Méndez
Editorial Director, Santillana Puerto Rico

Luis Guillermo Bernal
Editorial Director, Santillana Guatemala

Cecilia Mejía
Editorial Director, Santillana Perú

Graciela Pérez de Lois
Editorial Director, Santillana Argentina

Manuel José Rojas
Editorial Director, Santillana Chile

Mario Núñez
Director of Professional Development, Santillana USA

Reviewers

Dr. Tamara Alsace
Buffalo, NY

Dr. Josefa Báez-Ramos
Seattle, WA

Mercedes Bernal
West New York, NJ

Miguel Castro
New Orleans, LA

Yvonne Davault
Mansfield, TX

Dr. Frances S. Hoch
Raleigh, NC

Petra Liz-Morell
Ridgefield Park, NJ

James Orihuela
Whittier, CA

Ana Sainz de la Peña
Allentown, PA

Eugenia Sarmiento
Centennial, CO

Thomasina White
Philadelphia, PA

Writers

Dr. Miguel Santana
received his PhD in Hispanic literature at the University of Texas–Austin. Dr. Santana has taught Spanish at the elementary, high school, and college levels, and has worked as a Spanish editor and writer for numerous educational publishers in the United States. Miguel Santana is also an author of several novels.

Dr. Lori Langer de Ramírez
received her doctorate in curriculum and teaching from Teacher's College, Columbia University. She is chairperson of the ESL and World Language Department for Herricks Public Schools, New York. Dr. Langer de Ramírez is the recipient of many prestigious awards.

Eduardo Fernández Galán
received his *Licenciatura en Lingüística Hispánica* from the Universidad Complutense de Madrid. He has taught Spanish at Montgomery High School in Montgomery, New Jersey, and The College of New Jersey in Ewing.

Dr. Michele Guerrini
received her PhD in Romance languages from the University of Pennsylvania. She has worked as director of bilingual and EFL departments at Richmond Publishing in Spain and as an adjunct assistant professor of Spanish at The George Washington University in Washington, DC.

Cristina Núñez Pereira
received her *Licenciatura en Filología Hispánica* from the Universidad Nacional de Educación a Distancia and is a *Licenciada en Periodismo* from the Universidad Carlos III de Madrid.

Belén Saiz Noeda
received her *Licenciatura en Filología Hispánica* from Universidad de Alicante. She was a professor of Spanish language and culture and was in charge of Spanish teacher education at the Universidad de Alcalá and at other institutions.

María Inés García
received her masters in Spanish from Texas A & I University. She is a former director of the Languages Other Than English program for the Texas Education Agency, and was the Spanish specialist with the agency for 26 years.

María J. Fierro-Treviño
received her MA from the University of Texas–San Antonio. She was the director of Languages Other Than English program for the Texas Education Agency. She has taught Spanish at the secondary and college levels, and has worked as an instructional specialist, and as a presenter of professional-development seminars.

Contributors

Janet L. Glass
Dwight-Englewood School, Englewood, NJ

Dr. Frances S. Hoch
Raleigh, NC

Jan Kucerik
Pinellas County Schools Largo, FL

Dr. Dave McAlpine
University of Arkansas–Little Rock, Little Rock, AR

Maria Elena Messina
Adrian C. Wilcox High School, Santa Clara, CA

Dr. Gerardo Piña-Rosales
North American Academy of the Spanish Language, The City University of New York (CUNY) Lehman and Graduate Center, New York, NY

Advisers

Trina M. Gonzales-Alesi
John Glenn Middle School of International Studies, Indio, CA

Paula Hirsch
Windward School, Los Angeles, CA

María Orta
Kennedy High School, Chicago, IL

Nina Wilson
Murchison Middle School, Austin, TX

Developmental Editor	Editorial Coordinator	Editorial Director
Susana Gómez	Anne Smieszny	Enrique Ferro

Welcome to

The pairs

Andy Douglas y su hermana Janet Douglas

Nosotros somos fans del español por la música. La música latina es muy divertida.

Tess Williams y su madre Patricia Williams

Hay lugares fantásticos en el mundo hispano.

Español Santillana

Who we are

We are four pairs of fans of the Spanish language and of Hispanic cultures. Our objective is to get to know the Spanish-speaking world: its people, its landscapes, its cities, its customs, and its traditions. That's why we've created the website Fans del Español.

What we do

To reach our goal, we are going to travel to different Spanish-speaking countries with special missions: to find the most surprising place, the most fun customs and traditions, the most original recipe, and so on. In each country, we will take on Desafíos (challenges) that each pair will try to complete. Will we succeed?

You can follow our adventures through this book and on the website www.fansdelespañol.com.

Rita Delgado y su sobrina
Diana Robles

Tim Taylor y su abuelo
Mack Taylor

Hummm. Nosotras somos fans de la cocina hispana. Es deliciosa.

La gente hispana es maravillosa.

The countries of the challenges

What countries are the pairs going to visit? Let's find out. Do these activities.

1. Look at the photos and investigate. In which countries are these places located?

2. Look at the map and answer. What countries share borders with the countries represented by the photos?

3. Leaf through the book. What color corresponds to each country?

CANADÁ

OCÉANO ATLÁNTICO

ESTADOS UNIDOS

MÉXICO

BAHAMAS

CUBA

REPÚBLICA DOMINICANA

HAITÍ

PUERTO RÍCO

JAMAICA

BELICE

GUATEMALA   HONDURAS

EL SALVADOR   NICARAGUA

COSTA RICA   PANAMÁ

VENEZUELA

GUYANA

SURIN

COLOMBIA

ECUADOR

PERÚ

BOLIVIA

PARAGUAY

CHILE

URUGUAY

ARGENTINA

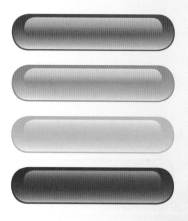

(1) Sevilla.

(2) Misión de Santa Bárbara.

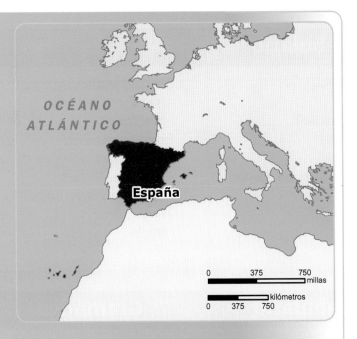

OCÉANO ATLÁNTICO

España

| 0 | 375 | 750 |
millas

kilómetros
| 0 | 375 | 750 |

uayana Francesa

BRASIL

(3) Buenos Aires.

(4) Isla de Pascua.

Fans del Español

Your participation counts!

1. Your vote decides the winner

In these challenges, you are going to play an important role. You will accompany us to each country. Pay close attention, because you are going to form part of the judging panel. In each country, you will evaluate which pair has done the best job or which task is the most interesting. Each time, you will help to decide the winning team.

2. Your challenge

You will also have your own challenge: TU DESAFÍO. During the course of the year, you will be able to accumulate points toward your challenge. To do this, watch for this symbol:

🚩→ TU DESAFÍO

When you see it, go to the *Fans del español* website. Just by participating, you will earn points. If at the end of the course you have accumulated enough points, you too will have won your challenge!

Contents

Gramática

- Expressing place, movement, and existence
  - Adverbs and expressions of place
  - The verb *ir*
  - The verb *haber*
- Expressing habitual actions in the present:
  - Regular verbs
  - Adverbs of frequency
- Expressing habitual actions in the present. Stem-changing verbs

- Expressing likes:
  - The verb *gustar*
  - Adverbs of quantity
  - Comparison
- Object pronouns
- Expressing habitual actions in the present:
  - Irregular verbs in the *yo* form
  - Demonstratives

Gramática

Cultura

- The verb *sentirse*
- Affirmative *tú* commands. Regular verbs

- *Mapa cultural*: Spain
  - Atlantic Spain: the cradle of the Spanish language
  - The plateau: territory of *La Mancha*

- Madrid: a painter's paradise
- The south: an arabic heritage
- *Lectura: El* Guernica, *de Pablo Picasso*

- The present participle
- Stem-changing verbs (*u > ue*)

- *Mapa cultural*: United States
  - Judy Baca and the murals of Los Angeles
  - Tex-mex food

- Little Havana
- *Lectura: Celebramos la Herencia Hispana*

- The preterite tense of the verbs *ser* and *ir*
- Negative commands

- *Mapa cultural*: Argentina
  - The tango
  - Mafalda
  - Buenos Aires

- Gnocchi Day
- *Lectura*: La vuelta al mundo de Cinthia Scoch

- Irregular verbs in the preterite. *Estar* and *tener*
- Expressing permission and prohibition

- *Mapa cultural*: Chile
  - Easter Island
  - Pablo Neruda
  - The Viña del Mar International Song Festival

- *Lectura*: Oda a la manzana

Unidad 5

España

Al otro lado del Atlántico

Video Program

Videos

- España. Al otro lado del Atlántico
- La Alhambra
- El monasterio de Silos
- Mapa cultural de España

Audiovisuales

En Madrid

Una vuelta ciclista

El azulejo perdido

El escudo de los reyes

Una receta antigua

www.fansdelespañol.com

Unidad 6

Estados Unidos

Desafíos en casa

DESAFÍO 3

DESAFÍO 4

Video Program

Videos

- Estados Unidos. Desafíos en casa
- La Calle Ocho (Miami)
- Los Grammy latinos
- Mapa cultural de los Estados Unidos

Audiovisuales

En Washington DC

Una partida de dominó

Una noche en el museo

Fotos de famosos

¡Vamos a jugar!

www.fansdelespañol.com

Unidad 7

Argentina

En tierra de gauchos

DESAFÍO ①

DESAFÍO ②

Video Program

Videos

- Argentina. En tierra de gauchos
- El tren a las nubes
- Las cataratas del Iguazú
- Mapa cultural de Argentina

Audiovisuales

En Buenos Aires

El tren a las nubes

Un gaucho de la Pampa

Las cataratas del Iguazú

Sobres en la calle

www.fansdelespañol.com

Unidad 8

Chile

De vuelta a los Andes

Video Program

Videos

- Chile. De vuelta a los Andes
- Isla de Pascua
- Maratón de las Escaleras (Valparaíso)
- Mapa cultural de Chile

Audiovisuales

En Santiago de Chile

Las estrellas de Atacama

Una estatua falsa

El Maratón de las Escaleras

La famosa Ruta W

www.fansdelespañol.com

XVII

Unidad
puente

¿Recuerdas?

You already know Spanish. You know how to introduce yourself, to greet people, to describe people, and to talk about your house and household chores. You can also buy items, ask for food in a restaurant, and express your likes and preferences.

This year, you are going to learn to do many other things in Spanish. You'll learn to express your feelings, to talk about your hobbies and free-time activities, and to give directions. But before we begin, let's review what you already know.

¿Estás preparado para el desafío?

¡Buena suerte!

1. Identificar y describir

Vocabulario

Las presentaciones
La familia
¿Cómo es?
¿Cómo está?

Gramática

Describir personas:
– El verbo *ser* y el verbo *estar*
– Los adjetivos

Expresar posesión:
– El verbo *tener*
– Los adjetivos posesivos

Identificar personas y cosas:
– Los nombres
– Los artículos

2. Expresar acciones habituales

Vocabulario

La casa
Tareas domésticas y actividades
de ocio

Gramática

Expresar lugar, movimiento
y existencia:
– Adverbios y expresiones de lugar
– El verbo *ir*
– El verbo *haber*

Expresar acciones habituales
en el presente:
– Verbos regulares
– Adverbios de frecuencia

Expresar acciones habituales
en el presente. Verbos con raíz
irregular

3. Expresar gustos y preferencias

Vocabulario

Las tiendas
La ropa
La comida

Gramática

Expresar gustos en distinto grado:
– El verbo *gustar*
– Adverbios de cantidad
– La comparación

Pronombres de objeto

Expresar acciones habituales
en el presente:
– Verbos irregulares en la primera
persona
– Los demostrativos

1. IDENTIFICAR Y DESCRIBIR

Vocabulario

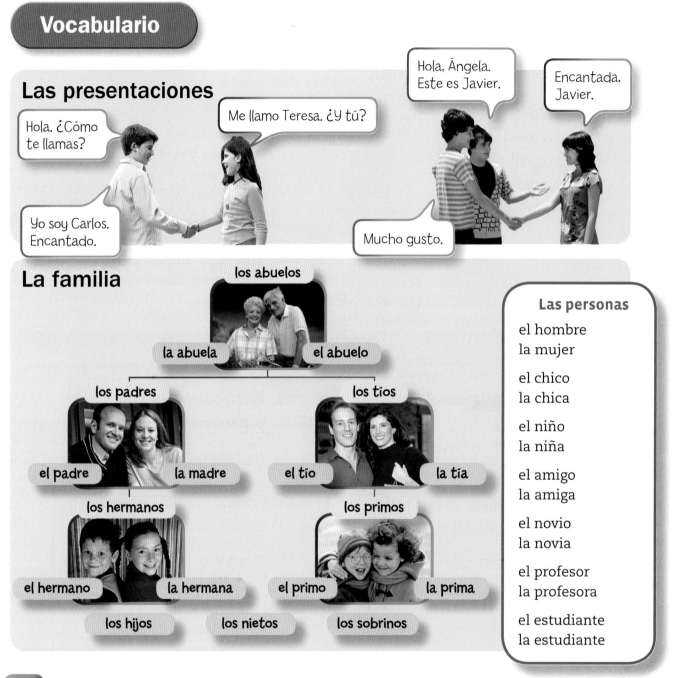

Las presentaciones

Hola. ¿Cómo te llamas?

Yo soy Carlos. Encantado.

Me llamo Teresa. ¿Y tú?

Hola, Ángela. Este es Javier.

Encantada, Javier.

Mucho gusto.

La familia

los abuelos

la abuela · el abuelo

los padres · los tíos

el padre · la madre · el tío · la tía

los hermanos · los primos

el hermano · la hermana · el primo · la prima

los hijos · los nietos · los sobrinos

Las personas

el hombre
la mujer

el chico
la chica

el niño
la niña

el amigo
la amiga

el novio
la novia

el profesor
la profesora

el estudiante
la estudiante

---

1 **Mucho gusto**

▶ **Completa.** Choose the words that complete each conversation.

| Esta es | ¿Cómo te llamas? | Mucho gusto. | ¿y tú? | Te presento a |

1. **A.** ¿Cómo estás, Tess?
   B. Bien, ¿ __1__ ?

2. **A.** __2__ Ana López.
   B. Encantado, Ana.

3. **A.** __3__ mi novia Sara.
   B. __4__ .

4. **A.** ¿ __5__ ?
   B. Me llamo Alan.

2 La familia de Alicia

▶ **Escucha y corrige.** Listen to Alicia's description of her family and correct the information below.

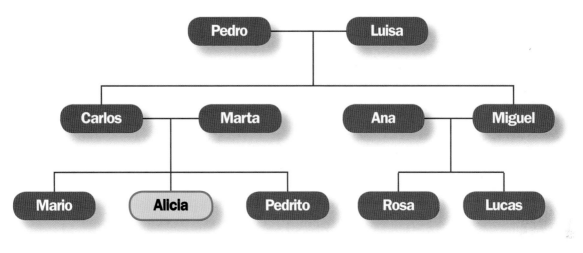

- Pedro — Luisa
- Carlos — Marta
- Ana — Miguel
- Mario
- Alicia
- Pedrito
- Rosa
- Lucas

3 ¿Quién es?

▶ **Escribe.** Write the relationship between the characters.

Modelo Rita ⟶ Diana

Rita es la tía de Diana.

1. Diana ⟶ Rita
2. Patricia ⟶ Tess
3. Tess ⟶ Patricia
4. Andy ⟶ Janet
5. Mack ⟶ Tim
6. Tim ⟶ Mack

4 ¿Qué tal?

▶ **Habla.** Get to know your classmates. Introduce yourself to a partner and find out how he or she is doing.

Modelo A. *Hola. Me llamo Tom. ¿Y tú?*
B. *Yo me llamo Alan. ¿Cómo estás, Tom?*
A. *Bien, gracias. Te presento a Clara.*
B. *...*

Vocabulario

¿Cómo es?

Características físicas

La señora es mayor, baja y rubia.

El chico es joven, alto y moreno. No es gordo. Es delgado y atlético.

Rasgos de personalidad

Lara es graciosa y simpática. Es espontánea y atrevida.

Tom es serio y tímido. Es inteligente y estudioso.

¿Cómo está?

contenta   triste   emocionado   enojada   cansado   enfermo

Tengo hambre.   Tengo sed.   Tengo frío.   Tengo calor.   Tengo miedo.

5 ¿Cómo están?

▶ **Escucha y escribe.** Listen to the conversations and write how each person feels.

contenta   cansado   enojado   triste   emocionada   enfermo

1. Janet   2. Andy   3. Diana   4. Rita   5. Mack   6. Tim

Modelo 1. *Janet está emocionada.*

6 No es cierto

▶ **Habla.** Your partner isn't wearing his or her glasses today and is having trouble seeing. Help him or her describe the people in the photos.

Modelo Pedrito: guapo/feo
        A. *Pedrito es* **guapo**.
        B. *No, Pedrito no es guapo. Es* **feo**.

1

Carlos:
moreno/rubio

2

Don Luis:
joven/mayor

3

Toni:
alto/bajo

4

Paco:
delgado/gordo

7 ¿Qué siento cuando...?

▶ **Escribe.** Describe how you would feel in each situation.

miedo   frío   sed

calor   hambre

Modelo Estoy en el Polo Norte. ⟶ *Tengo frío.*

1. Estoy en el desierto del Sahara. No tengo agua.
2. Nieva mucho. La temperatura es −5 °F.
3. Voy a pedir una pizza con jamón y queso.
4. ¡Tengo un examen de Matemáticas!
5. Hace sol. La temperatura es 100 °F.

Describir personas

El verbo *ser* y el verbo *estar*

VERBO SER (*TO BE*). PRESENTE

Singular		Plural	
yo	soy	nosotros nosotras	somos
tú	eres	vosotros vosotras	sois
usted él ella	es	ustedes ellos ellas	son

VERBO ESTAR (*TO BE*). PRESENTE

Singular		Plural	
yo	estoy	nosotros nosotras	estamos
tú	estás	vosotros vosotras	estáis
usted él ella	está	ustedes ellos ellas	están

- The verb ser is used mainly to identify and to describe physical characteristics and personality traits.

  José **es** mi profesor de español. Él **es** alto, inteligente y simpático.

- The verb estar is used to express conditions and feelings.

  Ellos no **están** contentos.

Los adjetivos

- Spanish adjectives can be masculine or feminine, singular or plural.
- The **feminine** form is developed from the masculine form:

Masculine form	Feminine form	Examples
Ends in -o.	Changes -o to -a.	El niño es alto. → La niña es alta.
Ends in -e or in a consonant.	Does not change.	Mi padre es joven. → Mi madre es joven.

- The **plural** form is developed from the singular form:

Singular form	Plural form	Examples
Ends in a vowel.	Adds -s.	Ella es simpática. → Ellas son simpáticas.
Ends in a consonant.	Adds -es.	El profesor es joven. → Los profesores son jóvenes.

---

8 **¿Y tú cómo eres?**

▶ **Escucha y elige.** Choose the adjective that corresponds to each description you hear.

1. joven/jóvenes
2. altos/alta
3. simpática/simpático
4. atlético/atléticas

9 **Yo no estoy cansado**

▶ **Escribe.** Use the verb *estar* to say how the people in the photos feel.

Modelo *Marta está emocionada.*

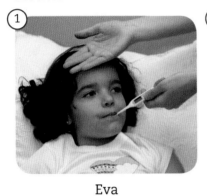

1

Eva

2

Manuel y Martín

3

Javier

4

Liliana

5

Paula

6

Teresa

10 **Es simpática y está contenta**

▶ **Escribe.** Fill in a chart, like the one below, describing the people in the photos.

Modelo

¿Quién es?	¿Cómo es?	¿Cómo está?
María	Es morena y delgada. Es simpática.	Está contenta.

1 María 2 Carlos 3 Julia 4 Alberto 5 Luisa

Gramática

Expresar posesión

El verbo *tener*

Verbo tener (to have). Presente

Singular		Plural	
yo	tengo	nosotros nosotras	tenemos
tú	tienes	vosotros vosotras	tenéis
usted él ella	tiene	ustedes ellos ellas	tienen

Tengo dos hijos. Mis hijos **tienen** cinco y diez años.

- The verb tener usually means *to have*. And it also means *to be* when it expresses age or feelings.

    Yo **tengo** una computadora.   **Tengo** doce años.   **Tengo** miedo.

- To express obligation we can use tener que + infinitive.

    Tenemos que estudiar español.

Los adjetivos posesivos

- Possessive adjectives are used to show ownership. They agree with the noun they accompany, that is, they agree with the thing possessed, not with the owner.

    Nuestros amigos son simpáticos.

Adjetivos posesivos

mi mis	*my*	nuestro, nuestra nuestros, nuestras	*our*
tu tus	*your (informal)*	vuestro, vuestra vuestros, vuestras	*your (informal)*
su sus	*his, her, your*	su sus	*their, your*

---

11 ### ¿Qué tienes tú?

▶ **Escribe.** Write sentences using the verb *tener*.

Modelo Jorge - 2 computadoras → *Jorge tiene dos computadoras.*

1. Tú - 16 años
2. Ustedes - 5 perros
3. Yo - 8 primos
4. Mis abuelos - 9 nietos
5. Mi hermana - 21 años
6. Usted - 3 gatos

12 Tengo una fiesta de quinceañera

▶ **Completa.** Janet received an e-mail from a Mexican fan. Fill in the blanks with the correct form of the verb *tener*.

Para:
Cc:
Asunto:
Mensaje nuevo

¡Hola, Janet!

Soy Rosa. ___1___ catorce años, pero mañana es mi cumpleaños. ¡Estoy muy emocionada y quiero invitarte a mi quinceañera! Es una fiesta muy divertida, con muchos invitados. Mis padres y yo ___2___ muchos amigos.

¿Ustedes ___3___ fiestas como la quinceañera en los Estados Unidos? En México es una tradición familiar. Mi prima también ___4___ quince años y celebramos juntas la fiesta de quinceañera. ¿Y tú, cuántos años ___5___, Janet?

¡Hasta pronto!

Rosa

---

13 ¿De quién es el primo?

▶ **Une y escribe.** Match the description in column A with the family member in column B to form a complete sentence.

Ⓐ

1. El hijo de tu tío es
2. Los sobrinos de mi padre son
3. Las hijas de mi tía son
4. Luis es mi primo y el primo de mis hermanos; es
5. Pedro es el primo de mi amiga; es
6. Ana es la prima de Elena; es

Ⓑ

a. mis primos.
b. su prima.
c. mis primas.
d. nuestro primo.
e. tu primo.
f. su primo.

14 Mi mejor amigo es simpático

▶ **Habla.** Can you describe your best friends? Talk to a partner about your best friends and those of your classmates.

Modelo   A. *Mi mejor amigo es simpático.*
                ¿Cómo es tu mejor amigo?
            B. *Mi mejor amigo es serio.*
                ¿Cómo es la mejor amiga de Andrea?
            A. *Su mejor amiga es muy simpática.*

Identificar personas y cosas

Los nombres

- Spanish nouns can be **masculine** or **feminine**. Almost all nouns that end in -o are masculine, and those that end in -a are feminine.

- Nouns that refer to people usually have a masculine and a feminine form. The feminine form is developed from the masculine form:

Masculine form	Feminine form	Examples
Ends in -o.	Changes -o to -a.	el niño ⟶ la niña
Ends in a consonant.	Adds -a.	el profesor ⟶ la profesora

- Most Spanish nouns can be **singular** (one) or **plural** (more than one). The plural form is developed from the singular form:

Singular form	Plural form	Examples
Ends in a vowel.	Adds -s.	el primo ⟶ los primos
Ends in a consonant.	Adds -es.	el profesor ⟶ los profesores

Los artículos

- Spanish nouns are usually used with a definite or indefinite article. Articles agree with nouns in gender and number.

	SINGULAR		PLURAL	
	Masculino	Femenino	Masculino	Femenino
Definite articles	el	la	los	las
Indefinite articles	un	una	unos	unas

- Articles, like adjectives, agree in **gender** and **number** with the noun they accompany.

El niño es alto. Es **una** niña muy simpática.
Los niños son altos. Son **unas** niñas muy simpáticas.

---

15 **En buena compañía**

▶ **Escucha, elige y escribe.** Choose the article that agrees with the words you hear, then write the word with its corresponding article.

1. un/unas 2. los/las 3. la/los 4. una/unos 5. el/las

16 Rita y Alan

▶ **Escucha y escribe.** Rita and her friend Alan have discovered that their relatives are identical in all except gender. Listen and describe Alan's relatives based on Rita's descriptions of her family.

Modelo RITA: *Mi sobrina es alta.*
          ALAN: *Mi sobrino es alto también.*

1. hermano **2.** abuelo **3.** tía **4.** primo **5.** padre

▶ **Escribe.** Now write the plural of Alan's descriptions.

Modelo *Mis sobrinos son altos.*

17 En la foto

▶ **Escribe.** Write the captions for these photos using the appropriate form of the indefinite article.

Modelo 1. *Una mujer y un niño.*

▶ **Habla.** Now, with a partner, describe the people in the photos using the appropriate form of the definite article.

Modelo 1. *La mujer es bonita y simpática. El niño es gracioso y está contento.*

2. EXPRESAR ACCIONES HABITUALES

La casa

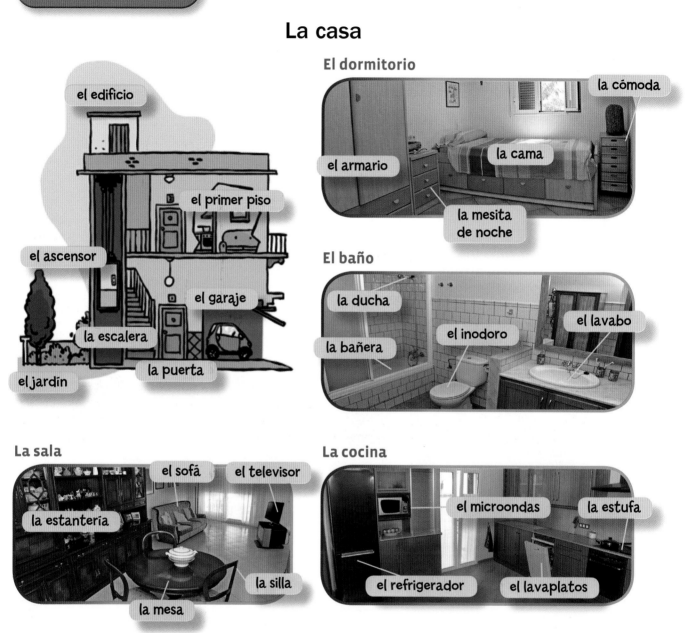

El dormitorio

- la cómoda
- la cama
- el armario
- la mesita de noche

el edificio

el primer piso

el ascensor

el garaje

la escalera

la puerta

el jardín

El baño

- la ducha
- el lavabo
- el inodoro
- la bañera

La sala

- el sofá
- el televisor
- la estantería
- la silla
- la mesa

La cocina

- el microondas
- la estufa
- el refrigerador
- el lavaplatos

---

18 **¿Dónde está?**

▶ **Escucha y une.** Everyone has lost something. Listen and match each person with the part of the house where his or her lost item can be found.

A	B
1. Andy	a. el dormitorio
2. Tess	b. la cocina
3. Tim	c. el garaje
4. Rita	d. el baño
5. Janet	e. la sala

19 Busca el intruso

▶ **Identifica.** Identify the item that doesn't belong in each room.

A
1. la estufa
2. el lavaplatos
3. el sofá
4. el refrigerador
5. el microondas

B
1. el inodoro
2. la cómoda
3. el lavabo
4. la ducha
5. la bañera

C
1. el armario
2. el sofá
3. la cómoda
4. la cama
5. la mesita de noche

D
1. el sofá
2. la mesa
3. la silla
4. la estantería
5. la bañera

20 ¿Qué tienes en tu dormitorio?

▶ **Habla.** What does your partner have in his or her bedroom? Ask five questions.

Modelo A. ¿Tienes una computadora?
B. Sí, tengo una computadora en mi dormitorio.

▶ **Escribe.** Write a paragraph comparing both bedrooms.

Modelo

El dormitorio de mi amiga Anne tiene una cama, un armario y una estantería grande.
Mi dormitorio tiene...

¡Hoy **tengo que** lavar los platos!

¡Yo **tengo ganas de** escuchar música!

Vocabulario

Tareas domésticas y actividades de ocio

limpiar el baño

pasar la aspiradora

barrer el suelo

sacudir los muebles

sacar la basura

cortar el césped

pasear al perro

cuidar a la mascota

ver la televisión

leer una revista

hablar por teléfono

21 **Cada actividad en su sitio**

▶ **Relaciona.** Match each activity with the part of the house where we do it.

1. lavar los platos
2. cortar el césped
3. cuidar a la mascota
4. leer una revista
5. ver la televisión

Ⓐ   Ⓑ   Ⓒ

22 **Primero las tareas domésticas**

▶ **Escucha y relaciona.** Listen and match the characters with their chores.

1. Tess   2. Andy   3. Tim   4. Rita   5. Janet

23 **¡Más tareas!**

▶**Habla.** Talk to a partner about what you have to do to solve each problem.

Modelo El baño no está limpio. (nosotros)
→ *Nosotros tenemos que limpiar el baño.*

pasear al perro   leer una revista

pasar la aspiradora   hablar por teléfono   lavar los platos

1. El suelo no está limpio. (yo)
2. Es el cumpleaños de tu amigo. (tú)
3. No funciona el lavaplatos. (nosotros)
4. Necesitan una receta para la fiesta. (ustedes)
5. El perro está muy nervioso. (ellos)

24 **¿Qué tienes que hacer los fines de semana?**

▶**Habla.** Talk to a partner about what chores you have to do on the weekends.

Modelo A. *Yo tengo que ordenar mi dormitorio. Y tú, ¿qué tienes que hacer?*
B. *Yo tengo que…*

▶ **Dibuja.** Draw a Venn diagram to compare your chores.

Expresar lugar, movimiento y existencia

Expresar lugar. Adverbios y expresiones de lugar

- To say where things are located, use the verb estar with words that express place.

  El coquí **está en el jardín.**

- These words and phrases are also used to show location.

¿Dónde están los coquíes?

aquí ahí allí

al lado de **la flor**

lejos de **la flor**

cerca de **la flor**

detrás de **la flor**

encima de **la flor**

a la izquierda de **la flor**

delante de **la flor**

debajo de **la flor**

a la derecha de **la flor**

Expresar movimiento. El verbo ir

- To express where someone is going, use the verb ir *(to go)* and this formula:

  $\boxed{ir\ a + \text{place}}$ **Voy al** cine.

  Remember: a + el = al

Expresar existencia. El verbo haber

- To say that someone or something exists, use the form hay *(there is, there are).*

  Hay libros en la estantería.
  ¿Hay un lavaplatos en la cocina?

VERBO IR (TO GO). PRESENTE

Singular		Plural	
yo	voy	nosotros nosotras	vamos
tú	vas	vosotros vosotras	vais
usted él ella	va	ustedes ellos ellas	van

25 ¿De quién hablan?

▶ **Escucha e identifica.** Listen and identify the person being described.

Modelo Está a la izquierda de Ana.
       → *Es Marta.*

26 ¿Vienes a la fiesta?

▶ **Escribe.** Complete the letter with the correct form of the verb *ir*.

> Hola, Nuria:
>
> Mañana mis amigos y yo **vamos** a una fiesta. ¿ ___1___ tú también? ___2___ mucha gente nueva. Por ejemplo, ___3___ Sandra y Jenny, las primas de Javier.
>
> Bueno, te escribo mañana. Ahora me ___4___ de compras con mi madre. Siempre ___5___ juntas a comprar.
>
> Un beso.
>
> Charo

27 ¿Cuántos hay?

▶ **Habla.** With a partner, take turns asking about the number of objects below.

Modelo computadoras - 5
       A. *¿Cuántas computadoras hay?*
       B. *Hay cinco computadoras.*

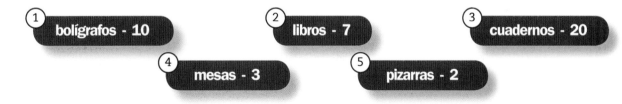

1 bolígrafos - 10
2 libros - 7
3 cuadernos - 20
4 mesas - 3
5 pizarras - 2

28 ¿Dónde están?

▶ **Habla.** Talk to a partner about the items in your classroom. Say how many there are and where they are located in the classroom.

Modelo A. *¿Hay pizarras en la clase?*
       B. *Sí, hay dos pizarras.*
       A. *¿Dónde están?*
       B. *Están detrás de la mesa del profesor.*

Expresar acciones habituales en el presente

Verbos regulares

VERBOS LAVAR (TO WASH), PRENDER (TO SWITCH ON) Y ABRIR (TO OPEN). PRESENTE

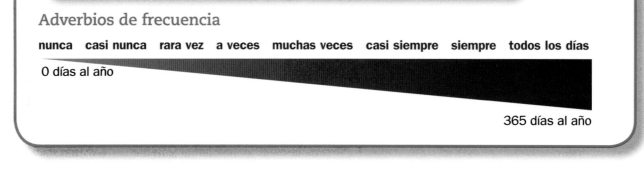

		Lavar	Prender	Abrir
Singular	yo	**lav**o	**prend**o	**abr**o
	tú	**lav**as	**prend**es	**abr**es
	usted, él, ella	**lav**a	**prend**e	**abr**e
Plural	nosotros, nosotras	**lav**amos	**prend**emos	**abr**imos
	vosotros, vosotras	**lav**áis	**prend**éis	**abr**ís
	ustedes, ellos, ellas	**lav**an	**prend**en	**abr**en

Adverbios de frecuencia

nunca   casi nunca   rara vez   a veces   muchas veces   casi siempre   siempre   todos los días

0 días al año

365 días al año

---

29   **¿Quién cuida el jardín?**

▶ **Escucha y une.** Listen and match each chore with the person or group.

Yo cuido el jardín.

Ⓐ	Ⓑ
1. cortar el césped	a. ustedes
2. sacudir los muebles	b. yo
3. pasear al perro	c. ellas
4. barrer el suelo	d. nosotros
5. limpiar el garaje	e. tú

▶ **Escribe.** Now write who does each chore in complete sentences and using the correct form of the verb.

▶ **Habla y escribe.** Tell your partner who does the chores at your house. Make a list of the chores people do at your partner's house.

Modelo

En mi casa	En casa de mi compañero(a)
Mi padre lava los platos.	Su hermana y él lavan los platos.

30 Tareas domésticas para el fin de semana

▶ **Completa.** Tess is writing an e-mail to her friend Pancho about her chores.
Complete the e-mail by using the correct form of the verbs in the boxes.

pasar	sacudir	pasear	limpiar
sacar	barrer	cortar	lavar

```
○ ○ ○                           Mensaje nuevo
      Para: _____
        Cc: _____
▼  Asunto: _____

¿Qué tal, Pancho?
Mi familia y yo tenemos muchas tareas domésticas los fines de semana.
Mi padre siempre  corta  el césped los sábados. Mi hermano ___1___
la basura y ___2___ al perro. Mis hermanos y yo normalmente ___3___
los platos y ___4___ el baño.
Mi madre ordena la casa. ¿Tú ___5___ el suelo de tu dormitorio?
Yo barro el suelo o ___6___ la aspiradora y mi hermano ___7___
los muebles.
¡Buen fin de semana!
Tess
```

31 ¿Con qué frecuencia?

▶ **Habla y escribe.** How often do you do each activity? Interview
four classmates and record your answers in a chart like the one below.

lavar los platos	cortar el césped	ver la televisión	limpiar el baño
usar la computadora	hablar por teléfono	leer una revista	pasear al perro

Modelo A. *¿Con qué frecuencia lavas los platos?*
              B. *Todos los días.*

	nunca	casi nunca	rara vez	a veces	muchas veces	casi siempre	todos los días
lavar los platos	✔			✔ ✔			✔
...							

Expresar acciones habituales en el presente

Verbos con raíz irregular: *e > ie*

VERBO CERRAR (TO CLOSE). PRESENTE

Singular		Plural	
yo	**cierro**	nosotros nosotras	**cerramos**
tú	**cierras**	vosotros vosotras	**cerráis**
usted él ella	**cierra**	ustedes ellos ellas	**cierran**

- Other verbs *e > ie*:

  empezar *(to begin)* ⟶ yo empiezo
  entender *(to understand)* ⟶ yo entiendo
  pensar *(to think)* ⟶ yo pienso
  preferir *(to prefer)* ⟶ yo prefiero
  querer *(to want)* ⟶ yo quiero

Verbos con raíz irregular: *o > ue*

VERBO PODER (TO BE ABLE). PRESENTE

Singular		Plural	
yo	**puedo**	nosotros nosotras	**podemos**
tú	**puedes**	vosotros vosotras	**podéis**
usted él ella	**puede**	ustedes ellos ellas	**pueden**

- Other verbs *o > ue*:

  costar *(to cost)* ⟶ cuesta(n)
  contar *(to count)* ⟶ yo cuento
  recordar *(to remember)* ⟶ yo recuerdo
  volar *(to fly)* ⟶ yo vuelo
  volver *(to return)* ⟶ yo vuelvo

Verbos con raíz irregular: *e > i*

VERBO PEDIR (TO ASK FOR). PRESENTE

Singular		Plural	
yo	**pido**	nosotros nosotras	**pedimos**
tú	**pides**	vosotros vosotras	**pedís**
usted él ella	**pide**	ustedes ellos ellas	**piden**

- Other verbs *e > i*:

  repetir *(to repeat)* ⟶ yo repito
  competir *(to compete)* ⟶ yo compito
  medir *(to measure)* ⟶ yo mido
  servir *(to serve)* ⟶ yo sirvo
  vestir *(to dress)* ⟶ yo visto

32 ¿Quién hace cada cosa?

▶ **Escucha y relaciona.** Listen and match each statement with its pronoun.

Modelo 1. → **e.** nosotros

a. ellos　　**b.** yo　　**c.** tú　　**d.** ella　　**e.** nosotros　　**f.** ustedes　　**g.** él

33 ¿Quieres leer una revista?

▶ **Habla.** Tess would like to make plans with her partners, but everyone has something else to do. Use the photos to give Tess an excuse for each character.

Modelo Andy, ¿quieres ver la televisión?
　　　　　→ *No puedo. Tengo que cortar el césped.*

1. Andy, Janet, ¿ustedes quieren ir al centro?
2. Mack, ¿Tim quiere visitar un museo?
3. Tim, ¿Diana y Janet quieren leer revistas?
4. Rita, ¿quieres ir al teatro?
5. Mamá, ¿quieres hablar por teléfono con los Estados Unidos?

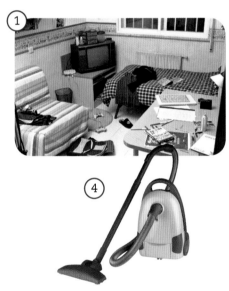

34 Unas preguntas

▶ **Escribe.** Answer the questions in complete sentences.

Modelo ¿Entienden ustedes el español?
　　　　　→ *Sí, nosotros entendemos el español.*

1. ¿Prefieres barrer o pasar la aspiradora?
2. ¿Piensas hablar por teléfono con tus amigos hoy?
3. ¿Qué clase prefieres?
4. ¿Quieren ustedes ver la televisión?
5. ¿Los profesores repiten las preguntas en clase?

3. EXPRESAR GUSTOS Y PREFERENCIAS

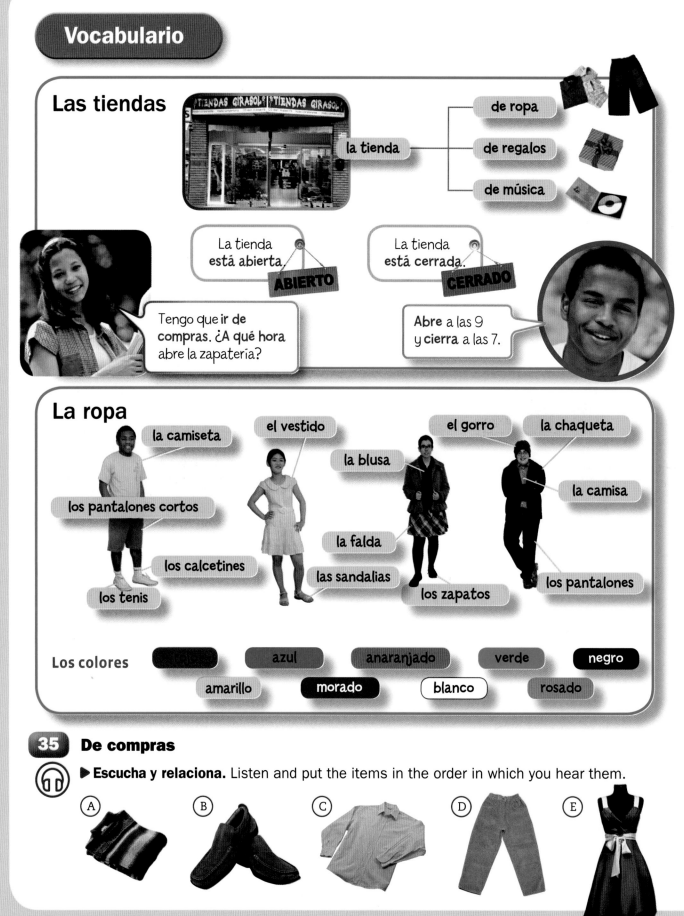

Vocabulario

Las tiendas

la tienda
- de ropa
- de regalos
- de música

La tienda está abierta. **ABIERTO**

La tienda está cerrada. **CERRADO**

Tengo que **ir de compras**. ¿A qué hora abre la zapatería?

Abre a las 9 y **cierra** a las 7.

La ropa

- la camiseta
- el vestido
- el gorro
- la chaqueta
- la blusa
- la camisa
- los pantalones cortos
- los calcetines
- la falda
- las sandalias
- los tenis
- los zapatos
- los pantalones

Los colores
rojo · azul · anaranjado · verde · negro
amarillo · morado · blanco · rosado

35 De compras

▶ **Escucha y relaciona.** Listen and put the items in the order in which you hear them.

Ⓐ Ⓑ Ⓒ Ⓓ Ⓔ

36 **¿Está abierta o cerrada?**

▶ **Lee y escribe.** Each store has different hours. Use the information below to say if they are open or closed at the times indicated.

Modelo Tienda de ropa. 10:00 a. m. - 8:00 p. m. Ahora son las doce.
→ *Está abierta.*

Tienda	Horario	Ahora...
1. Tienda de regalos	9:00 a. m. - 6:00 p. m.	son las cuatro y media.
2. Tienda de música	8:30 a. m. - 5:00 p. m.	son las nueve de la mañana.
3. Tienda de ropa	9:00 a. m. - 8:00 p. m.	son las diez de la noche.
4. Zapatería	10:00 a. m. - 8:00 p. m.	son las tres de la tarde.

37 **¿Cuánto cuesta?**

▶ **Habla.** With a partner, talk about the prices of the following items.

Modelo A. *¿Cuánto cuesta la falda amarilla?*
B. *La falda amarilla cuesta veinticuatro dólares.*

(A) $ 35
(B) $ 98
(C) $ 18
(D) $ 40
(E) $ 69

38 **¿Quién es?**

▶ **Escribe.** Can you identify someone by his or her clothing? Choose a classmate and write a short description of their clothes.

Modelo

> Lleva una camiseta azul de algodón, unos pantalones cortos azules y unos tenis blancos.

 ▶ **Lee y habla.** Read your description aloud and see if your classmates can guess who is being described.

La comida

el mesero

Señores, la **carta**.

la servilleta

el cuchillo

el tenedor

el mantel

la cuchara

el plato

la botella

la sal

el vaso

la taza

la pimienta

el azúcar

Comidas

la sopa

los frijoles

el pan

los huevos

Postres

el helado

la torta

las verduras

el pollo con papas

la carne con arroz

el pescado con maíz

las frutas

Bebidas

el agua

el refresco

la leche

el jugo de naranja

Sabores

dulce

salado

picante

agrio

amargo

La sopa está **caliente** y el refresco está **frío**.

39 **De compras en el supermercado**

▶ **Escucha y escribe.** Diana and Rita have to do some shopping. Listen and write what they buy.

40 En el restaurante

▶**Lee y decide.** Read this conversation between a waiter and a client at a restaurant and decide if each statement is true *(cierto)* or false *(falso)*.

A la carta

MESERO: ¿Quiere ver la carta, señor?

CLIENTE: Sí, gracias. ¿Hay algún plato especial?

MESERO: Nuestra especialidad es la paella. Es arroz con carne o pescado.

CLIENTE: Pues quiero la paella.

MESERO: ¿Y para beber?

CLIENTE: Una botella de agua, por favor.

MESERO: ¿Quiere tomar postre?

CLIENTE: ¿Tienen helado?

MESERO: No, señor. Hay frutas y torta de chocolate.

CLIENTE: Entonces prefiero un café.

MESERO: ¿Cómo quiere el café?

CLIENTE: Con leche.

Aquí tiene la carta, señor.

1. El cliente no quiere ver la carta.
2. La paella lleva pescado.
3. El cliente pide un refresco.
4. De postre hay torta y helado.
5. El cliente pide un postre.
6. Al cliente no le gusta el café.

▶**Representa.** Act out this situation with a partner.

41 ¿Qué uso para cada comida?

▶**Escribe.** Write a sentence explaining what utensils you use to eat or drink each item.

Modelo *Para beber un jugo de naranja uso un vaso.*

Expresar gustos en distinto grado

El verbo *gustar*

- To express likes or dislikes, use the verb gustar.

VERBO GUSTAR (TO LIKE). PRESENTE

	Singular	Plural	
(A mí)	**me gusta**	**me gustan**	*I like*
(A ti)	**te gusta**	**te gustan**	*you like*
(A usted) (A él/a ella)	**le gusta**	**le gustan**	*you like he/she likes*
(A nosotros/as)	**nos gusta**	**nos gustan**	*we like*
(A vosotros/as)	**os gusta**	**os gustan**	*you like*
(A ustedes) (A ellos/a ellas)	**les gusta**	**les gustan**	*you like they like*

Note: To speak about one thing or an action, use the singular form gusta.

A María le **gusta** la sopa.

To speak about two or more things, use the plural form gustan.

A mí me **gustan** los postres.

Adverbios de cantidad

nada

poco

bastante

mucho

No me gusta **nada** el pescado, pero me gusta **mucho** el chocolate.

La comparación

- To express inequality regarding one characteristic, use these structures:

más + adjective + *que*	La torta es **más dulce que** la fruta.

menos + adjective + *que*	Los refrescos son **menos sanos que** el agua.

- To express equality, use this structure:

tan + adjective + *como*	Este sándwich está **tan bueno como** ese.

---

42 **¿A quién le gusta?**

▶ **Escucha y escribe.** Listen and write the food each person likes.

1. yo   **2.** mi hermano   **3.** ustedes   **4.** nuestros amigos   **5.** tú

▶ **Escribe.** Now write complete sentences with your answers, using the correct form of the verb *gustar*.

43 **¿Qué prefieres?**

▶ **Habla.** What do you prefer to eat? Use the prompts below to act out three dialogues with a partner.

Modelo ensalada / arroz

A. ¿Quieres una ensalada?
B. No, gracias. No me gusta nada la ensalada. Prefiero el arroz.
A. A mí me gusta mucho la ensalada.

1. refresco / agua

2. pescado / carne

3. verduras / frijoles

RECUERDA

Los verbos *querer* y *preferir* tienen la irregularidad *e > ie* en el presente, como el verbo *cerrar*.

– querer (to want) ⟶ yo quiero,
                        tú quieres,
                        él quiere...

– preferir (to prefer) ⟶ yo prefiero,
                           tú prefieres,
                           él prefiere...

44 **¿Más o menos?**

▶ **Escribe.** Compare the foods and drinks below using an adjective from the box.

dulce	salado
picante	agrio
frío	caliente

Modelo

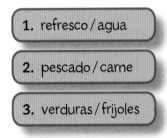
la carne   el pescado

La carne es más salada que el pescado.

① la sopa   la ensalada

② el maíz   las papas

③ la pimienta   el azúcar

④ el limón   la banana

▶ **Habla.** Give a partner your opinion about the foods and drinks above.

Modelo A. ¿Qué te gusta más, el maíz o las papas?
             B. Me gustan más las papas porque no son tan dulces como el maíz.

Pronombres de objeto

Pronombres de objeto directo

- To avoid repeating words that have already been mentioned, you can replace the direct object with a pronoun.

SINGULAR		PLURAL	
Masculino	Femenino	Masculino	Femenino
lo *him, it*	la *her, it*	los *them*	las *them*

- Direct object pronouns go normally before the conjugated verb and attached at the end of the infinitive.

> Quiero **la camisa**. → La quiero.
> Quiero comprar **ese suéter**. → Quiero comprar**lo**.

Pronombres de objeto indirecto

- Indirect object pronouns are the same as those used with the verb gustar.

Singular		Plural	
me	*to me*	nos	*to us*
te	*to you (informal)*	os	*to you (informal)*
le	*to him, to her, to you (formal)*	les	*to them, to you*

- Indirect object pronouns go before the conjugated verb and attached at the end of the infinitive.

> Traigo el desayuno **a Juan**. → **Le** traigo el desayuno.
> Tengo que pedir la carta **al mesero**. → Tengo que pedir**le** la carta.

---

45 **¿Quién lo barre?**

▶**Escribe.** You are eager to help out today. Volunteer to do each chore.

Modelo Hay que barrer el suelo. → *Yo lo barro.*

(1) limpiar
el baño

(2) pasar la
aspiradora

(3) cerrar las
ventanas

(4) preparar
el pescado

(5) comprar frutas
y verduras

46 ¿Quién lo hace?

▶ **Habla.** Discuss who does the following chores at your home with a partner.

Modelo

A. ¿Quién pone la mesa en tu casa?
B. **La** ponemos mis hermanos y yo.

①

preparar la comida

②

lavar los platos

③

comprar las frutas

④

hacer la ensalada

⑤

servir el café

Yo le sirvo la comida al cliente.

47 ¿A quién?

▶ **Escribe.** Rewrite the sentences using the indirect object pronouns from the box.

me	te	le	nos	os	les

Modelo El mesero sirve la comida.   (a mí)
→ El mesero **me** sirve la comida.

1. Yo pido la tarjeta de crédito.   (a usted)
2. El mesero repite la pregunta.   (a nosotros)
3. Ellos piden agua.   (a la señora López)
4. ¿Tu madre sirve el desayuno?   (a ti)
5. Nosotros pedimos más helado.   (a ellas)

Gramática

Expresar acciones habituales en el presente

Verbos irregulares en la primera persona

- Some verbs are irregular in the present tense only in the first person. The rest of the forms follow the same pattern as the regular verbs.

VERBOS HACER (TO MAKE, TO DO), PONER (TO PUT), TRAER (TO BRING) Y SALIR (TO LEAVE). PRESENTE

		Hacer	Poner	Traer	Salir
Singular	yo	hago	pongo	traigo	salgo
	tú	haces	pones	traes	sales
	usted, él, ella	hace	pone	trae	sale
Plural	nosotros, nosotras	hacemos	ponemos	traemos	salimos
	vosotros, vosotras	hacéis	ponéis	traéis	salís
	ustedes, ellos, ellas	hacen	ponen	traen	salen

- Other verbs that are irregular only in the first person are:

    saber *(to know how)* ⟶ yo **sé**, tú sabes, él sabe…
    conocer *(to be acquainted)* ⟶ yo **conozco**, tú conoces, él conoce…
    ver *(to see)* ⟶ yo **veo**, tú ves, él ve…

Los demostrativos

- To indicate where something or someone is located in relation to the person speaking, use demonstratives.

DEMOSTRATIVOS

Distance from speaker	SINGULAR		PLURAL	
	Masculino	Femenino	Masculino	Femenino
Near	este	esta	estos	estas
At a distance	ese	esa	esos	esas
Far away	aquel	aquella	aquellos	aquellas

Me gusta **esta** camisa y **esa** falda.

---

48 **¿Quién pone la mesa?**

▶ **Escribe.** Answer the following questions using a direct object pronoun.

Modelo ¿Quién pone la mesa? (yo) ⟶ Yo la pongo.

1. ¿Quién pone los platos? (ellos)
2. ¿Quién trae el postre? (tú)
3. ¿Quién hace la cena? (papá)
4. ¿Quién corta la carne? (ella)
5. ¿Quién conoce al mesero? (nosotros)
6. ¿Quién sabe su nombre? (yo)

49 **Salimos a cenar**

▶ **Completa.** Two friends are having dinner at a restaurant in downtown Lima. Complete their conversations using a demonstrative from the box.

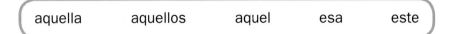

| aquella | aquellos | aquel | esa | este |

LUISA: Aquí está el restaurante El limeño. ¿Entramos?
EVA: A mí no me gusta ___1___ restaurante. Prefiero ___2___ de allí.
LUISA: ¿El restaurante El Inca?
EVA: Sí. Es muy famoso por la comida indígena.

MESERO: ¿Quieren sentarse en ___3___ mesa, señoras?
LUISA: Yo prefiero ___4___, más cerca de la ventana.

EVA: ¡Tengo hambre! ¿Dónde está nuestro mesero?
LUISA: Un momento. Está con ___5___ clientes.
EVA: ¡Aquí viene el mesero!

▶ **Escribe y representa.** With a partner, write a conversation similar to one of the ones above using at least three demonstrative adjectives.

50 **No, yo no la pongo**

▶ **Habla.** Talk to a partner about who does the following activities.

Modelo poner la mesa (mi madre)
     A. ¿Tú pones la mesa en tu casa?
     B. No, yo no pongo la mesa en mi casa. La pone mi madre.

1. saber hacer paella (mis padres)
2. conocer buenas recetas (mi hermana)
3. traer la cena (Pedro)

4. hacer la comida (mi padre)
5. servir la sopa (mi madre)
6. hacer la compra (todos)

España

Al otro lado del Atlántico

DESAFÍO 2

DESAFÍO 1

▶ **To talk about the body and the senses**

Vocabulario
Partes del cuerpo

Gramática
Los verbos *ver*, *oír*, *oler* y *decir*

La Vuelta Ciclista a España

La Alhambra

▶ **To express daily routine**

Vocabulario
La higiene personal

Gramática
Los verbos reflexivos

DESAFÍO 3

▶ **To express physical conditions**

Vocabulario
Síntomas
y enfermedades

Gramática
El verbo *doler*
El verbo *sentirse*

El monasterio
de Silos

DESAFÍO 4

▶ **To give commands and advice**

Vocabulario
Remedios básicos
Hábitos saludables

Gramática
El imperativo
afirmativo de *tú*.
Verbos regulares

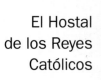

El Hostal
de los Reyes
Católicos

La llegada

En Madrid

The four pairs meet in Madrid. They visit a hospital to find Dr. Galdón, their Spanish host. Dr. Galdón will assign a task to each pair. But they are in for a surprise!

Perdón, señora. ¿Es usted la doctora Galdón?

No. Yo trabajo en el hospital, pero no soy la doctora Galdón. Soy enfermera. ¿Te sientes mal?

Yo soy médica, pero no soy la doctora Galdón. ¡Lo siento!

Sí. Yo soy la doctora Galdón. Espera un minuto... ¿Te duele la cabeza, mi amor?

1 ¿Comprendes?

▶ **Escoge y escribe.** Choose the correct answer for the questions, then write a complete sentence for each.

1. ¿Dónde están las parejas?   a. En un parque.   b. En un hospital.
2. ¿Dónde trabaja la doctora Galdón?   a. En un hospital.   b. En una escuela.
3. ¿Cómo es la doctora Galdón?   a. Es muy tímida.   b. Es muy graciosa.
4. ¿Qué hace la doctora?   a. Se afeita.   b. Se maquilla.
5. ¿A quién le duele la cabeza?   a. A Diana.   b. A la niña.

Modelo 1. *Las parejas están en un hospital.*

EXPRESIONES ÚTILES

To ask how someone feels:

¿Cómo estás?
¿Qué te pasa?
¿Cómo te sientes?
¿Te sientes bien/mal?

To say how you feel:

Me siento bien/mal.
Estoy enfermo(a).

To wish someone to feel better:

Que te mejores.
Cuídate.

To say where something hurts:

Me duele la cabeza.
Me duelen los pies.

¡Me duele la cabeza!

2 ¿Cómo se sienten?

▶ **Escucha y une.** Listen to the dialogue between Dr. Galdón and her patients. Match the people (column A) with how they feel (column B).

A	B
1. A María	a. se siente bien.
2. A Javier	b. le duele la cabeza.
3. Pedro	c. está enferma.
4. Rosalía	d. le duelen los pies.

3 ¿Qué dicen?

▶ **Elige.** Choose the right expression for each picture.

a. ¿Cómo se siente?   **b.** Cuídate.   **c.** Me duelen los pies.   **d.** Me duele la cabeza.

¿Quién ganará?

4 **Los desafíos**

▶ **Habla.** What will be the challenge for each pair? Think about this question and discuss it with your classmates.

DESAFÍO ①

Una vuelta ciclista

Tess y Patricia

DESAFÍO ②

El azulejo perdido

Andy y Janet

DESAFÍO ③

El escudo de los reyes

Rita y Diana

DESAFÍO ④

Una receta antigua

Mack y Tim

5 **Las votaciones**

▶ **Decide.** You decide. You will vote to choose the most exciting challenge. Who do you think will win?

Emocionante

Una vuelta ciclista

Tess and Patricia are at the Asturias stage of the *Vuelta Ciclista a España* (Bicycle Tour of Spain). Their task is to get an autographed T-shirt from the leader of the race. First, they have to figure out who he is!

¿Quién gana la etapa, Tess? No puedo ver nada.

Yo tampoco veo nada y no oigo al comentarista.

Mira, el líder tiene problemas. Le duele la pierna izquierda.

¡Cuidado! ¡Un accidente!

Un golpe fuerte en la cabeza. ¿Puede ver? ¿Me oye?

Me duele la cabeza. ¡Qué dolor!

Continuará...

6 Detective de palabras

▶ **Completa.** Use words from the *fotonovela* to complete these sentences.

1. ¿Quién _____ la etapa, Tess?
2. Yo tampoco _____ nada.
3. Le _____ la pierna izquierda.
4. ¿Puede ver? ¿Me _____?
5. Me _____ la cabeza.

▶ **Habla y representa.** With a partner, decide who said each line and act out the dialogue.

¿Comprendes?

▶ **Escribe.** Answer the questions in complete sentences.

1. ¿Qué problema tiene Patricia?
2. ¿Qué problema tiene Tess?
3. ¿Qué problema tiene el líder?
4. ¿Qué le duele al ciclista del accidente?

8 **¿Qué ves?**

▶ **Habla.** Patricia took these photos in Spain. Take turns describing the people, their physical characteristics, and their clothes.

Modelo A. *¿Qué ves?*
          B. *Veo a un ciclista. Lleva una camiseta amarilla*
              y unos zapatos amarilllos.

CULTURA

La Vuelta Ciclista a España

La Vuelta Ciclista a España es una carrera por etapas (*stages*). Durante tres semanas, ciclistas internacionales participan en una carrera por las ciudades, los campos y las montañas de España. El líder lleva un jersey amarillo.

La Vuelta Ciclista a España es una competición tan importante como el *Tour de France* y el *Giro d'Italia*.

9 **Piensa.** Why do you think the leader wears a yellow jersey?

▶ **TU DESAFÍO** Visit the website to learn more about the *Vuelta Ciclista a España*.

treinta y nueve 39

Vocabulario

Partes del cuerpo

la cabeza

el cuello

el brazo

la mano

los dedos

la pierna

el pie

los dedos

el pelo

los ojos

las orejas

la nariz

la cara

la boca

los dientes

Acciones

ver   oír   oler   saborear   tocar

10 Acciones habituales

▶ **Completa.** What do these people enjoy doing? Complete the captions with the appropiate infinitive.

oír

oler

saborear

ver

tocar

1 _____ una comida.

2 _____ un perfume.

3 _____ un cuadro.

4 _____ música.

5 _____ un instrumento.

11 Características físicas

▶ **Habla.** With a partner, describe this character.
Use the words in the boxes.

Modelo *Tiene las orejas grandes.*

piernas	pies
brazos	nariz
cabeza	ojos
manos	orejas

largo	corto
grande	pequeño
alto	bajo
gordo	delgado

12 ¿Fátima, Armando o la doctora Galdón?

▶ **Escucha y escribe.** Patricia meets three special people in Spain.
Listen and write the name of the person who has each of these physical traits.

1. ojos azules
2. nariz grande
3. pelo negro
4. piernas largas

5. cara bonita
6. cuerpo delgado
7. pelo rubio
8. cuello largo

13 Autorretrato

▶ **Escribe.** Write a paragraph describing at least three of your physical characteristics
and the things you like to see, hear, smell, and touch.

Modelo *Soy alta, morena y tengo los ojos negros. Me gusta oír música pop.*

CULTURA

El Angliru

El Angliru es un puerto de montaña muy alto. Está en el norte
de España, en Asturias. La Vuelta Ciclista a España pasa a veces
por El Angliru. El Angliru es una de las etapas más difíciles
de la carrera, pero también es una zona natural muy bonita.

14 **Piensa.** What body parts would need to be very
strong in order to bicycle up a mountain like *El Angliru*?

▶ **TU DESAFÍO** Visit the website to learn more about the Asturias region.

Gramática

Los verbos *ver*, *oír*, *oler* y *decir*

- The verbs ver *(to see)*, oír *(to hear)*, oler *(to smell)*, and decir *(to say, to tell)* express actions that our senses perform. All four verbs are irregular.

VERBO VER (TO SEE). PRESENTE

Singular		Plural	
yo	veo	nosotros nosotras	vemos
tú	ves	vosotros vosotras	veis
usted él ella	ve	ustedes ellos ellas	ven

VERBO OÍR (TO HEAR). PRESENTE

Singular		Plural	
yo	oigo	nosotros nosotras	oímos
tú	oyes	vosotros vosotras	oís
usted él ella	oye	ustedes ellos ellas	oyen

VERBO OLER (TO SMELL). PRESENTE

Singular		Plural	
yo	huelo	nosotros nosotras	olemos
tú	hueles	vosotros vosotras	oléis
usted él ella	huele	ustedes ellos ellas	huelen

VERBO DECIR (TO SAY, TO TELL). PRESENTE

Singular		Plural	
yo	digo	nosotros nosotras	decimos
tú	dices	vosotros vosotras	decís
usted él ella	dice	ustedes ellos ellas	dicen

Note:
1. In Spanish, the letter h is always silent. Do not pronounce it in the irregular forms of oler.
2. Spanish words that start with the sound ue are spelled hue.

15 **Piensa.** Although the verbs tocar *(to touch)* and saborear *(to taste)* refer to the senses, they are not included here. Why do you think that is?

16 **¿Qué haces?**

▶ **Habla.** What do you do with these things? Ask your partner using direct object pronouns in your responses.

Modelo
A. *¿Qué haces con una flor?*
B. *La veo, la huelo, la toco.*

1. una televisión
2. una radio
3. una guitarra
4. un perfume
5. un trabalenguas *(tongue twister)*
6. un perro

17 **¿Qué hacen los participantes?**

 ▶ **Escucha y contesta.** Tess and Patricia are talking about their experiences in Spain. Listen and answer the questions in complete sentences.

1. ¿Quién no puede oler ni oír bien? ¿Por qué?
2. ¿Por qué apaga la radio Patricia?
3. ¿Adónde va Patricia?
4. ¿Quién quiere ver un espectáculo de flamenco?

18 **Un día difícil**

▶ **Completa.** Tess is not having a great day. Fill in the blanks with the appropriate form of the verbs *oler*, *oír*, *ver*, and *decir*.

> **Un mal día**
>
> Estamos en un restaurante típico, pero no me siento bien.
> No ___1___ la carta porque tengo los ojos irritados, y no ___2___
> al mesero porque la música está muy alta. Además, no ___3___
> la comida porque tengo la nariz roja. Mamá me ___4___:
> «No estás enferma». Pero yo me siento mal.

19 **Una encuesta**

▶ **Escribe.** Write five questions using the sense verbs.

Modelo *¿Qué programas de televisión ves?*

 ▶ **Habla.** Use your questions to interview five classmates. Report your findings to the class.

CULTURA

¿Lo ves o no lo ves?

El cubismo es un estilo artístico de principios del siglo xx. Los artistas cubistas representan los objetos desde distintas perspectivas. El español Pablo Picasso es un famoso pintor cubista. Fíjate en el cuadro de la fotografía. ¿Qué ves en él?

20 **Dibuja y habla.** Draw a picture of a partner using Picasso's cubist style. Compare your picture with your partner's. Talk about what you see in each drawing.

Pablo Ruiz Picasso.
Retrato de Dora Maar.

▶ **TU DESAFÍO** Use the website to learn more about Pablo Picasso.

Comunicación

21 El ciclista Antonio López

▶ **Lee y escribe.** In his blog, Antonio López wrote about his experiences during the *Vuelta Ciclista a España*. Read the text and list his problems.

La etapa de El Angliru

22 de septiembre. Asturias

Hoy es un día difícil. Desde mi cuarto veo El Angliru y, lo confieso, estoy nervioso. Tengo los ojos rojos, me duele el cuello, tengo las piernas y los pies cansados... Pero hoy es un día importante. ¡Quiero ganar esta etapa! Gracias a todos los fans por sus mensajes electrónicos. ¡Nos vemos en la carrera!

▶ **Escucha y escribe.** An organizer of the *Vuelta* is describing services available for cyclists. Listen and take notes about the services that Antonio López could use.

▶ **Escribe.** Using the blog entry and the listening activity above, write an e-mail to Antonio López. Suggest services that could help him.

22 Personaliza tus sentidos

▶ **Escribe.** Write an e-mail describing things you like to do with your five senses. Write a sentence for each one and explain your reasons.

Modelo

Para:		
Cc:		
Asunto:	Me gusta...	

OÍR. Me gusta oír música en español porque aprendo vocabulario nuevo.

▶ **Habla.** Read your e-mail to several classmates. Fill in a chart like the one below to compare your likes.

Modelo

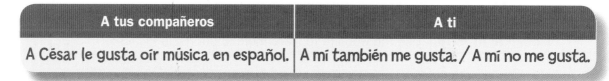

A tus compañeros	A ti
A César le gusta oír música en español.	A mí también me gusta. / A mí no me gusta.

23 **Adivinanzas con sentido**

▶ **Crea y escribe.** Create a monster by drawing or making a collage. Then write a paragraph to describe your monster's body and how it sees, hears, smells, tastes, touches, and walks. Notice that Spanish does not use possessive adjectives with body parts.

> ## Mi monstruo
>
> El monstruo tiene tres ojos. Tiene tres dedos en las manos...

▶ **Habla.** In a group, display your artwork along with that of your classmates. Then take turns describing your monsters. Who can be the first to guess which monster is being described?

Final del desafío

24 **¿Qué pasa en la historia?**

▶ **Escribe.** Write a caption for each photograph using the five senses. Include details about what the participants hear from the crowd, see, smell, taste, and touch, and what the people are wearing.

Modelo 1. *Patricia y Tess buscan al ciclista con el jersey amarillo.*

 Earn points for your own challenge! Listen to the questions for your *Minientrevista Desafío 1* on the website and write your answers.

El azulejo perdido

Andy and Janet are at the Alhambra in Granada, Spain. Their task is to find an *azulejo* (tile) among the hundreds of tiles that decorate this fortress. Where will they find it?

La higiene personal era muy importante en los tiempos de la Alhambra.

Sí, Andy, en esa época los baños eran un evento social.

Necesito afeitarme.

Mira, los baños de la Alhambra. ¿Ves un azulejo similar a este?

¿Afeitarte? Tú no tienes pelo en la cara.

Lo sé. Es una broma. Pero necesito lavarme las manos.

Yo tengo jabón, pasta de dientes y desodorante en mi mochila. ¿Los necesitas?

Continuará...

25 **¿Comprendes?**

▶ **Completa.** Look at the *fotonovela* to choose the best option to complete the sentences.

1. Andy dice que necesita _____   **a.** afeitarse   **b.** bañarse
2. Andy quiere _____   **a.** lavarse las manos   **b.** lavarse los pies
3. Janet tiene en su mochila _____   **a.** jabón   **b.** champú
4. Janet tiene que encontrar _____   **a.** un baño   **b.** un azulejo

26 **Hotel Baños Reales**

 ▶ **Escucha y escribe.** Andy and Janet are staying at the *Hotel Baños Reales*. Listen to the radio advertisement and combine phrases from columns A and B to write true statements.

Ⓐ

1. El hotel
2. Para la higiene personal
3. En los baños
4. La crema de afeitar
5. Para relajarse

Ⓑ

a. hay jabón gratis.
b. huele muy bien.
c. el hotel tiene un *spa*.
d. hay productos en las habitaciones.
e. está cerca de la Alhambra.

27 **La mochila de Janet**

▶ **Habla.** With your partner, say what Janet has in her bag. Take turns.

Modelo

Tiene jabón.

Sí. Y tiene desodorante.

CULTURA

La Alhambra

La Alhambra es una fortaleza (*fortress*) árabe. Está en la ciudad de Granada, en el sur de España. Tiene más de 700 años. La fortaleza tiene varios edificios y grandes jardines. Los edificios están decorados con diseños geométricos.

En los palacios árabes los baños eran (*were*) muy importantes. Como en las termas romanas (*roman baths*), los baños de la Alhambra tienen una zona fría, una zona caliente y salas de descanso.

28 **Piensa y compara.** What do you think are the similarities and differences between the personal-hygiene habits of the 1300s and those of today?

▶→ **TU DESAFÍO** Learn more about the Alhambra on the website.

Vocabulario

La higiene personal

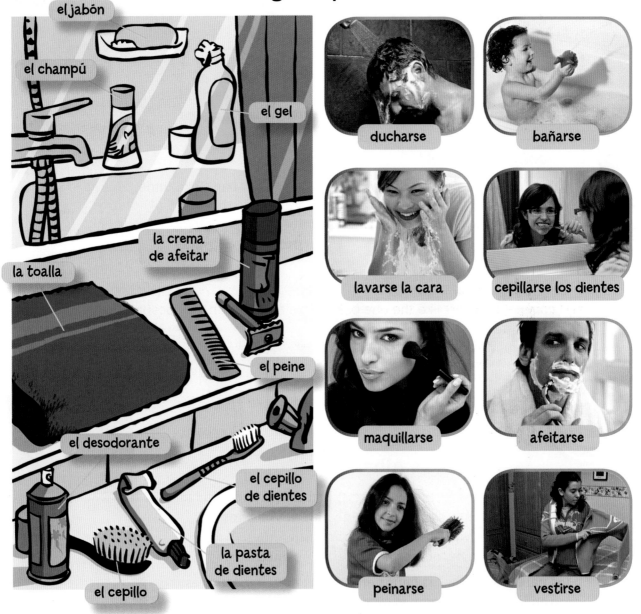

el jabón

el champú

el gel

la crema de afeitar

la toalla

el peine

el desodorante

el cepillo de dientes

la pasta de dientes

el cepillo

ducharse

bañarse

lavarse la cara

cepillarse los dientes

maquillarse

afeitarse

peinarse

vestirse

29 **La rutina de Janet**

▶ **Escucha y escribe.** Andy is describing Janet's daily routine. Listen and put her routine in order. Then write sentences.

Modelo 1. *Janet tiene que levantarse antes de las ocho.*

    a. vestirse para la excursión

    b. cepillarse los dientes

    c. ponerse desodorante

    d. peinarse

    e. maquillarse

    f. ducharse

30 **En el *spa* del hotel**

▶ **Escribe.** Janet has answered this survey requested by the hotel. Write a note saying which of the options she prefers.

Modelo *Para ducharse prefiere…*

Su opinión es importante	HOTEL BAÑOS REALES

Estimado(a) cliente:
Nos gusta conocer sus preferencias.
Gracias por responder a esta encuesta.

HOTEL BAÑOS REALES
* * * *
GRANADA

1. ¿Qué prefiere para ducharse? ☑ jabón   ☐ gel de ducha
2. ¿Qué prefiere para peinarse? ☑ peine   ☐ cepillo
3. ¿Qué prefiere para cepillarse los dientes?   ☐ pasta de dientes de menta   ☑ pasta de dientes de frutas

31 **Mis obligaciones durante el día**

▶ **Escribe.** What three things do you usually do at each time of day? Copy and complete a chart like the one below. Use the verbs in the vocabulary.

Modelo

7:00 a. m. – 12:00 p. m.	12:00 p. m. – 5:00 p. m.	5:00 p. m. – 9:00 p. m.
Ducharme		

COMPARACIONES

Los productos de higiene personal

Los productos de higiene personal cambian con los tiempos. En la época de la Alhambra, había (*there were*) jabón y perfumes, pero no había desodorante ni pasta de dientes.

Cada cultura tiene una idea diferente de la higiene personal. Por eso, en otras culturas usan productos que nosotros no usamos.

32 **Compara.** Do you know of any unusual personal-hygiene products or practices from other cultures or other historical periods?

Gramática

Los verbos reflexivos

- Sometimes an action is reflected back onto the subject. In Spanish, this idea is expressed with a reflexive verb.

    Juan se lava. (Juan performs the action, and he receives the effects of the action.)

    The verbs ducharse, bañarse, maquillarse, peinarse, and vestirse are reflexive verbs.

- Reflexive verbs are conjugated with a reflexive pronoun: me, te, se, nos, os, se.
  The pronoun is placed as follows:
  – In front of the conjugated verb: Yo me lavo.
  – Attached to the end of the infinitive: Quiero lavarme.

VERBO LAVARSE (TO WASH ONESELF). PRESENTE

Singular		Plural	
yo	me lavo	nosotros nosotras	nos lavamos
tú	te lavas	vosotros vosotras	os laváis
usted él ella	se lava	ustedes ellos ellas	se lavan

- Many verbs related to habits are reflexive verbs.
    – despertarse *(ie) (to wake up)* → Yo **me despierto** a las seis de la mañana.
    – levantarse *(to get up)* → Yo **me levanto** a las siete.
    – acostarse *(ue) (to go to bed)* → Ellos **se acuestan** muy tarde.
    – dormirse *(ue) (to fall asleep)* → Tú **te duermes** pronto.

33 **Piensa.** The verb lavarse means *to wash oneself* while the verb lavar means *to wash*. How can you explain the difference between the two meanings?

34 **Un día para descansar**

▶ **Escucha y escribe.** Andy and Janet are taking a day off to relax. Listen and write who does each of these actions.

1. vestirse con ropa cómoda
2. bañarse en el *jacuzzi*
3. lavarse la cara con agua mineral
4. ducharse con un gel hidratante
5. afeitarse con una crema de maracuyá
6. lavarse las manos con un jabón de frutas

▶ **Escribe.** Write sentences to summarize what Janet and Andy do.

Modelo *Janet se lava la cara.*

35 Rutinas de la mañana

▶ **Habla.** What do the four pairs do each morning? Talk with a partner to compare their morning routines with yours.

Modelo 1. A. *Diana y yo nos levantamos a las siete de la mañana. ¿Y tú?*
B. *Yo me levanto a las siete y media.*

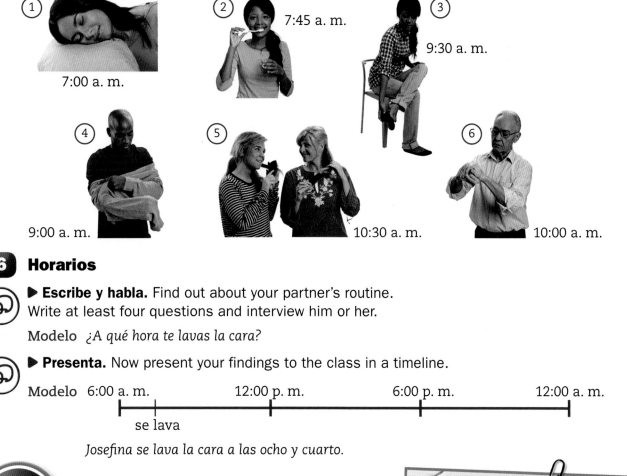

① 7:00 a. m.

② 7:45 a. m.

③ 9:30 a. m.

④ 9:00 a. m.

⑤ 10:30 a. m.

⑥ 10:00 a. m.

36 Horarios

▶ **Escribe y habla.** Find out about your partner's routine. Write at least four questions and interview him or her.

Modelo *¿A qué hora te lavas la cara?*

▶ **Presenta.** Now present your findings to the class in a timeline.

Modelo

| 6:00 a. m. | | 12:00 p. m. | | 6:00 p. m. | | 12:00 a. m. |

se lava

Josefina se lava la cara a las ocho y cuarto.

CONEXIONES: SALUD

La adolescencia

La adolescencia es un período de cambios mentales y físicos. Durante la adolescencia es muy importante mantener una rutina sana. Acostarte y levantarte temprano, comer una dieta equilibrada (*balanced*) y mantener buenos hábitos de higiene puede ayudarte a sentirte bien.

37 Piensa. How do you feel when you skip breakfast or when you don't sleep enough? Can you concentrate at school?

Comunicación

38 Una persona organizada

▶ **Habla.** Read the schedule Janet has prepared for tomorrow morning. Tell your partner how this schedule compares with your own daily schedule.

Modelo *Janet se levanta a las siete menos cuarto, pero yo me levanto a las siete.*

6:45 a. m.	7:15 a. m.	7:30 a. m.	7:45 a. m.	7:50 a. m.	8:00 a. m.
Levantarme	Ducharme	Vestirme	Cepillarme los dientes	Peinarme	Maquillarme

39 Para descansar en Granada

▶ **Escucha y escribe.** Lanjarón is a spa resort in the Sierra Nevada. Listen to the spa's radio advertisement and list three special features you would like.

▶ **Escribe.** According to what you heard, write an e-mail to a nearby resort. Ask if they offer the same features.

Modelo

De:

Para:

Asunto:

Cuerpo del texto   Anchura variable

Estimados señores:

Quiero descansar y relajarme unos días. ¿Ustedes tienen baños de aguas termales en su hotel? ¿Y tienen…

Atentamente,

40 Así lo hago yo

▶ **Escribe y habla.** Write your schedule, then compare it with a partner's. Report your findings to the class.

Modelo *Yo me levanto a las siete. Sandra se levanta a las siete y media. Las dos nos duchamos a las ocho.*

41 Tu higiene diaria

▶ **Escribe.** Write sentences describing when you use each item.

Modelo 1. *Uso el desodorante todos los días.*

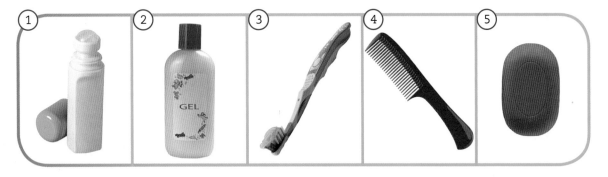

Final del desafío

Nuestro desafío en Granada

Lunes

Tenemos un plan: acostarnos a las nueve
de la noche para levantarnos a las seis de la mañana.
¡Es un buen plan! No nos duchamos por la mañana
porque nos duchamos por la noche. Por la mañana
nos lavamos las manos y la cara, nos ponemos
desodorante y nos cepillamos los dientes.
Después vamos a la Alhambra.

Martes

¿Y nuestro plan? Janet no está en el dormitorio.
Tampoco está en el autobús turístico. ¿Dónde está?
¡Está en el *spa* del hotel! ¿Y el azulejo? No lo
tenemos. ¡Adiós al desafío en España! Es la primera
prueba fallada. ¡Qué mal!

42 ¿Qué pasa en la historia?

▶ **Lee y escribe.** Andy is not very happy with Janet at the end of this challenge.
Read his blog for the beginning and end of the *Desafío*, and find out why. Then write
Janet's blog entry for the same days.

El escudo de los reyes

Diana and Rita are in Santiago de Compostela at the famous *Hostal de los Reyes Católicos*. Their task is to find the *escudo* (coat of arms) of the royal family on the side of this old hospital. Can they find it?

¿Cómo te sientes, Diana? ¿Estás enferma? ¿Necesitas ir al médico?

No... solo estoy un poco débil y cansada. Y me duelen los pies.

¿Quieres descansar?

No, no es nada serio, no te preocupes. ¡Hay que buscar el escudo!

¿Ves el escudo?

Veo algo en esa pared...

Continuará...

43 Detective de palabras

▶ **Completa.** Complete the questions.

1. ¿Cómo te _____?

2. ¿_____ enferma?

3. ¿Necesitas _____ al médico?

4. ¿Quieres _____?

▶ **Escribe.** Write the answers to each question according to the dialogue.

Modelo   ¿Estás enferma? → *No, no estoy enferma.*

44 **¿Comprendes?**

▶ **Escribe.** Decide whether each statement is true *(cierto)* or false *(falso)*. If it is false, make it true.

1. Diana se siente bien.
2. A Diana le duele la cabeza.
3. Diana no quiere ir al médico.
4. Diana no quiere descansar.

45 **¡Me duele!**

▶ **Habla.** Does it hurt? Look at the pictures and ask a partner. Take turns asking and answering.

Modelo A. *¿Te duele la espalda?*
B. *Sí, me duele la espalda.*

46 **Una visita al médico**

▶ **Habla.** Imagine you don't feel well and you go to the doctor. With a partner, take turns playing the role of doctor and patient.

Modelo DOCTOR(A): *Buenos días, ¿cómo está?*
PACIENTE: *Buenos días, doctor(a). No me siento bien. Me duele la cabeza.*

CULTURA

El Hostal de los Reyes Católicos

El Hostal de los Reyes Católicos está en Santiago de Compostela, en Galicia, en el noroeste de España. Tiene más de 500 años. Originalmente era *(it was)* un hospital y un parador *(state-run hotel)* para los peregrinos *(pilgrims)* del famoso Camino de Santiago. Hoy muchos peregrinos y turistas descansan allí.

47 **Piensa.** How do you feel after a long trip? Where do you rest? What do you do to rest?

→ TU DESAFÍO Visit the website to learn more about the *Hostal*.

Vocabulario

Síntomas y enfermedades

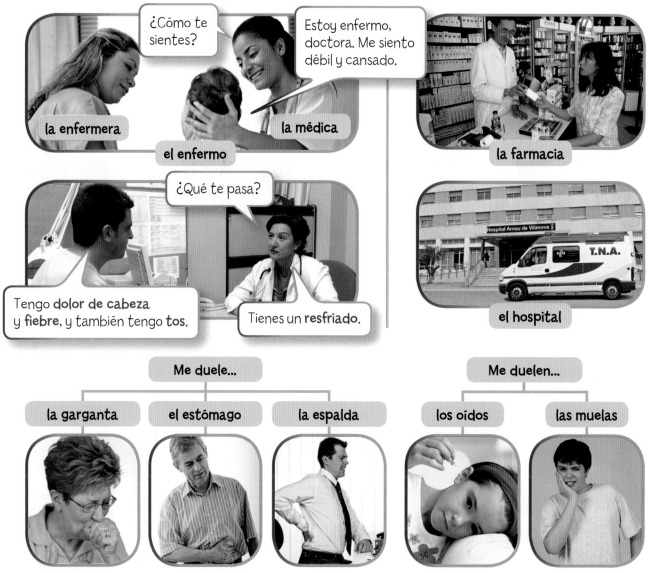

¿Cómo te sientes?

Estoy enfermo, doctora. Me siento débil y cansado.

la enfermera

el enfermo

la médica

la farmacia

¿Qué te pasa?

Tengo **dolor de cabeza** y **fiebre**, y también tengo **tos**.

Tienes un **resfriado**.

el hospital

Me duele...

la garganta · el estómago · la espalda

Me duelen...

los oídos · las muelas

48 ¿A la farmacia, al médico o al hospital?

▶ **Escribe.** Decide whether you would go to the pharmacy, to the doctor, or to the hospital for each problem.

¿Adónde vas?

Modelo Voy a la farmacia.

1. tienes dolor de cabeza
2. tienes tos
3. tienes fiebre
4. te sientes débil

5. tienes un resfriado
6. te duelen los oídos
7. te sientes mal
8. te duele el brazo

49 **Los dolores de mi amiga**

 ▶ **Escucha y decide.** Listen to the conversation between Dr. Galdón and her patient. Tell which of these problems the patient has.

1. dolor de cabeza   2. fiebre   3. tos   4. dolor de estómago   5. dolor de espalda

50 **Una encuesta de salud**

▶ **Escribe.** You are at a doctor's office. Fill out this health survey with information about how you feel today.

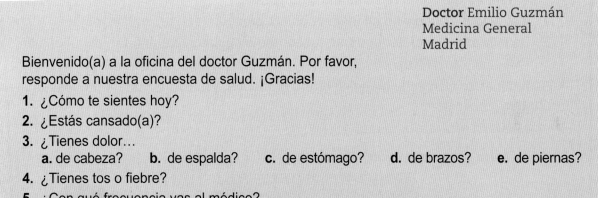

Doctor Emilio Guzmán
Medicina General
Madrid

Bienvenido(a) a la oficina del doctor Guzmán. Por favor, responde a nuestra encuesta de salud. ¡Gracias!

1. ¿Cómo te sientes hoy?
2. ¿Estás cansado(a)?
3. ¿Tienes dolor…
   a. de cabeza?   **b.** de espalda?   **c.** de estómago?   **d.** de brazos?   **e.** de piernas?
4. ¿Tienes tos o fiebre?
5. ¿Con qué frecuencia vas al médico?
6. ¿Qué haces para mantenerte sano(a)?

51 **¿Qué te pasa?**

▶ **Habla.** In pairs, take turns being a doctor and a patient and role-play different health problems. The patient mimes the problem and the doctor guesses.

Modelo   A. [softly coughs]
         B. Tienes tos.

CULTURA

El Camino de Santiago

Desde el siglo X, miles de peregrinos de todo el mundo recorren cada año el Camino de Santiago.
El Camino lleva (leads) a la catedral de Santiago de Compostela, en el noroeste de España. Santiago de Compostela, Roma y Jerusalén son los principales lugares de peregrinación para los cristianos.

52   **Compara.** The Camino de Santiago is a Christian pilgrimage. Do you know of any pilgrimage sites from other religions?

Gramática

El verbo *doler*

- To say that something hurts, use the verb doler *(to hurt, to ache)*.

    Me duele la cabeza.

- The verb doler is an irregular verb with an o > ue stem change (like poder).

- Doler follows the same rules as the verb gustar:
    1. It is always paired with an indirect object pronoun: me, te, le, nos, os, les.
    2. Usually only two of its forms are used: the singular duele and the plural duelen.

        Me duele la cabeza.   **Me duelen** los pies.

- Sometimes to clarify the meaning of the pronouns, you can include a prepositional phrase.

    A María le duele la mano.

VERBO DOLER (TO HURT, TO ACHE). PRESENTE

	Singular	Plural
(A mí)	me **duele**	me **duelen**
(A ti)	te **duele**	te **duelen**
(A usted) (A él/a ella)	le **duele**	le **duelen**
(A nosotros/as)	nos **duele**	nos **duelen**
(A vosotros/as)	os **duele**	os **duelen**
(A ustedes) (A ellos/a ellas)	les **duele**	les **duelen**

53 **Piensa.** Why do you think Spanish uses a definite article when referring to a body part, and not a possessive adjective like *my* or *his*? Why is it necessary to use the possessive adjective in English?

54 **¡Ay, qué dolor!**

▶ **Habla.** With a partner, take turns saying what aches and pains each person has.

Modelo   Rita - los pies ⟶ A Rita le duelen los pies.

1. Tim - los brazos
2. Janet y Diana - las piernas
3. Nosotros - el estómago
4. Tú - los ojos
5. Yo - los oídos
6. Ellos - la cabeza
7. Ustedes - la mano
8. Mack - la espalda

55 Una visita al hospital

▶ **Escucha, dibuja y escribe.** Rita tells the nurse at the hospital what is bothering her. Draw a picture of Rita and label the part that hurts.

56 ¿A ti qué te duele?

▶ **Escribe.** Write a sentence to say what part of the body hurts each person.

Modelo Carlos → *A Carlos le duelen los pies.*

① Pepe ② Luis ③ Jaime ④ Sofía ⑤ Elena

▶ **Habla.** Now interview a classmate to see if these body parts ache.

Modelo

¿A ti te duelen los pies?

Sí, me duelen los pies.

¿Y la cabeza?

No, no me duele la cabeza.

CONEXIONES: ARTE

El Obradoiro

La fachada (*front*) del Obradoiro es la parte más característica de la catedral de Santiago de Compostela. Está en la Plaza del Obradoiro. Allí llegan (*arrive*) los peregrinos que hacen el Camino de Santiago.

57 Investiga.
Use the Internet to find out when the *catedral de Santiago de Compostela* and the *fachada del Obradoiro* were built.

Gramática

El verbo *sentirse*

- In order to express physical and emotional states, use the verb sentirse *(to feel)*.

  Me **siento** bien. Juanita **se siente** contenta.

- Sentirse is an e > ie stem-changing verb (like cerrar) used with a reflexive pronoun.

VERBO SENTIRSE (TO FEEL). PRESENTE

Singular		Plural	
yo	**me siento**	nosotros nosotras	**nos sentimos**
tú	**te sientes**	vosotros vosotras	**os sentís**
usted él ella	**se siente**	ustedes ellos ellas	**se sienten**

- The verb encontrarse can be used to express the same meaning as sentirse. Encontrarse is an o > ue stem-changing verb (like poder).

  Hoy **me encuentro** muy bien. Patricia **se encuentra** enferma hoy.

Sentences with si

- To express what you do if something happens, use this construction:

  | Si + condition ... | Si me siento enfermo, voy al médico.

58 **Piensa.** What do the words sí and si mean in Spanish? Can you think of any other word pairs that are differentiated by only an accent mark?

59 **¿Cómo se sienten?**

▶ **Escribe.** Write sentences about how these people feel. Use the verb *sentirse* and the words in the boxes.

Modelo Yo *me siento bien.*

enfermo(a)

emocionado(a)

cansado(a)

bien

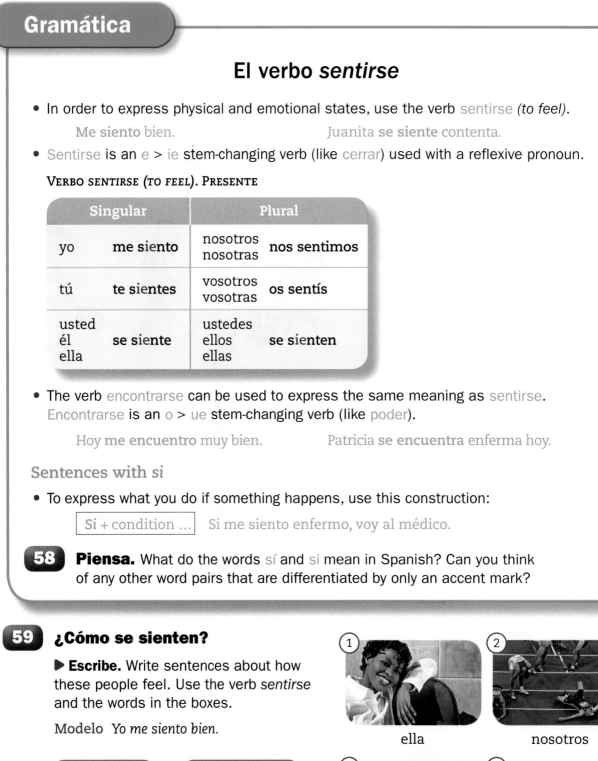

① ella

② nosotros

③ ellos

④ tú

60 **¿Cómo se sienten?**

▶ **Escribe.** How do the people below feel if they do the activities indicated?

Modelo   Voy al parque.
→ *Si voy al parque, me siento bien.*

1. Mi madre hace deporte.
2. Nosotros visitamos a un amigo.
3. Tú haces un regalo.
4. Tus amigos duermen poco.
5. Ustedes comen mucho.

61 **En la consulta de la doctora**

▶ **Escucha y elige.** Diana and Rita explain their symptoms to Dr. Galdón. Choose the answer that summarizes the situation at the doctor's office.

1. a. A Diana le duele la cabeza.
   b. Diana tiene un resfriado.
   c. Diana tiene sueño.

2. a. A Rita le duele un brazo.
   b. Rita tiene hambre.
   c. Rita tiene fiebre.

3. a. A Rita le duele el estómago.
   b. A Diana le duele el estómago.
   c. Diana come mucho.

4. a. Tienen un resfriado.
   b. Tienen tos.
   c. Están fuertes.

5. a. Tienen que ir al hospital.
   b. Tienen que beber refrescos.
   c. Tienen que descansar.

▶ **Habla.** In small groups, discuss what the doctor said and say whether you agree or disagree with her.

62 **¿Qué hacer si te encuentras mal?**

▶ **Escribe y habla.** With your partner, prepare a presentation about five common health problems and their remedies. Then report your findings to the class.

Modelo   *Si tienes fiebre, toma una ducha fría.*

CONEXIONES: CIENCIAS

Los gérmenes y la salud

Vivimos en un mundo lleno de gérmenes *(germs)*.
La mejor forma de evitar la gripe *(influenza)* y otras enfermedades es lavarse las manos con frecuencia. Si quieres mantenerte fuerte *(strong)* y sano *(healthy)*, tienes que beber mucha agua, comer alimentos saludables y descansar bien.

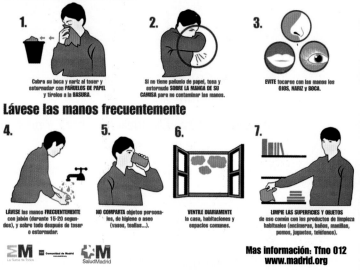

63 **Escribe.** What are some ways that you try to keep yourself healthy?
Make a poster to illustrate the benefits of living a healthy life. For example: *Cuando como bien, tengo mucha energía.*

Comunicación

64 **¿Cómo te encuentras?**

 ▶ **Escucha y relaciona.** Some people went to the nurse's office today. Listen and match the statements you hear with the pictures.

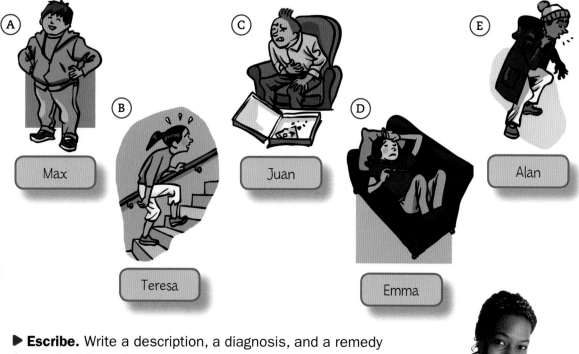

(A) Max

(B) Teresa

(C) Juan

(D) Emma

(E) Alan

▶ **Escribe.** Write a description, a diagnosis, and a remedy for each picture above.

Modelo *A Teresa le duele la cabeza y tiene fiebre. Tiene gripe. Tiene que descansar.*

65 **Problemas de salud**

▶ **Decide.** The school nurse is collecting information. Answer the questions about yourself to help her.

1. ¿Te duele la cabeza?	**a.** casi siempre	**b.** a veces	**c.** nunca
2. ¿Comes alimentos sanos?	**a.** casi siempre	**b.** a veces	**c.** nunca
3. ¿Vas al médico?	**a.** casi siempre	**b.** a veces	**c.** nunca
4. ¿Haces deporte?	**a.** casi siempre	**b.** a veces	**c.** nunca
5. ¿Te acuestas temprano?	**a.** casi siempre	**b.** a veces	**c.** nunca
6. ¿Bebes más de un litro de agua al día?	**a.** casi siempre	**b.** a veces	**c.** nunca

 ▶ **Habla.** Compare your responses to the questions with a partner. Do you both have the same answers?

66 El Camino de Santiago

▶ **Habla.** You and a friend are going to walk the *Camino de Santiago*. With a partner, talk about the possible problems below and suggest solutions.

Modelo A. ¿Qué hacemos si tenemos sed?
          B. Si tenemos sed, bebemos agua.

1. tener un resfriado
2. tener frío
3. sentirse mal
4. tener tos
5. doler los pies
6. estar débiles

Final del desafío

¡Ay, tía, ___1___ mucho los pies! Hoy no me encuentro ___2___.

Por allí hay un ___3___. ¿Vamos al ___4___?

¡Tía, mira! ¡El ___5___ está en la otra pared!

67 ¿Qué pasa en la historia?

▶ **Escribe y representa.** Complete the dialogue above. Then in groups act out the ending of the *Desafío*.

 **→ TU DESAFÍO**   Earn points for your own challenge! Listen to the questions for your *Minientrevista Desafío 3* on the website and write your answers.

Una receta antigua

Tim and Mack are in Silos, in the province of Burgos. They have to find the old pharmacy of the Silos Monastery and ask for a remedy to cure a stomachache. Will they do it?

> Mira, abuelo. Aquí está el monasterio de Silos...

> Bien. Está lejos, pero estamos en forma, ¿verdad?

> Y tú también. Eres joven, comes bien y te cuidas.

> Claro. Tú eres una persona muy sana, abuelo. Haces deporte y comes alimentos saludables.

> ¡Mira, el monasterio! Camina rápido, abuelo. Dentro está la farmacia.

Continuará...

68 **Detective de palabras**

▶ **Completa.** Using the *fotonovela*, fill in the missing verb to complete each statement.

1. _____, abuelo.   a. Mirar   b. Mira

2. _____ en forma.   a. Estamos   b. Tenemos

3. Tú _____ deporte.   a. hago   b. haces

4. _____ alimentos saludables.   a. Come   b. Comes

5. _____ rápido, abuelo.   a. Camina   b. Caminas

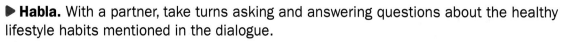

▶ **Habla.** With a partner, take turns asking and answering questions about the healthy lifestyle habits mentioned in the dialogue.

Modelo A. ¿Estás en forma?
        B. Sí, estoy en forma.

69 **Camino del monasterio**

▶ **Completa.** These are signs that Tim and Mack see on the way
to the monastery. Complete them with the verbs in the box.

cuida
toma
bebe

1 _____ alimentos
saludables: come
frutas y
verduras.

2 _____
agua
mineral:
sana y
natural.

3 _____
tu cuerpo:
visita al médico
regularmente.

70 **Una vida sana**

▶ **Escucha y elige.** Mack is telling Tim what he must do to stay healthy.
Select the recommendations that Mack makes to Tim.

1. Tienes que comer bien.
2. Tienes que acostarte temprano.
3. Tienes que dormir doce horas al día.
4. Tienes que hacer deporte.
5. Tienes que ver poca televisión.

▶ **Habla.** Check off the things that you do to stay healthy
and compare your answers with a partner's. Who lead
a healthier lifestyle? Explain.

Modelo *Yo estoy sano. Como bien, me acuesto temprano...*

CULTURA

El monasterio de Silos

El monasterio de Silos está en Burgos, en el norte
de España. Es del siglo XI y es famoso por su arquitectura.
Uno de los lugares más interesantes del monasterio
es la antigua farmacia.

El coro (*choir*) de los monjes (*monks*) del monasterio
es muy famoso.

71 **Piensa.** How do you think that the concept of health and medicine has changed
since the pharmacy of the monastery was built?

▶ **TU DESAFÍO** Use the website to learn more about the Benedictine monks of Silos.

Vocabulario

Remedios básicos

los medicamentos

tomar medicamentos

Hábitos saludables

beber mucha agua

comer bien

descansar

¡Estás en forma!

Sí, hago ejercicio y me cuido mucho.

correr

caminar

hacer deporte

72 **Hábitos sanos**

▶ **Escribe y habla.** How well do you take care of yourself? Write questions for each answer. Then interview your partner.

Modelo No, no tomo medicamentos. → *¿Tomas medicamentos?*

1. Sí, como bien.
2. No, no hago deporte.
3. No, no camino.
4. Sí, me cuido mucho.
5. Sí, corro todos los días.
6. No, descanso poco.

73 Un gimnasio nuevo

▶ **Escucha y escribe.** A new gym is advertising on the radio. Listen and decide whether you can or cannot do these activities there.

Modelo hacer deportes → *Sí puedo hacer deportes.*

1. llevar a mi perro
2. comer bien
3. beber jugos naturales
4. correr
5. comprar medicamentos
6. caminar

74 Una encuesta

▶ **Escribe y habla.** Write five questions using words from page 66. Then interview four classmates. Record their answers in a table like the one below. Do they live healthy?

Modelo

	Todos los días	A veces	Casi nunca	Nunca
¿Con qué frecuencia haces deporte?	John	Ellen Brad	Emily	

CONEXIONES: CIENCIA Y SALUD

Mi pirámide

La pirámide de nutrición es un esquema para seguir una dieta equilibrada. Según la pirámide, hay seis tipos de comidas: cereales (*grains*), verduras, frutas, leche, carnes y legumbres, y aceites. La pirámide también recomienda hacer ejercicio y beber agua.

El gobierno de los Estados Unidos tiene una página en Internet donde (*where*) puedes diseñar tu plan. ¡Visítala!

MiPirámide
PASOS HACIA UNA MEJOR SALUD
MyPyramid.gov

GRANOS   VERDURAS   FRUTAS   PRODUCTOS LÁCTEOS   CARNES y FRIJOLES

75 Investiga.
Create your own personalized food pyramid online. Does anything surprise you about the recommended daily portions of each food?

▶ **TU DESAFÍO** Visit the website to learn more about food and health.

Gramática

El imperativo afirmativo de *tú*. Verbos regulares

- To tell someone what to do, use a command.

    Camina más rápido, por favor.

- These are the command forms that we use when talking to one person:

IMPERATIVO AFIRMATIVO. VERBOS REGULARES

Caminar	Comer	Escribir
camina	come	escribe

- Notice that for regular verbs, the tú command is the same as the tú form in the present tense without the final -s.

    tú caminas → camina
    tú comes → come
    tú escribes → escribe

Imperativos y pronombres objeto

- Object and reflexive pronouns are placed attached to the end of the tú command.

    Dame ese libro.   Lávate las manos.

76 **Piensa.** Devise a simple rule to form the tú command from the usted form of the present tense.

77 **¿Qué hago?**

▶ **Escribe.** The people below need some directions. Tell them what to do, using the verbs in the boxes.

Modelo 1. *¡Camina más rápido!*

| caminar | comprar | beber | comer | tomar |

78 **Buenos consejos**

► **Une y escucha.** Tim and Diana are talking about what they do to lead a healthy life. Match Tim's advice with Diana's excuses. Then listen and check.

CONSEJOS
1. Corre.
2. Camina.
3. Pasea al perro por el parque.
4. Come bien.

EXCUSAS
a. Tengo alergia a las flores.
b. No me gusta caminar.
c. No me gustan las verduras.
d. Es muy aburrido.

79 **Para vivir mejor...**

► **Lee y completa.** Read this poster with tips to living a healthy lifestyle and complete it using the *tú* commands.

cepillarse

beber

practicar

comer

lavarse

cuidarse

HÁBITOS SALUDABLES

1. Las frutas y verduras son muy saludables. <u>Cómelas</u> todos los días.
2. Los jugos naturales tienen muchas vitaminas. <u>1</u> para desayunar o para almorzar.
3. <u>2</u> las manos siempre antes de comer.
4. <u>3</u> los dientes después de comer.
5. El deporte es muy bueno para ti. <u>4</u> habitualmente.
¡<u>5</u> **más y vive mejor!**

► **Escribe.** With a partner, write three more health tips.

CONEXIONES: ARTE

La belleza física

Las ideas sobre la belleza humana no son iguales para todos. Mira estos dos cuadros.
La pintura de la izquierda es la original, del español Diego Velázquez (1599–1660); la pintura de la derecha es del pintor colombiano Fernando Botero (1932). ¿Te parecen bonitas?

Diego Velázquez.
La infanta Margarita de Austria.

Fernando Botero.
La princesa Margarita.

80 **Piensa.** What is considered beautiful in your culture? What do people do to meet that ideal?

Comunicación

81 **Los remedios de la abuela**

 ▶ **Escucha y elige.** Tim isn't feeling well, and Mack's feet hurt. Tim decides to call his grandmother. Listen and choose the advice she gives for each problem.

El problema es...

El remedio es...

▶ **Habla.** In small groups, discuss the advice that Tim's grandmother gave him. Use the images above to assist you.

Modelo *Si te duele la cabeza, descansa.*

▶ **Escribe.** While in Burgos, Mack made a new friend: Agustín Ramos.
Write a story about Agustín's lifestyle change.

Final del desafío

a. Perdón, señor, buscamos un remedio para el dolor de estómago.

b. Termina la manzana, abuelo. ¡Ya estamos en el monasterio!

c. ¡Vaya! Té de menta. ¿Es todo?

d. El mejor remedio es el té de menta.

e. Tengo que estar en forma. Comer frutas es bueno para la salud.

Para el dolor de estómago bebe té de menta.

83 ¿Qué pasa en la historia?

▶ **Escribe y representa.** Rewrite the speech bubbles in the correct order according to the scenes above. Then act out the ending of the *Desafío* with a partner.

Todo junto

HABLAR

84 **Un juego de mesa**

 ▶ **Habla.** You and your partner are playing Operation. Point to different parts of the patient's body and say what hurts or what problem he has. Your partner will "operate" by telling you how to fix or prevent the problem.

Modelo   A. *Doctor, me duele el estómago.*
         B. *Bebe jugo de frutas.*
         A. *También me duele la cabeza.*
         B. *Tienes que descansar.*

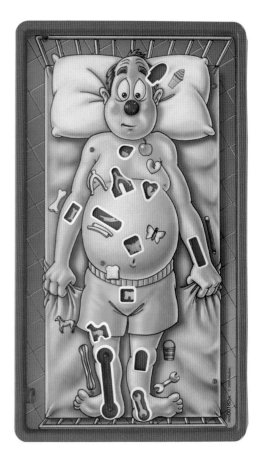

ESCUCHAR Y ESCRIBIR

85 **Esmeralda está enferma**

▶ **Escucha y escribe.** Esmeralda, the main character from a radio soap opera, is feeling sick today, and her boyfriend, Rodrigo, is trying to find out what's wrong with her. Listen and write Rodrigo's suggestions for each problem.

Problemas de Esmeralda	Sugerencias de Rodrigo
1. Sentirse débil.	
2. Dolor de cabeza.	
3. Dolor de espalda, brazos y piernas.	
4. Dolor de manos y pies.	

▶ **Escribe y representa.** According to what you heard, write your own ending to the scene. Perform your original ending for the class.

ESCRIBIR Y HABLAR

86 **Mi rutina**

▶ **Escribe.** Indicate your daily routine by filling in a chart like this one.

MI HORARIO	
7:00 a. m.	Me levanto.
8:00 a. m.	
_____ a. m.	

▶ **Habla.** Compare your daily routine with your partner's. Then explain the differences.

Modelo

> Carlos se levanta a las siete y yo me levanto a las siete y cuarto.

ESCRIBIR Y HABLAR

87 **Anuncios**

▶ **Escribe.** With your partner, write slogans for these products using the *tú* command.

Modelo *Lávate las manos con el jabón POMPAS.*

| lavarse | cepillarse | bañarse | afeitarse |

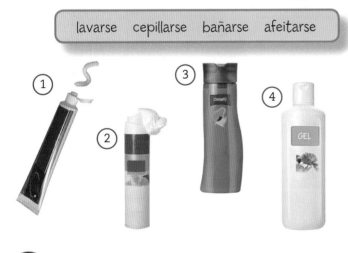

▶ **Habla.** With your classmates, vote to decide the most original slogans.

CULTURA

Los horarios de los españoles

Los horarios de los españoles con frecuencia sorprenden a los visitantes.

En general, los españoles se levantan entre las 7 y las 8 de la mañana, y se acuestan entre las 11 y las 12 de la noche.

Muchas tiendas cierran a mediodía. ¡Pero en España «mediodía» significa las 2 p. m., no las 12 p. m.! Después del descanso para la comida, las tiendas abren a las 5 y cierran sobre (*about*) las 8 de la tarde. Los españoles comen y cenan tarde.

ABIERTO

Horario Comercial
Mañana de 9 a 1´30
Tarde de 5 a 9
Sábado tarde abierto

La siesta es una costumbre española muy popular. Pero los españoles no duermen la siesta a diario. ¡Tienen que trabajar y estudiar!

88 **Compara.** What are the similarities and differences between your community's schedules and Spanish habits?

En la Plaza Mayor

The four pairs meet in Madrid after attempting their individual tasks.
Did the characters complete their tasks successfully?

¡Tenemos el jersey del líder de la Vuelta Ciclista!

Perdona, Andy. ¡Me siento muy mal!

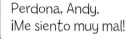

¡El té de menta es el mejor remedio para el dolor de estómago!

Este es el escudo. Está en el Hostal de los Reyes Católicos.

89 **Al llegar**

▶ **Escribe.** At the meeting point in Madrid, the four pairs talk to Dr. Galdón. Choose one of the characters and write a script for their conversation. Be sure to include the following points:

- How he or she feels.

> DOCTORA GALDÓN: ¿Cómo te encuentras, Diana?
> DIANA: No me siento bien, doctora.

- What body parts hurts him or her.

> DOCTORA GALDÓN: ¿Te duele la cabeza?
> DIANA: Sí, un poco. Y también me duele la garganta.

- What he or she has to do to feel better.

> DOCTORA GALDÓN: Tienes un resfriado, Diana. Tienes que ir a la farmacia y comprar estos medicamentos.
> DIANA: Gracias, doctora.

▶ **Representa.** In pairs, act out your script for the class, or videotape it to show to the class.

90 **Las votaciones**

▶ **Decide.** Which pair has done the most exciting challenge? Take a vote to decide.

¿Vamos al Museo del Prado?

¡Sí! ¡Buena idea!

Emocionante

España es una monarquía parlamentaria situada en el sur de Europa. Su territorio comprende la mayor parte de la Península Ibérica, los archipiélagos de Baleares y Canarias, y las ciudades de Ceuta y Melilla, en el norte de África. La capital de España es Madrid.

91 Disfruta España

▶ **Escribe.** Look at the map, read the statements, and write where these people should go. Use affirmative *tú* commands.

Modelo Paula quiere ir a una ciudad de la costa atlántica.
→ *¡Visita Cádiz!*

1. Juan quiere ver una ciudad en la costa del mar Cantábrico.
2. Luis quiere ir a una ciudad de la costa mediterránea.
3. Cristina quiere conocer la capital de España.
4. Susana quiere conocer el centro de España.

España es un país grande, pero es más pequeño que el estado de Texas.

Los paisajes de España

España es un país con una geografía y una cultura muy variadas.

1. La España atlántica

El norte del país es la **España atlántica**. Es una zona de paisajes verdes, entre el mar y la montaña, y pueblos marineros que viven de la pesca y el turismo.

(1) Lago Enol (Asturias).

(2) Paseo de la Castellana (Madrid).

(3) Playa en Cádiz (Andalucía).

2. La meseta y Madrid

El interior de España es una extensa **meseta** con campos de cereales y viñedos. La abundancia de castillos da nombre a dos de sus regiones: **Castilla y León** y **Castilla-La Mancha**.

3. El sur

Andalucía es la región de España situada en el sur de la Península Ibérica. Sus playas están bañadas por el **océano Atlántico** y el **mar Mediterráneo**. Sus paisajes, sus pueblos blancos y su clima convierten a esta región en un gran destino turístico.

92 Esto es España

▶ **Relaciona.** Match this photo with one of the three Spanish regions you have just read about.

▶ **Responde.** If you were to live in Spain, which region would you choose? Why? Make a chart with your reasons.

1. La España atlántica: la cuna del español

La lengua española nació en el norte de España. Desde allí se extendió hacia el sur y luego pasó a América.

(1) Monasterio de San Millán de la Cogolla (La Rioja), cuna del español.

(2) Molinos de viento en Consuegra (Toledo).

2. La meseta: territorio de La Mancha

En la meseta está **La Mancha,** una región que es el escenario de las aventuras de **don Quijote.** Él es el protagonista de la novela más famosa de la lengua española, *El ingenioso hidalgo don Quijote de La Mancha*, escrita por **Miguel de Cervantes.** Los molinos de viento son característicos del paisaje de **La Mancha.**

3. Madrid: paraíso de pintores

Madrid, la capital de España, es una ciudad moderna con una intensa vida cultural. En esta ciudad está el **Museo del Prado,** uno de los museos de pintura más importantes del mundo. Aquí hay obras de los más famosos pintores españoles, como **Francisco de Goya** y **Diego Velázquez.**

(3) Fachada del Museo del Prado (Madrid).

4. El sur: la herencia árabe

En España la influencia árabe es muy importante, especialmente en **Andalucía.** Las construcciones árabes más famosas son los jardines y palacios de la **Alhambra,** en **Granada,** y la **Mezquita de Córdoba.**

(4) La Alhambra (Granada).

(4) Mezquita de Córdoba.

93 **Investigación: Barcelona**

The eastern part of the Iberian Peninsula is the Mediterranean, where there are large cities such as Barcelona and Valencia.

▶ **Lee y completa.** Read the text and complete the graphic organizer by assigning the characteristics that correspond to Madrid, to Barcelona, or to both.

Madrid   Barcelona

gran ciudad

- [ ] edificios modernistas
- [ ] templo de la Sagrada Familia
- [ ] museo del Prado
- [ ] puerto mediterráneo
- [ ] grandes avenidas
- [ ] capital de España

Barcelona es una gran ciudad situada en la costa mediterránea. Tiene grandes avenidas, bellos edificios modernistas y un templo muy famoso: la Sagrada Familia.

La Casa Batlló (Barcelona).

Pablo Ruiz Picasso. *Guernica*.
Óleo sobre lienzo. 349,3 × 776,6 cm.

Pablo Ruiz Picasso.

El Guernica,
de Pablo Picasso

El *Guernica*, de Pablo Ruiz Picasso (1881–1973), es un famoso cuadro del Museo Reina Sofía de Madrid.

Picasso pinta esta obra en 1937, durante la Guerra Civil española (1936–1939), cuando los aviones destruyen el pueblo de Guernica. Picasso quiere representar en el cuadro el dolor, la muerte[1] y el horror de la guerra.

El *Guernica* es un cuadro lleno de simbolismo. A la izquierda hay un toro, símbolo de la brutalidad. Debajo del toro, una mujer llora con su hijo muerto en brazos. Más abajo hay un hombre muerto con una espada rota[2] y una flor en la mano como un símbolo de esperanza[3]. En el centro hay un caballo enloquecido[4]. A la derecha hay una mujer desesperada en medio del fuego.

---

1. death   **2.** broken sword   **3.** hope   **4.** crazy

ESTRATEGIA Hacer preguntas

94 **¡Cuántas preguntas!**

▶ **Responde.**

1. ¿Qué es el *Guernica*?
2. ¿Quién es Pablo Ruiz Picasso?
3. ¿Cuándo pinta Picasso el *Guernica*?
4. ¿Dónde está el *Guernica*?
5. ¿Qué representa el *Guernica*?

Museo Nacional Centro de Arte Reina Sofía

AMPLIACIÓN:
Pza. Emperador Carlos V s/n
28012 Madrid

Santa Isabel,52
28012 Madrid
www.museoreinasofia.es

COMPRENSIÓN

95 **¿Qué significa?**

▶ **Escribe.** What do these *Guernica* fragments represent? Write a sentence that explains the meaning of each one according to the information in the reading.

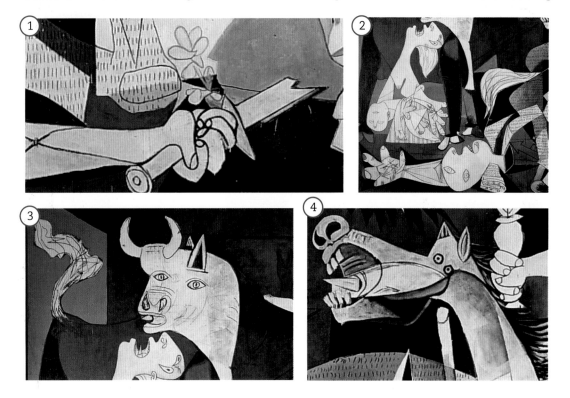

96 **¡Qué gran historia!**

▶ **Escribe.** Write another title for the reading. Then compare it with a partner's. Which title is clearer? Which is more original?

 **TU DESAFÍO** Earn points for your own challenge! Visit the website and get information about Picasso's work.

Partes del cuerpo

		La cabeza	
el brazo	*arm*	la boca	*mouth*
el cuerpo	*body*	la cara	*face*
la cabeza	*head*	la nariz	*nose*
el cuello	*neck*	los ojos	*eyes*
el dedo	*finger, toe*	las orejas	*ears*
los dientes	*teeth*	el pelo	*hair*
la espalda	*back*	**Acciones**	
el estómago	*stomach*	oír	*to hear*
la garganta	*throat*	oler	*to smell*
la mano	*hand*	saborear	*to taste*
las muelas	*teeth*	tocar	*to touch*
los oídos	*ears*	ver	*to see*
el pie	*foot*		
la pierna	*leg*		

La higiene personal

el cepillo	*hairbrush*
el cepillo de dientes	*toothbrush*
el champú	*shampoo*
la crema de afeitar	*shaving cream*
el desodorante	*deodorant*
el gel	*gel*
el jabón	*soap*
la pasta de dientes	*toothpaste*
el peine	*comb*
la toalla	*towel*

Acciones

acostarse	*to go to bed*
afeitarse	*to shave*
bañarse	*to take a bath*
cepillarse	*to brush (one's hair, teeth)*
ducharse	*to take a shower*
lavarse	*to get washed, wash (up)*
levantarse	*to get up*
maquillarse	*to make (oneself) up*
peinarse	*to comb (one's hair)*
vestirse	*to get dressed*

Síntomas y enfermedades

el dolor	*pain, ache*
la fiebre	*fever*
la gripe	*flu*
el resfriado	*cold*
la tos	*cough*
el hospital	*the hospital*
la farmacia	*the pharmacy*
el/la médico(a)	*doctor*
el/la enfermero(a)	*nurse*
el/la enfermo(a)	*patient*

¿Cómo te sientes?

Estoy enfermo(a).	*I am sick.*
Me siento débil.	*I feel weak.*
Me siento bien.	*I feel fine.*
Me siento mal.	*I don't feel well.*

¿Qué te pasa?

Me duele(n)…	*I have a … ache.*
Tengo dolor de…	*I have a … ache.*

Remedios básicos y hábitos saludables

los medicamentos	*medications, medicines*
tomar medicamentos	*to take medicine(s)*
beber mucha agua	*to drink a lot of water*
caminar	*to walk*
comer bien	*to eat well (a healthy diet)*
comer mal	*to eat badly (an unhealthy diet)*
correr	*to run*
cuidarse	*to take care of oneself*
descansar	*to rest*
estar en forma	*to be in shape*
hacer deporte	*to play sports*
hacer ejercicio	*to exercise*

DESAFÍO 1

1 **El cuerpo.** Match each action with the corresponding part of the body.

1. ver
2. tocar
3. oír
4. saborear
5. oler

a. las manos
b. la boca
c. la nariz
d. los oídos
e. los ojos

DESAFÍO 2

2 **La higiene.** What objects do you need to do the actions below? Write sentences.

Modelo *Para ducharte necesitas gel y una toalla.*

1. peinarte   2. lavarte el pelo   3. cepillarte los dientes   4. lavarte las manos

DESAFÍO 3

3 **¿Qué les pasa?** With a partner, take turns asking and answering about each person's problem.

Modelo 1. A. *¿Qué le pasa a Diana?*
             B. *Le duele la boca.*

| ① | ② | ③ | ④ | ⑤ |
| Diana | Mack | Tess | Tim | Janet |

DESAFÍO 4

4 **Tim está enfermo.** Rita is worried about Tim. Complete their conversation using the words from the box.

RITA: ¿Qué te pasa, Tim? ¿Te ___1___ bien?

TIM: No. Me ___2___ mal. Me ___3___ mucho las piernas y ___4___

RITA: Puede ser la gripe.

TIM: Además estoy ___5___ y no como bien.

RITA: Tienes que ir al ___6___

TIM: Sí, tienes razón. Tengo que ___7___

> encuentras
> cansado
> cuidarme
> la cabeza
> duelen
> médico
> siento

Los verbos *ver, oír, oler y decir* (pág. 42)

	VER	OÍR	OLER	DECIR
yo	veo	oigo	huelo	digo
tú	ves	oyes	hueles	dices
usted, él, ella	ve	oye	huele	dice
nosotros(as)	vemos	oímos	olemos	decimos
vosotros(as)	veis	oís	oléis	decís
ustedes, ellos(as)	ven	oyen	huelen	dicen

Los verbos reflexivos (pág. 50)

LAVARSE

yo	me lavo	nosotros nosotras	nos lavamos
tú	te lavas	vosotros vosotras	os laváis
usted él ella	se lava	ustedes ellos ellas	se lavan

El verbo *doler* (pág. 58)

	singular	plural
A mí	me duele	me duelen
A ti	te duele	te duelen
A usted A él A ella	le duele	le duelen
A nosotros A nosotras	nos duele	nos duelen
A vosotros A vosotras	os duele	os duelen
A ustedes A ellos A ellas	les duele	les duelen

El verbo *sentirse (e > ie)* (pág. 60)

SENTIRSE

yo	me siento	nosotros nosotras	nos sentimos
tú	te sientes	vosotros vosotras	os sentís
usted él ella	se siente	ustedes ellos ellas	se sienten

Oraciones con si (pág. 60)

To say what happens if a condition arises, use a clause with si.

Si tengo fiebre, no voy a clase.

El imperativo afirmativo de tú. Verbos regulares (pág. 68)

CAMINAR	COMER	ESCRIBIR
camina	come	escribe

DESAFÍO 1

5 **¿La hueles?** Answer the questions using the words in parentheses.

Modelo ¿Hueles la carne? (no - la pizza) → *No, no la huelo. Huelo la pizza.*

1. ¿Ven ustedes los partidos de fútbol? (no - los documentales)
2. ¿Oyes la radio por la noche? (no - mis CD)
3. ¿Hueles la fruta? (no - el café)
4. ¿Dices tu apellido en clase? (no - el nombre)

DESAFÍO 2

6 **Rutinas.** Write sentences using the appropriate form of the verbs.

Modelo tú - cepillarse los dientes con frecuencia
        → *Tú te cepillas los dientes con frecuencia.*

1. Mis padres - levantarse muy temprano siempre
2. Mis hermanos y yo - ducharse por la noche
3. Mi hermana mayor - maquillarse todos los días
4. Mi abuelo - afeitarse cuatro veces por semana

DESAFÍO 3

7 **¿Qué haces si...?** What do you do in these situations? Write sentences.

Modelo sentirse débil → *Si me siento débil, descanso y como bien.*

1. doler la cabeza   2. sentirse enfermo(a)   3. encontrarse mal   4. doler los oídos

DESAFÍO 4

8 **Órdenes.** What would you say to the characters in these situations? Use a verb from the box to write a command. Include a reflexive or direct object pronoun.

| ducharse |
| comprar |
| leer |
| acostarse |

Modelo Andy tiene un examen a las 9 de la mañana → *¡Levántate!*

1. Mack tiene un correo electrónico de la madre de Tim.
2. Tess tiene mucho sueño.
3. Tim está muy sucio: pelo, cara, manos...
4. Janet necesita unos medicamentos.

CULTURA

9 **Conoce España.** Answer the questions.

1. Where can you see the influence of Arabic culture in Spain today?
2. What do you know about the *Camino de Santiago*?
3. What historic event did Picasso want to reflect in his painting *Guernica*?

Un póster sobre
hábitos
de higiene

In this project you will make a healthy habits poster.

PASO 1 Escribe una lista de los principales hábitos de higiene

Make a chart of your hygiene habits, and indicate how often you practice each one.

PASO 2 Haz una encuesta para conocer los hábitos de higiene de tu grupo

- In a group, interview your classmates about their good hygiene habits (*hábitos de higiene*). Then make a list of what they do.

Modelo

A. *¿Qué hábitos de higiene tienes?*
B. *Ducharme, lavarme la cara…*

- Interview your classmates again to discover how often they do each activity and complete a chart like the one below. Use frequency expressions from the box.

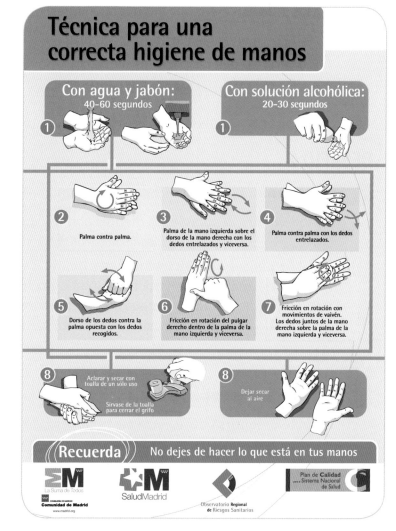

Técnica para una correcta higiene de manos

Con agua y jabón: 40–60 segundos

Con solución alcohólica: 20–30 segundos

② Palma contra palma.

③ Palma de la mano izquierda sobre el dorso de la mano derecha con los dedos entrelazados y viceversa.

④ Palma contra palma con los dedos entrelazados.

⑤ Dorso de los dedos contra la palma opuesta con los dedos recogidos.

⑥ Fricción en rotación del pulgar derecho dentro de la palma de la mano izquierda y viceversa.

⑦ Fricción en rotación con movimientos de vaivén. Los dedos juntos de la mano derecha sobre la palma de la mano izquierda y viceversa.

⑧ Aclarar y secar con toalla de un sólo uso. Sírvase de la toalla para cerrar el grifo

⑧ Dejar secar al aire

Recuerda No dejes de hacer lo que está en tus manos

EM La Suma de Todos · Comunidad de Madrid
SaludMadrid
Observatorio Regional de Riesgos Sanitarios
Plan de Calidad para el Sistema Nacional de Salud

¿Con qué frecuencia te lavas el pelo?

Yo me lavo el pelo tres veces a la semana.

Hábito de higiene	Frecuencia
Lavarse el pelo	Tres veces a la semana

Expresiones de frecuencia
nunca
a veces
todos los días
una vez a la semana
(dos) veces a la semana

PASO 3 Analiza los hábitos de tu grupo

- Find out the recommended frequency for each activity. Consult your school nurse or do research.

  A. *¿Con qué frecuencia hay que cepillarse los dientes?*

  B. *Dos o tres veces al día.*

- How healthy are your habits? Compare the information in your chart with your research to draw conclusions.

  Nosotros nos cepillamos los dientes una vez al día. Eso no está bien. Hay que cepillarse los dientes dos o tres veces al día.

PASO 4 Crea tu póster:
Diez hábitos de higiene

- Select the ten most important habits on your chart and illustrate them.
- Express each habit as a command. Include frequency expressions.

DIEZ HÁBITOS DE HIGIENE

1. Lavarse las manos

   Lávate las manos antes de comer.

2. Cepillarse los dientes

Unidad 5

Autoevaluación

¿Qué has aprendido en esta unidad?

Complete these activities to evaluate how well you can communicate in Spanish.

Evaluate your skills. For each item, say Very well, Well, or I need more practice.

a. Can you talk about your body?

  ▶ Ask your partner what part of the body he or she uses to smell a flower, hear a CD, or touch a pet.

  ▶ Ask your partner to say what body parts are used to eat a sandwich and to get dressed.

b. Can you talk about healthy habits?

  ▶ Ask your partner how often he or she takes a shower and goes to bed at midnight.

  ▶ Tell your partner three things he or she should do to stay healthy.

c. Can you report a pain or an ailment?

  ▶ Role-play with a partner. Pretend to be sick or have a pain in a part of your body.

  Look at your partner and ask how he or she feels. Ask what pain(s) or what ailment he or she has.

d. Can you suggest a remedy for common pains or ailments?

  ▶ Discuss with your partner what you usually do when you have a health problem.

Unidad 6

Estados Unidos

Desafíos en casa

DESAFÍO 2

DESAFÍO 1

▶ **To give commands and advice**

Vocabulario
El trabajo

Gramática
Imperativo afirmativo.
Verbos irregulares

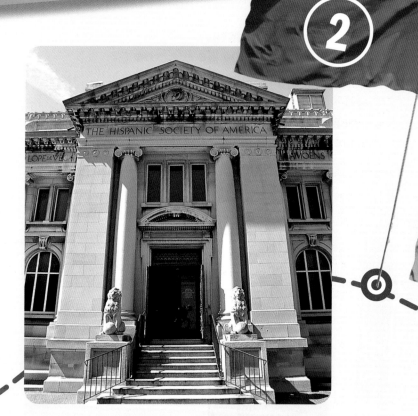

Museo de la Sociedad Hispánica
de Nueva York

Parque del
Dominó
de Miami

▶ **To express intention**

Vocabulario
Los pasatiempos

Gramática
Ir a + infinitivo.
Expresiones temporales
de futuro

El Dodger Stadium

DESAFÍO ③

▶ **To express the progress of an action**

Vocabulario
Tiempo libre

Gramática
El presente continuo
El gerundio

Los premios *Grammy* latinos

DESAFÍO ④

▶ **To talk about sports**

Vocabulario
Los deportes

Gramática
Verbos con raíz irregular (*u > ue*)

En Washington DC

The four pairs meet in Washington DC, where they will receive tasks from Mr. and Mrs. Goldberg, their American hosts.

¡Bienvenidos! Yo soy John Goldberg. Soy abogado. Trabajo en una oficina.

¡Hola! Yo soy Jane Goldberg. Me dedico a las computadoras. Soy ingeniera.

Hola. Yo también quiero ser ingeniera.

Yo quiero ser entrenador de fútbol americano y médico.

Diana quiere ser fotógrafa. Nos está tomando fotos.

Yo quiero jugar al tenis toda mi vida. Voy a ser un jugador profesional.

Una sonrisa, por favor. ¡Perfecto, Tess! ¡Muy bien, Patricia!

1 ¿Comprendes?

▶ **Une.** Match each question with the corresponding answer.

A

1. ¿Qué es el señor Goldberg?
2. ¿Dónde trabaja el señor Goldberg?
3. ¿A qué se dedica la señora Goldberg?
4. ¿Qué quiere ser Andy?
5. ¿Qué quiere ser Diana?

B

a. En una oficina.
b. A las computadoras.
c. Es abogado.
d. Fotógrafa.
e. Médico y entrenador.

EXPRESIONES ÚTILES

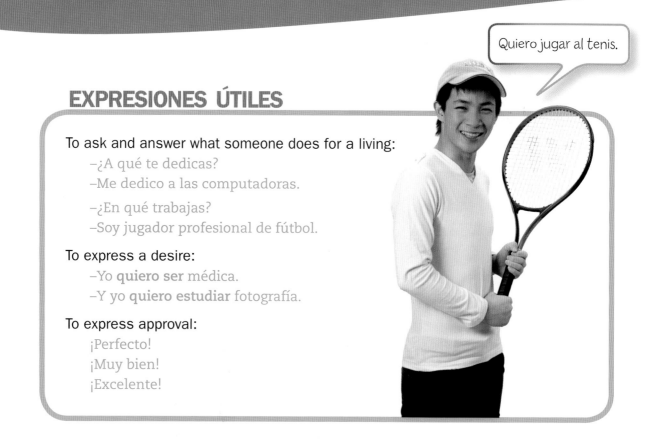

Quiero jugar al tenis.

To ask and answer what someone does for a living:
–¿A qué te dedicas?
–Me dedico a las computadoras.

–¿En qué trabajas?
–Soy jugador profesional de fútbol.

To express a desire:
–Yo **quiero ser** médica.
–Y yo **quiero estudiar** fotografía.

To express approval:
¡Perfecto!
¡Muy bien!
¡Excelente!

2 **¿Qué expresión usas?**

▶ **Completa.** Complete the dialogues with the missing words.

1. –¿A qué te ___1___ ?
–Soy ingeniera.

2. –¿En qué ___2___ ?
– ___3___ entrenador de tenis.

3. –Yo quiero ser ingeniero.
–Yo también. ___4___ estudiar Ingeniería.

4. –Hablo español, inglés y francés.
–¡ ___5___ !

3 **Mucho gusto, señor Goldberg**

▶ **Escribe.** Tim sits down for an interview with Mr. Goldberg. Use the expressions above and the dialogue to create a comic strip with Tim and Mr. Goldberg.

▶ **Representa.** With a partner, perform your comic strip for the class.

¿Qué quieres ser, Tim?

Quiero ser jugador de tenis.

¿Quién ganará?

4 **Los desafíos**

▶ **Habla.** What challenge will each pair face? Think about this question and discuss it with your classmates.

DESAFÍO ①

Una partida de dominó

Tim y Mack

DESAFÍO ②

Una noche en el museo

Diana y Rita

DESAFÍO ③

Fotos de famosos

Tess y Patricia

DESAFÍO ④

¡Vamos a jugar!

Andy y Janet

5 **Las votaciones**

▶ **Decide.** You decide. You will vote to choose the most multicultural challenge. Who do you think will win?

Multicultural

Una partida de dominó

Tim and Mack are in Miami. Their task is to win a dominoes game in a Little Havana competition. But they don't know most of the players are world-class contenders! What a difficult task!

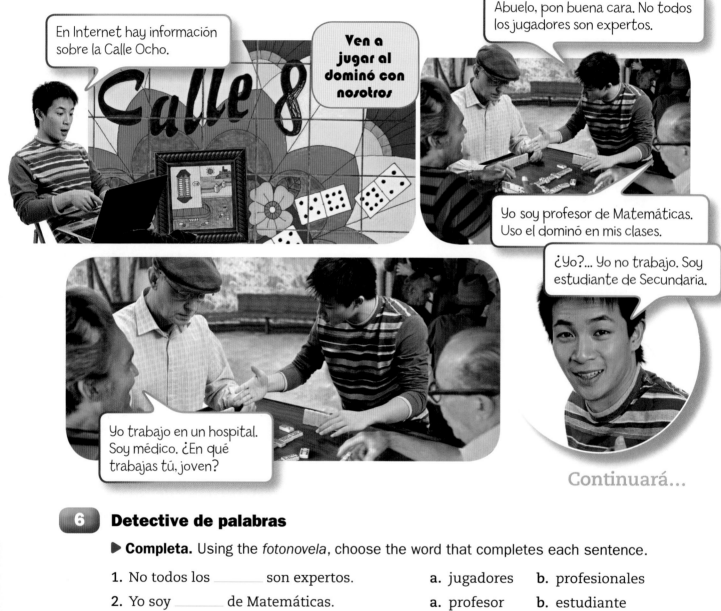

En Internet hay información sobre la Calle Ocho.

Ven a jugar al dominó con nosotros

Abuelo, pon buena cara. No todos los jugadores son expertos.

Yo soy profesor de Matemáticas. Uso el dominó en mis clases.

¿Yo?... Yo no trabajo. Soy estudiante de Secundaria.

Yo trabajo en un hospital. Soy médico. ¿En qué trabajas tú, joven?

Continuará...

6 ## Detective de palabras

▶ **Completa.** Using the *fotonovela*, choose the word that completes each sentence.

1. No todos los _____ son expertos.   a. jugadores   b. profesionales
2. Yo soy _____ de Matemáticas.   a. profesor   b. estudiante
3. Trabajo en un _____.   a. hospital   b. médico
4. Soy _____ de Secundaria.   a. jugador   b. estudiante

▶ **Responde.** Answer the questions according to the dialogue.

1. ¿Quién usa el dominó en sus clases?
2. ¿Dónde trabaja el médico de la foto?
3. ¿Quién no trabaja? ¿Por qué?

7   Las mujeres también juegan

 ▶ **Escucha y escribe.** In Miami, Tim and Mack meet an interesting group of players. Listen to the conversations and write the name of the person and her profession.

> **a.** mesera de un restaurante cubano

> **b.** profesora de Matemáticas

> **c.** empresaria de una tienda de ropa

> **d.** doctora de Medicina Familiar

8   Ven a la Calle Ocho

▶ **Completa.** Before the tournament, Tim writes a blog for domino lovers. Complete his text with the appropriate forms of the verb *ser*.

> El Parque del Dominó
>
> 5 de mayo. Miami
>
> Mi abuelo y yo ___1___ de California. Sabemos jugar al dominó, pero no ___2___ expertos. El Parque del Dominó ___3___ el escenario de nuestra prueba en Miami. Ustedes ___4___ muy buenos jugadores y yo no ___5___ un jugador profesional, ¡pero vamos a ganar!

 **CULTURA**

La Calle Ocho

La Calle Ocho es la calle principal de la Pequeña Habana, un importante barrio hispano de Miami. En esta calle hay restaurantes, teatros, galerías y negocios de personas de origen cubano. Muchos cubano-americanos se reúnen (*meet*) para conversar (*talk*) y jugar al dominó en el parque Máximo Gómez, conocido como «Parque del Dominó».

9   **Piensa.** Why do communities provide public forums for cultural entertainment such as Miami's Maximo Gomez Park?

Vocabulario

El trabajo

Las profesiones

¿En qué trabajas?

Soy **directora** de un hospital. Soy **médica**.

Lugares de trabajo

Trabajo en una **oficina**.

Somos empleadas de una **fábrica**.

Trabajo en una **escuela**.

Trabajo en una **obra**.

la abogada — el secretario — la entrenadora — el maestro — la ingeniera

10 ¿De quién es?

▶ **Habla.** With a partner, take turns asking and answering about the profession with which these items are associated.

Modelo 1. A. ¿De quién es el portafolios?
        B. Es de la abogada.

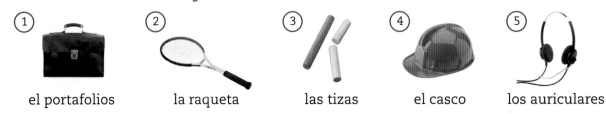

① el portafolios   ② la raqueta   ③ las tizas   ④ el casco   ⑤ los auriculares

▶ **Habla.** Now ask and answer questions with your partner about the places where the professions above are performed.

Modelo A. ¿Dónde trabaja la abogada?
        B. La abogada trabaja en una oficina.

11 Futuros profesionales

▶ Escucha y escribe. The characters are talking about their future careers. Listen to their statements and report the information.

Modelo 1. *Janet quiere ser maestra de Música.*

① Janet

② Tim

③ Diana

④ Andy

⑤ Tess

12 Tareas y profesiones

▶ Escribe. Write what professional would do each of the following tasks.

1. dirigir la construcción del aeropuerto
2. enseñar a los estudiantes
3. organizar la agenda del día
4. preparar a los atletas
5. defender a sus clientes
6. curar a los enfermos

▶ Escribe. Write sentences about each professional's job.

Modelo 1. el ingeniero
→ *Los ingenieros dirigen la construcción del aeropuerto.*

▶ Habla. Now talk with a classmate about the professions above. Which would you prefer to have and why? Which would you not like to have?

COMUNIDADES

PROFESIONES BILINGÜES

En muchas profesiones es necesario hablar dos o más lenguas. Abogados, enfermeros, médicos y policías son ejemplos de personas que pueden usar el español en su trabajo diario. Si hablas varias lenguas, puedes tener más y mejores trabajos.

13 Piensa. What jobs in your community require speaking a second language? How might you use Spanish in your future profession?

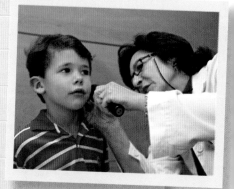

Gramática

Imperativo afirmativo. Verbos irregulares

- Some common tú commands have irregular conjugations.

VERBOS IRREGULARES. IMPERATIVO

tener (to have)	hacer (to do)	poner (to put)	venir (to come)	salir (to leave)	ser (to be)	decir (to say)	ir (to go)
ten	haz	pon	ven	sal	sé	di	ve

Ten un buen día.	**Sal** de tu cuarto, por favor.
Haz una ensalada.	**Sé** responsable.
Pon el libro en la estantería.	**Di** la verdad.
Ana, **ven** a la cocina, por favor.	**Ve** a casa de tus abuelos.

- To form the tú command of tener, hacer, poner, venir, and salir, detach the infinitive ending:

  ten-~~er~~ → ten   hac-~~er~~ → haz   pon-~~er~~ → pon
  ven-~~ir~~ → ven   sal-~~ir~~ → sal

- If the tú form of a verb is irregular in the present tense, it is also irregular in the tú command.

  tú empiezas → empieza   tú duermes → duerme

- Remember that object and reflexive pronouns follow and are attached to the command.

  Hay que poner la mesa. Pon**la**, por favor.   Haz**le** una hamburguesa.

14   **Piensa.** How would you know if someone was using sal to mean *salt* or *leave*?

15   **Consejos de los profesionales**

▶ **Completa.** Using the verbs above, complete these professional recommendations with the appropriate command form.

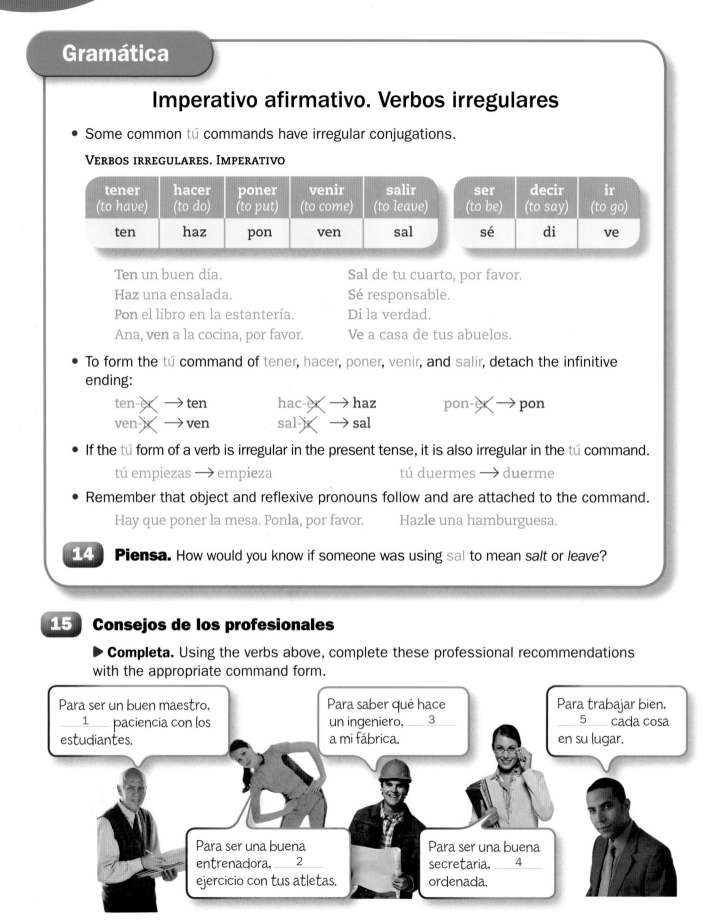

Para ser un buen maestro, ___1___ paciencia con los estudiantes.

Para ser una buena entrenadora, ___2___ ejercicio con tus atletas.

Para saber qué hace un ingeniero, ___3___ a mi fábrica.

Para ser una buena secretaria, ___4___ ordenada.

Para trabajar bien, ___5___ cada cosa en su lugar.

16 La jueza Estrella Rodríguez

▶ **Escucha y decide.** Listen to Judge Rodríguez talking to Tim at a school Career Fair, and point out which pieces of advice Tim receives.

1. Sé honesto.
2. Ve a los eventos culturales de la Calle Ocho.
3. Sé una persona responsable.
4. Pon atención a las personas de tu comunidad.
5. Haz tus tareas todos los días.
6. Di siempre la verdad.

Estudia mucho, Tim.

17 Consejos para la vida diaria

▶ **Escribe.** Some friends ask you for advice. In each case, answer their question using a command form and an object pronoun.

1. ¿Dónde pongo los libros? - en la estantería
2. ¿Cuándo hago mis tareas? - después de clase
3. ¿Cuándo saco la basura? - antes de cenar
4. ¿Dónde hago deporte? - en el gimnasio de la escuela
5. ¿Dónde compro la ropa? - en el centro comercial
6. ¿Cuándo ordeno mi dormitorio? - durante el fin de semana

¿Dónde pongo los libros?

Ponlos en la estantería.

CULTURA

Cristina Saralegui

La periodista *(journalist)* Cristina Saralegui es famosa en todo el mundo hispano gracias a su programa de televisión *El show de Cristina*. Cristina es de origen cubano y vive en Miami. Para ella la clave del éxito es «hablar claro, hablar con mi acento, con mi corazón...».

18 Piensa. How does being a talk-show host and a magazine editor contribute to Cristina's influence on Hispanic Americans? Would you like to be in her position?

▶ **TU DESAFÍO** Use the website to learn more about Cristina Saralegui.

Comunicación

19 **Héroes de la comunidad**

▶ **Lee y habla.** A middle school in Miami is hosting a Career Day. Read the announcement, then talk with a partner about why you would attend this event. Which professionals would you like to talk to? What questions would you ask?

Modelo A. ¿Quieres asistir al evento?
B. Sí, quiero asistir porque quiero hablar con un ingeniero...

Héroes de la comunidad visitan la escuela

Hoy, martes 23, trabajadores de la comunidad visitan nuestra escuela. El evento «Todos podemos ser héroes» es a las doce del mediodía en el gimnasio. Ven y habla con médicos, enfermeras, ingenieros, secretarios, empresarios y empleados de fábricas. ¡Aprovecha esta oportunidad para empezar a decidir tu futuro!

▶ **Escucha y escribe.** Some of the guests for this event have left messages for the principal. Listen and note who is attending and who is not.

1. Elena Rosas
2. Fabián Candelas
3. Esperanza Esparza
4. Juan Hernández
5. Cristóbal Barrios
6. Marisa Jiménez

20 **Un estudiante organizado**

▶ **Escribe.** You are organizing a Career Fair in your school. Draw up a schedule for seven community workers.

Modelo

Agenda para el evento

1. Maestro de español. Cafetería, a las 10 de la mañana.
2. Ingeniero. Biblioteca, a las 11:15 de la mañana.

¿Quieres hablar con el maestro de Español?

Sí, quiero trabajar con niños y me gusta el español.

Ve a la cafetería. El maestro habla a las diez de la mañana.

▶ **Habla.** With a partner, role-play host and student. Use your schedule and make sure to include informal commands in your conversation.

21 El consejero informal

▶ **Lee y escribe.** You write the advice column in your class's newspaper. Read the e-mail that a classmate has sent you and take notes on the student's problems.

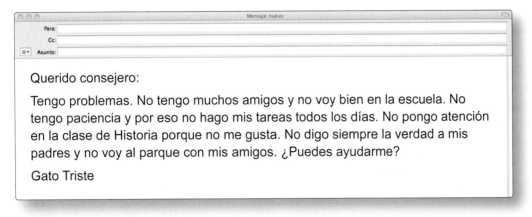

Mensaje nuevo

Para:
Cc:
Asunto:

Querido consejero:

Tengo problemas. No tengo muchos amigos y no voy bien en la escuela. No tengo paciencia y por eso no hago mis tareas todos los días. No pongo atención en la clase de Historia porque no me gusta. No digo siempre la verdad a mis padres y no voy al parque con mis amigos. ¿Puedes ayudarme?

Gato Triste

▶ **Escribe y representa.** Write a response to Gato Triste. Then role-play the situation with a partner using irregular commands.

Modelo A. *No voy bien en la escuela.*
           B. *Pon más atención y estudia más.*

Final del desafío

¿Qué hago, Tim? ¿Con qué ficha salgo?

Sal con la ficha nueve y ocho.

22 Juego de dominó

▶ **Crea y escribe.** You have to help Tim and Mack win the dominoes game! Create your own dominoes set, using professions and related words instead of numbers. Write the rules to your new game in Spanish, using the irregular *tú* commands (*pon, ten, haz,* etc.).

▶ **Juega.** Now play your dominoes game with a partner.

 → TU DESAFÍO Earn points for your own challenge! Listen to the questions for your *Minientrevista Desafío 1* on the website and write your answers.

Una noche en el museo

Diana and Rita are at The Hispanic Society of America Museum in New York City. Their task is to spend the whole night in the museum. What will they do to pass the time?

> ¡Toda la noche en el museo! ¡Me gusta la prueba! ¿Qué vamos a hacer?

> ¡Yo voy a ver muchas obras de arte! Mira este cuadro de Joaquín Sorolla.

> Yo voy a escribir mensajes a mis amigos y voy a hablar por teléfono con ellos.

> ¡¿Qué?! ¿No vamos a poder hablar por teléfono ni usar la computadora durante toda la noche?

> ¡Pero Diana, no podemos usar el teléfono ni la computadora!

Continuará...

23 Detective de palabras

▶ **Completa.** Diana and Rita want to do different things in the museum. What are their plans? Complete their statements.

RITA: Yo voy a ___1___ .

DIANA: Yo voy a ___2___ y voy a ___3___ .

▶ **Escribe.** What are your plans for today? Write three sentences to express them.

Modelo *Hoy voy a jugar al fútbol con mis amigos.*

24 **¿Qué quieren hacer?**

▶ **Escribe.** Using the *fotonovela*, write what Diana and Rita want to do, and tell whether they can do each activity or not.

Modelo *Rita quiere ver obras de arte. Puede ver muchas obras de arte en el museo.*

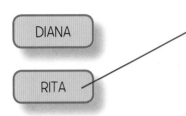

DIANA

RITA

ver obras de arte
escribir mensajes a sus amigos
hablar por teléfono con sus amigos
usar la computadora

25 **Vamos a pasear por Nueva York**

▶ **Escucha y une.** Diana and Rita are talking about their plans in New York. Listen and match the people in column A with the actions in column B.

Ⓐ

1. Diana y Rita
2. Diana
3. Rita
4. Los padres de Diana
5. Rita y Patricia
6. Tim

Ⓑ

a. va a tomar muchas fotos.
b. van a ir a Central Park.
c. va a ir a la Estatua de la Libertad.
d. va a visitar el Metropolitan Museum.
e. van a ir a Nueva York en verano.
f. van a ir de compras a Times Square.

CULTURA

La Sociedad Hispánica de América

La Sociedad Hispánica de América es una organización fundada en 1904 para promover las culturas hispanas. Tiene una importante colección de arte y objetos culturales de España, Portugal, Latinoamérica y las islas Filipinas. Entre los artistas más famosos con obras en el museo están Diego Velázquez, Bartolomé Murillo y Francisco de Goya. También hay libros y manuscritos raros y especiales.

26 **Piensa.** What items would you choose to put in a museum that promotes American culture, arts, and literature?

Vocabulario

Los pasatiempos

bailar

cantar

tocar
el piano

actuar

pintar

caminar

hacer deporte
practicar deportes

montar
en bicicleta

nadar

viajar

escuchar
música

leer
un libro

escribir
mensajes

27 **Una chica muy interesante**

▶ **Escucha y clasifica.** Listen as Diana talks about her likes and dislikes and classify her activities and pastimes in a table like the one below.

Me gusta mucho	Me gusta	No me gusta	No me gusta nada
	bailar		

▶ **Escribe y habla.** Use a similar table to classify your own likes and dislikes. Then talk with a partner about them.

Modelo *No me gusta nada pintar. ¿A ti te gusta?*

28 ¿Adónde voy?

▶ **Habla.** Ask your partner about the places below, using the verb *poder*, and say whether you like or don't like the activity mentioned. Take turns.

Modelo A. ¿Qué podemos hacer en el jardín?
           B. Podemos leer.
           A. ¡Qué bueno! Me gusta mucho leer.

1. En Times Square…
2. En Central Park…
3. En la Estatua de la Libertad…
4. En la Manhattan Artistic Academy…
5. En el jardín del hotel…

▶ **Escribe.** When, where, and with whom do you do the activities above in your city? Write sentences.

Modelo En verano, leo buenos libros en la biblioteca con mis hermanos.

29 Tu favorito

▶ **Escribe.** Choose and rank some activities from the *Vocabulario* according to your preference. Write five sentences.

Modelo Me gusta más bailar que hacer deporte.

▶ **Habla.** In a group, talk with your classmates and compare your choices.

Modelo A. A mí me gusta más bailar que hacer deporte. ¿Y a ustedes?
           B. A mí me gusta mucho hacer deporte. Me gusta jugar al tenis…

CONEXIONES: INGLÉS

Las palabras prestadas

El español y el inglés intercambian palabras y expresiones. Por ejemplo, los nombres de algunos deportes, como el *golf*, el *voleibol* y el *fútbol*, vienen del inglés. En cambio, las palabras en inglés *rodeo*, *lasso* y *salsa* tienen su origen en el español.

30 **Piensa.** Do you know any other words in English that come from Spanish? What can we learn about the culture of a place whose words we have borrowed?

Gramática

Ir a + infinitivo

- To express the intention to do something, use this structure:

  | ir a + infinitivo | Ellos **van a trabajar** en Nueva York.   Yo **voy a viajar** a México.

  The structure ***ir a*** + infinitive is one way to express the future.

- Notice that only ir is conjugated; the second verb remains in the infinitive.

  Nosotras **vamos a escuchar** música.

Expresiones temporales de futuro

- When you express intention or future plans, you can use some adverbs:

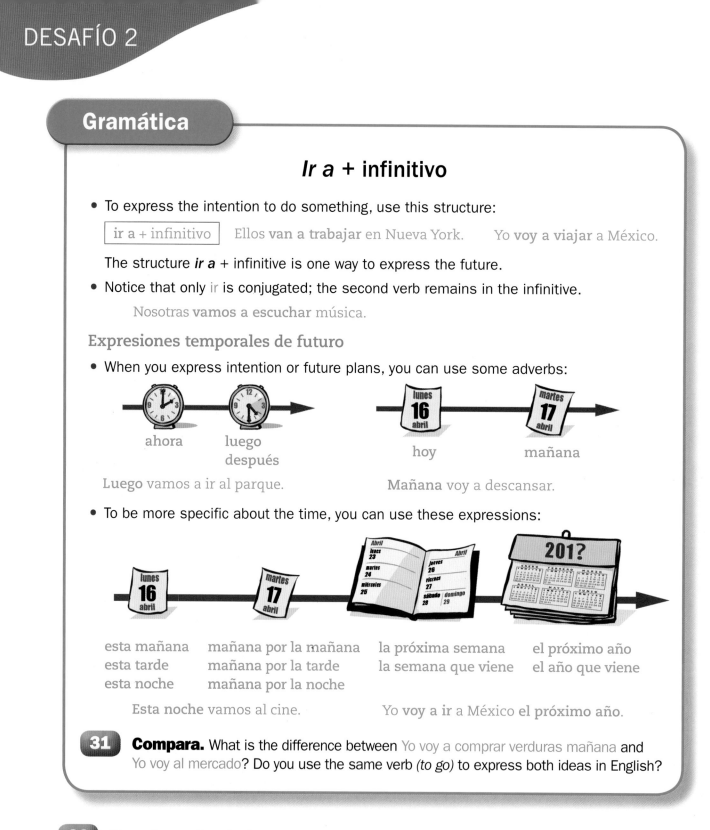

ahora   luego   hoy   mañana
          después

Luego vamos a ir al parque.   **Mañana** voy a descansar.

- To be more specific about the time, you can use these expressions:

esta mañana   mañana por la mañana   la próxima semana   el próximo año
esta tarde   mañana por la tarde   la semana que viene   el año que viene
esta noche   mañana por la noche

Esta noche vamos al cine.   Yo **voy a ir** a México **el próximo año**.

31 **Compara.** What is the difference between Yo voy a comprar verduras mañana and Yo voy al mercado? Do you use the same verb *(to go)* to express both ideas in English?

32 **Nuestro calendario**

▶ **Escribe.** Read Diana's notes and write what people are going to do.

Modelo Próxima semana. Tess al parque.
        → *La próxima semana Tess va a ir al parque.*

1. Hoy, 2:00 p. m. Todos al restaurante.
2. Hoy, 7:00 p. m. Yo al gimnasio.
3. Mañana, 8:00 p. m. Tim a la biblioteca.
4. Esta tarde, 6:00 p. m. Rita y yo al cine.

33 **Los planes de Rita**

▶ **Escucha e identifica.** What activities will Rita be doing in New York?
Listen and write the letter of each activity in the order you hear.

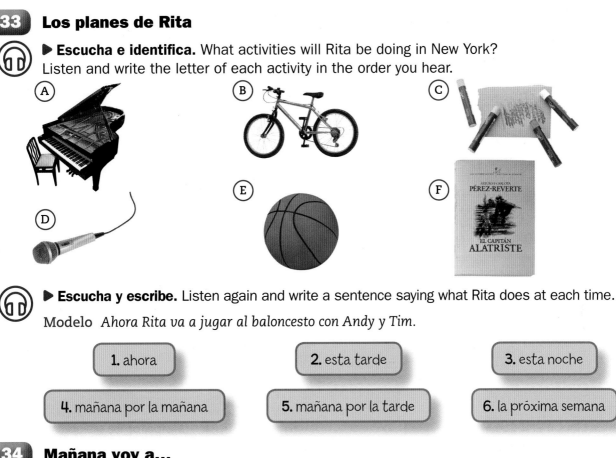

(A) (B) (C) (D) (E) (F)

▶ **Escucha y escribe.** Listen again and write a sentence saying what Rita does at each time.

Modelo *Ahora Rita va a jugar al baloncesto con Andy y Tim.*

1. ahora

2. esta tarde

3. esta noche

4. mañana por la mañana

5. mañana por la tarde

6. la próxima semana

34 **Mañana voy a...**

▶ **Escribe.** What are your plans for tomorrow morning, afternoon, and evening?
Write sentences telling two things you will do at each time.

▶ **Habla.** Now talk with two classmates about your plans. Who else is going to do
the same things as you?

COMUNIDADES

CENTRAL PARK

Central Park es un famoso parque de Nueva York. Ofrece
muchas actividades para jóvenes y mayores. Visitantes
de todo el mundo pasan tiempo allí, porque pueden
caminar, ver animales, asistir al teatro o a conciertos.
Central Park es un oasis en medio de la ciudad.

35 **Compara.** Do you have something like Central Park where you live?
Where do people go in your community for outdoor activities?
Do visitors from other countries ever go there?

Comunicación

36 Actividades en el parque

▶ **Lee y escribe.** Read the advertisement. Then write an itinerary for Diana at the celebration. Make sure to tell her what she is going to do at each place.

Modelo *Esta noche vas a…*

▶ **Escucha y escribe.** Listen to the message Diana left for Rita. Decide which Hispanic Day activities they are going to do.

Modelo *Diana y Rita van a ir al concierto de música tropical para bailar y escuchar música latina.*

LOS HISPANOS ♥ NY

¡La Gran Manzana está de fiesta!

¡Celebra el Día de la Hispanidad en Central Park! Esta noche vamos a celebrar un concierto de música tropical. ¡Vas a mover tu cuerpo con los ritmos del merengue y la salsa! Mañana por la mañana vamos a asistir a una exposición de esculturas de formas y colores extraordinarios.

También vamos a celebrar un torneo de juegos de mesa. Después vamos a tener un almuerzo con comida latinoamericana.

¿Quieres venir? Puedes comprar tus boletos en el Museo de la Sociedad Hispánica de América.

---

37 Un guía neoyorquino

▶ **Habla.** You are volunteering as a guide in New York. Your partner will tell you what a group of tourists are going to do this afternoon. Use the information to suggest where they can go.

Modelo señora López - leer un libro

1. patricia - pintar
2. los empresarios - bailar
3. yo - nadar
4. la profesora de música - caminar y ver animales
5. nosotros - ver cuadros de pintores hispanos
6. todos - escuchar música latina

La señora López va a leer un libro esta tarde.

Ella puede leerlo en Central Park.

38 Tengo curiosidad

▶ **Escribe.** What are your classmates' future plans? Write five interview questions about the things they intend to do in the near and distant future. Use a different time expression in each.

Modelo *¿Vas a escribir correos electrónicos hoy?*

▶ **Habla.** Use your questions to interview three classmates. Report your findings to the class.

39 **Las vacaciones ideales**

▶ **Habla.** In a small group, talk about where you are going to travel during your next vacation and what you are going to do there. Tell when you will do each thing.

¿Qué van a hacer el próximo verano?

Vamos a ir a California.

Yo voy a nadar en el océano.

Mi hermano y yo vamos a hacer deportes acuáticos.

▶ **Escribe.** Write an e-mail summarizing the plans for your friends.

Modelo

Mensaje nuevo
Para:
Cc:
Asunto:

¡Hola a todos!

El próximo verano yo voy a…

Final del desafío

Esta noche voy a…

Y yo…

También vamos a…

40 **¡Qué museo más interesante!**

▶ **Escribe.** Complete the speech bubbles according to the photos. Then add yourself into the scenes of the challenge. What will you do in the museum all night?

▶ **Representa.** Act out this ending for your classmates.

Fotos de famosos

Tess and Patricia are at the Latin Grammy Awards in San Antonio, Texas. Their task is to take photos of the musicians at the event. Will they find all the musicians in time to take their pictures before the show begins?

¡No lo puedo creer! ¡Estamos en los *Grammy* latinos! ¡Hoy vamos a un gran concierto!

¡Es increíble! Yo veo los *Grammy* latinos en la televisión todos los años.

¡Mira, allí está Juanes. ¿Tienes la cámara?

¡Rápido, Tess! ¡Juanes está saliendo! ¡Estás perdiendo la oportunidad!

Sí, la tengo en la bolsa... creo... La estoy buscando...

Continuará...

41   Detective de palabras

▶ **Relaciona.** Match each phrase with a picture.

1. ver la televisión
2. ir a un concierto
3. tomar una foto

Ⓐ   Ⓑ   Ⓒ

▶ **Habla.** How much do you like to do these activities? How often do you do them? Compare your answer with a partner's.

Modelo   A. ¿Te gusta ver la televisión?   A. ¿Cuándo ves la televisión?
            B. Sí, *me gusta mucho ver la televisión.*   B. *La veo todas las tardes.*

42 ¿Comprendes?

▶ **Escribe.** Answer the questions.

1. ¿Dónde están Tess y Patricia?
2. ¿A qué espectáculo asisten hoy?
3. ¿De quién toman fotos?
4. ¿Qué está buscando Tess en su bolsa?

43 ¿Qué estás haciendo?

▶ **Escribe.** Tess thinks that the people below are doing a certain thing, but Patricia disagrees. Write a sentence based on each picture.

Modelo   TESS: *Marcos está comiendo **una empanada**.*
PATRICIA: *¡No! Marcos está comiendo **una hamburguesa**.*

La familia está paseando en **coche**.

Sara está tocando **la guitarra**.

Rafa está jugando en **el parque**.

Susi está bebiendo **agua**.

Tom está apagando **la computadora**.

CULTURA

Los *Grammy* latinos

Desde el año 2000, el *Grammy* latino es un premio muy prestigioso para los cantantes, músicos o grupos musicales latinos. La gala de los *Grammy* latinos se celebra todos los años en otoño. El músico más premiado es el cantante colombiano Juanes, con 17 *grammys*.

44 **Piensa.** Have you ever seen the Latin Grammy Awards? Which Latin singer is your favorite?

▶→ TU DESAFÍO   Visit the website to learn more about the Latin Grammy Awards.

Vocabulario

Tiempo libre

A mí me gusta **escuchar la radio**. Y a ustedes, ¿qué les gusta hacer en su tiempo libre?

A mí me gusta mucho **tomar fotos** y **grabar** con mi cámara.

Yo prefiero **jugar a los videojuegos** y **escribir correos** a mis amigos.

A mí me gusta mucho **ir al cine**. Me gusta **ver películas** de terror.

tomar fotos
la cámara de fotos

grabar
la cámara de video

ver una película
la película

jugar a los videojuegos
el videojuego

45 **En mi tiempo libre**

▶ **Relaciona.** Match each activity with the related object.

1. grabar
2. escuchar
3. tomar
4. ver
5. jugar

Ⓐ Ⓑ Ⓒ Ⓓ Ⓔ

46 **¡Qué suerte!**

▶ **Escucha y escribe.** The local electronics store is giving away free gadgets to the first fifty customers. Listen and write what the characters say they will do with their item.

Modelo   las noticias → *Patricia quiere la radio para oír las noticias.*

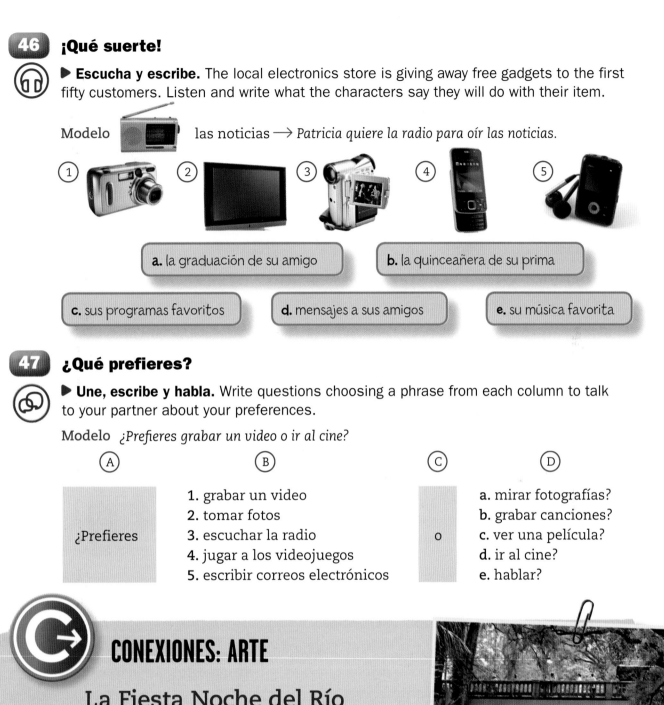

① ② ③ ④ ⑤

a. la graduación de su amigo   **b.** la quinceañera de su prima

c. sus programas favoritos   **d.** mensajes a sus amigos   **e.** su música favorita

47 **¿Qué prefieres?**

▶ **Une, escribe y habla.** Write questions choosing a phrase from each column to talk to your partner about your preferences.

Modelo   *¿Prefieres grabar un video o ir al cine?*

Ⓐ   Ⓑ   Ⓒ   Ⓓ

¿Prefieres	1. grabar un video		a. mirar fotografías?
	2. tomar fotos		b. grabar canciones?
	3. escuchar la radio	o	c. ver una película?
	4. jugar a los videojuegos		d. ir al cine?
	5. escribir correos electrónicos		e. hablar?

CONEXIONES: ARTE

La Fiesta Noche del Río

San Antonio es una ciudad del sur de Texas con mucha influencia hispana. La ciudad es famosa por su *River Walk*, o Paseo del Río. El *River Walk* es una zona para pasear y divertirse *(enjoy oneself)* a lo largo del río San Antonio. Hay hoteles, restaurantes, tiendas y teatros. Allí se celebra la Fiesta Noche del Río. Los actores bailan, cantan y actúan según las tradiciones de México, Argentina, España y los Estados Unidos.

48 **Relaciona.** What type of event would you like to attend at the River Walk?

Gramática

El presente continuo

- In Spanish we use the present progressive (presente continuo) to talk about actions that are happening at the moment of speaking.

   –¿Qué estás haciendo, Luis?
   –Estoy escuchando música.

Formación del presente continuo

- The present progressive is formed as follows:

   | estar + gerundio | Pablo **está haciendo** la comida y María **está escribiendo**.

- The gerundio (present participle) is formed by adding these endings to the verb stem:

   1. **-ando** for -ar verbs: escuch~~ar~~ → escuchando
   2. **-iendo** for -er and -ir verbs: hac~~er~~ → haciendo   escrib~~ir~~ → escribiendo

- Notice that in the present progressive, only estar is conjugated.

   VERBO TRABAJAR (TO WORK). PRESENTE CONTINUO

	Singular		Plural
yo	estoy trabajando	nosotros nosotras	estamos trabajando
tú	estás trabajando	vosotros vosotras	estáis trabajando
usted él ella	está trabajando	ustedes ellos ellas	están trabajando

49 **Piensa.** What are some uses of the present progressive in English? How are those similar to or different from the present progressive in Spanish?

50 **Una escuela de arte**

▶**Escucha y escribe.** Listen and write what the people below are studying in performing arts school.

Modelo *Alicia está estudiando baile.*

1. Nelson
2. Beatriz
3. Teresa y Kate
4. Elena
5. Sergio y Héctor

a. fotografía
b. radio
c. televisión
d. música
e. cine

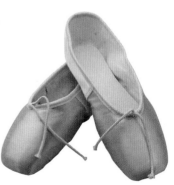

51 Sin palabras

▶ **Representa.** Act out an action from page 112 and see if your classmates can guess what you are doing.

Modelo *¡Estás escuchando música!*

52 Tess, la fotógrafa

▶ **Escribe y habla.** At the Latin Grammys, Tess took this photo for her school newspaper. Write sentences to caption what each person is doing. Then talk with a classmate about each person's actions.

Modelo A. *¿Qué está haciendo María?*
        B. *María está hablando por teléfono.*

CONEXIONES: MÚSICA

La música tejana

Un tipo de música muy popular en Texas y en otros lugares de los Estados Unidos es la música tejana. Los instrumentos principales en la música tejana son el acordeón, el piano eléctrico y la guitarra eléctrica. Un cantante muy famoso de música tejana es Jay Pérez.

53 Piensa y compara.
Have you ever heard *Tejano* music? What are the primary instruments in the music that you like to listen to?

Gramática

El gerundio

- Remember that the present participle (gerundio) is formed by adding the endings -ando or -iendo to the stem of the verb.

  trabaj-ar → trabajando   hac-er → haciendo   escrib-ir → escribiendo

Verbos irregulares en gerundio

- Most present participles are regular. The only irregular ones occur in verbs that have e > i or o > u stem changes.

VERBOS IRREGULARES EN GERUNDIO

E > I		O > U
decir → diciendo	servir → sirviendo	dormir → durmiendo
medir → midiendo	vestir → vistiendo	morir → muriendo
pedir → pidiendo		poder → pudiendo

- When the stem of an -er or -ir verb ends in a vowel, the ending -iendo is written -yendo.

  leer → leyendo   Estoy **leyendo** un libro.
  oír → oyendo   Estamos **oyendo** música.

El gerundio con pronombres objeto y reflexivos

- Object pronouns and reflexive pronouns can either be placed before estar or attached to the present participle.

  Luis **se** está vistiendo.   Luis está vistiéndo**se**.
  Ellas **lo** están diciendo.   Ellas están diciéndo**lo**.

54 **Piensa.** Why might -yendo be a better ending than -iendo for verbs like creer and traer?

55 **¡Está durmiendo!**

▶ **Escucha y completa.** Tess can hear but she can't see what is going on in the crowd. Listen and complete the following sentences to describe the situation. Use the present progressive form of the verbs in the box.

1. Un fotógrafo _____.

2. Un fan _____ una foto a Shakira.

3. Una chica _____ una canción muy bonita.

4. Los chicos del grupo Maná _____.

> dormir
> oír
> vestirse
> pedir

56 **¿Qué estás haciendo?**

▶ **Completa.** Tess and Diana are on the phone talking about their plans for the evening. Fill in the missing present participles in the dialogue.

> TESS: ¡Hola, Diana! ¿Cómo estás? ¿Qué estás ___1___ ?
>   hacer
>
> DIANA: Me estoy ___2___ . ¿Y tú?
>   vestirse
>
> TESS: Estoy ___3___ un libro muy interesante... ¿Cómo está Rita?
>   leer
>
> DIANA: Está mejor, gracias. Es solo un resfriado. Ahora está ___4___ .
>   dormir
> ¿Quieres salir a comer conmigo?
>
> TESS: Hoy no puedo. Mi madre está ___5___ una pizza... ¿Quieres venir?
>   pedir
> Estamos ___6___ el último disco de Juanes. ¡Es fantástico!
>   escuchar

57 **Haciendo todo a la vez**

▶ **Habla.** With a partner, say the things that each person is doing in the photos below.

1. Patricia...   2. Andy...   3. Mack y Tim...

CONEXIONES: HISTORIA Y GEOGRAFÍA

La influencia latina en los Estados Unidos

En los Estados Unidos hay muchos lugares con nombres españoles: ciudades como Los Ángeles, Santa Fe y San Diego; y estados como Florida, Colorado y California. Estos lugares pertenecieron (*belonged*) a España o a México. Hoy conservan los nombres y muchas costumbres latinas.

58 **Piensa.** What are some other place names that have Spanish origins? What do some of these names mean in English?

Comunicación

59 Correos a casa

▶ **Lee y completa.** While traveling around the United States, Tess and Patricia send e-mails to their friends and family. Read the e-mail below and fill in how they are doing. Use the present progressive form.

	Mensaje nuevo	
Para:		
Cc:		
Asunto:		

Queridos papá y hermanos:

¿Cómo estáis? Nosotras lo ___1___ muy bien en este Desafío y ___2___ mucho sobre la
                  pasar   aprender
cultura hispana en los Estados Unidos. Yo ___3___ mucho en español y mamá ___4___
                               hablar   comer
platos muy interesantes.

Todos los compañeros ___5___ muchas fotos. Tim y Andy también ___6___ videos.
                               tomar   grabar

Nos vemos pronto. Estas semanas nos ___7___ con más frecuencia. ¡Qué bien!
                                     comunicarse
Con mucho cariño,

Tess y mamá

60 Hablar de los otros

▶ **Escribe y habla.** Write sentences ordering the clues below. Then ask your partner what each person is doing.

Modelo	💿	El señor Ramírez	escuchar

A. ¿Qué está haciendo el señor Ramírez?
B. El señor Ramírez está escuchando música.

1.		Isabel	ver		4.		ellos	leer	
2.	Elisa		lavarse		5.	tú		cepillarse	
3.		usted	grabar		6.		Teresa	preparar	

61 Adivina qué

▶ **Escucha e identifica.** Listen as the people give clues about what they are doing. According to the clues, guess what each person is doing.

Final del desafío

¡Aquí está mi cámara!

¡Tess, rápido, toma la foto!

Perdón, Juanes, ¿podemos sacarle una foto?

Están esperándome en el teatro. ¡Es muy tarde!

¡Por favor, por favor! Estamos participando en un desafío cultural...

62 ¿Qué pasa en la historia?

▶ **Escribe y representa.** What happens in the last scene? Did Tess and Patricia get the last photo they needed? Write the dialogue and act out the final scene.

¡Vamos a jugar!

Andy and Janet are in Dodger Stadium in Los Angeles, the home of the LA Dodgers. One of them will play with the team and try to hit a home run before time runs out. Who will play? Will he or she hit the ball out of the park?

> ¡Qué difícil, Andy! No juego bien al béisbol.

> Vamos, Janet. Tú juegas mejor que yo.

> ¿Por qué no juegas tú? No tengo ganas de jugar.

> Vale, Janet. ¡Yo juego!

> ¡Voy a jugar! Hay que hacer un jonrón.

> ¡Oh, no!

Continuará...

63 ### Detective de palabras

▶ **Completa.** The sentences below summarize the *fotonovela*. Complete each one with a word from the boxes.

1. Janet _____ al béisbol mejor que Andy.
2. Janet no tiene ganas de _____.
3. Andy _____ primero.
4. Janet va a _____ para hacer un jonrón.

jugar	jugar
juega	juega

64 **¿De qué tiene ganas?**

▶ **Escribe.** What do the people below feel like doing? Write a sentence according to the pictures.

Modelo ¿Andy tiene ganas de comer empanada?
    → *No, Andy **no tiene ganas de** comer empanada.*

1. ¿El entrenador quiere perder tiempo? → 😠

2. ¿Tú y yo queremos jugar en el estadio? → 😋

3. ¿Andy y Tim quieren llevar sus guantes de béisbol? → 😋

4. ¿Los jugadores tienen ganas de ver la televisión? → 😠

5. ¿Tú quieres ver un partido de béisbol hoy? → 😋

6. ¿Ese fan del béisbol tiene ganas de jugar al fútbol? → 😠

> 😠 = no
> 😋 = sí

65 **Para estar en forma**

▶ **Escucha y escribe.** Listen to Janet's fitness plan and write down the advice she gives. You may find help in the box.

Modelo *Janet tiene que hacer ejercicio.*

dormir ocho horas	hacer ejercicio	comer bien
beber agua	tomar jugos de frutas	montar en bicicleta

▶ **Habla.** Now talk with a partner about the advice in the box. Which pieces of advice do you agree with? Which do you follow?

Modelo A. *¿Tú haces ejercicio?*
       B. *Sí, hago ejercicio todos los días.*

 **CULTURA**

El béisbol

El béisbol es un deporte muy popular en los Estados Unidos y en varios países de Latinoamérica, como Venezuela, Cuba y la República Dominicana. Por eso, muchos de los jugadores del Salón de la Fama del Béisbol son hispanos, como Roberto Clemente (Puerto Rico), Orlando Hernández (Cuba) y Rod Carew (Panamá).

66 **Piensa.** What other Spanish-speaking sports figures do you know? What other sports do you enjoy watching?

Vocabulario

Los deportes

Jugar al...

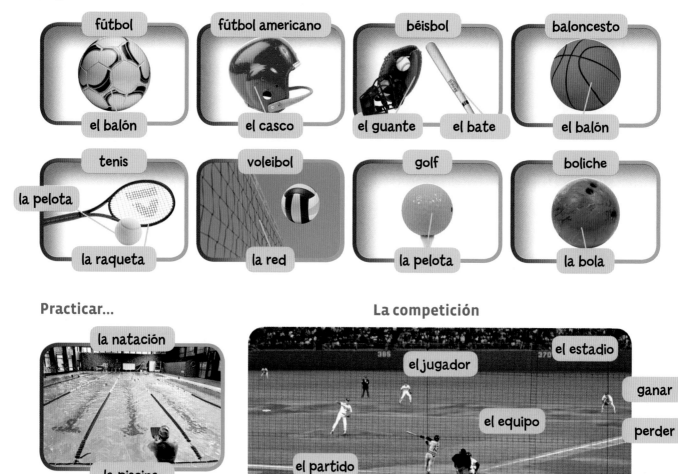

fútbol — el balón

fútbol americano — el casco

béisbol — el guante — el bate

baloncesto — el balón

tenis — la pelota — la raqueta

voleibol — la red

golf — la pelota

boliche — la bola

Practicar...

la natación — la piscina

La competición

el estadio — el jugador — ganar — el equipo — perder — el partido

67 **¿A qué están jugando?**

▶ **Escribe.** Andy and Janet play many sports. Write a sentence for each picture. Use the present progressive.

Modelo *Andy y Janet están jugando al fútbol americano.*

1   2   3   4

68 **¿Qué deporte?**

▶ **Escribe.** Andy and Janet are volunteering as P. E. teachers in a kindergarten class. Help them explain to the children which piece of equipment goes with each sport.

Modelo béisbol - bate ⟶ *Para jugar al béisbol necesitamos un bate.*

1. fútbol americano - casco
2. tenis - raqueta
3. voleibol - red
4. béisbol - guante
5. boliche - bola
6. baloncesto - balón

69 **¿Ver o jugar?**

▶ **Escucha y escribe.** Listen and fill in a chart like the one below with the sports the characters like to watch or play.

	①	②	③	④	⑤	⑥
ver						
jugar						

▶ **Escribe.** Now write sentences to tell which sports each participant likes to watch and which he or she likes to play.

Modelo *A Mack le gusta ver **el baloncesto** y le gusta jugar **al fútbol**.*

▶ **Habla.** Talk with a partner about the sports you like to watch and the ones you play. Share the information with your class.

CULTURA

La popularidad de los deportes

El fútbol es el deporte más popular del mundo. Según las estadísticas, el fútbol tiene millones de fans en todo el mundo. En los Estados Unidos, el deporte más popular es el fútbol americano y el fútbol es el deporte número cuatro.

70 **Compara.** Why do you think soccer is so popular around the world? Why do you think soccer is not as popular in the United States as it is in the rest of the world?

Gramática

Verbos con raíz irregular *(u > ue)*

- In the verb jugar *(to play)*, the u in the stem changes to ue in the present tense:

VERBO JUGAR (TO PLAY). PRESENTE

Singular		Plural	
yo	juego	nosotros nosotras	jugamos
tú	juegas	vosotros vosotras	jugáis
usted él ella	juega	ustedes ellos ellas	juegan

Note: As with other stem-changing verbs, all forms in the present tense are irregular except for nosotros, nosotras and vosotros, vosotras. This is another *boot* verb.

- The preposition a is used with jugar to talk about playing a sport or game.

> yo + jugar + a + el tenis   → Yo **juego al tenis**.
> nosotros + jugar + a + el fútbol → Nosotros **jugamos al fútbol**.

- Jugar means "to play a sport or a game". It isn't used to refer to playing a musical instrument, as in English. Tocar *(to play)* is used for an instrument.

> Ellos **juegan** al tenis.   Yo **juego** al voleibol.
> Ellos **tocan** el piano.   Yo **toco** la guitarra.

71 **Piensa.** Why do you think that Spanish uses different verbs to refer to playing sports vs. playing a musical instrument?

---

72 **¿A qué juegas?**

▶ **Habla.** Andy plays tennis. With your partner, take turns asking and answering whether you play the following sports. If you don't play a sport, refer to someone you know that does.

Modelo   A. *¿Juegas al baloncesto?*
           B. *Sí, juego al baloncesto en la escuela.*
           B. *No, no juego al baloncesto. Mi hermano*
              juega al baloncesto.

1. el tenis
2. el golf
3. el fútbol americano

4. el béisbol
5. el fútbol
6. el boliche

73 **Adivina…**

 ▶ **Escucha y decide.** Listen and decide which sport the four pairs are going to play.

A

B

C

D

▶ **Escribe.** Now write a sentence to tell what sport each person plays, and where.

Modelo *Andy juega al béisbol en el parque.*

74 **Deportes en familia**

▶ **Escribe.** You and your family plan to play several sports over the next three days. Write what sports you will play, and when you will play them.

Modelo *Hoy mi familia juega al fútbol por la tarde.*
    Mañana jugamos a…

▶ **Habla y presenta.** Now create a poster and present your schedule to the class.

CULTURA

El jai alai

El *jai alai* viene del País Vasco, del norte de España. Es conocido como «el deporte más rápido del mundo», por la velocidad (*speed*) de la pelota. Los jugadores juegan al *jai alai* con una pelota de cuero y una canasta (*basket*) atada (*tied*) al brazo. La cancha (*court*) de *jai alai* tiene tres paredes. En los Estados Unidos hay partidos de *jai alai* en el estado de Florida y en Connecticut.

75 **Investiga.** Go online and find out the rules of *jai alai*. When was it invented?

→ TU DESAFÍO Visit the website to learn more about *jai alai*.

Comunicación

76 **Primero las tareas**

▶ **Escucha y relaciona.** Andy wants to play sports this weekend, but Janet reminds him of the household chores he has to do. Listen and match each sport with the chore that will replace it.

77 **Temporada de deportes**

▶ **Habla y escribe.** Talk with a partner about the sports you play or would play during the different seasons. What sports do you both play? Write a short summary.

Modelo   A. ¿A qué juegas en invierno?
B. En invierno yo juego al baloncesto. ¿Y tú?
A. Yo practico la natación.

> En invierno, yo practico la natación y Sonia juega al baloncesto.

78 **En la tienda de deportes**

▶ **Habla.** Andy and Janet go to the sporting goods store to buy some new equipment. With your partner, take turns pointing to the different equipment and saying what they will buy to play different sports.

Modelo   Andy juega al béisbol. Va a comprar un bate nuevo.

79 Un día de deportes

▶ **Escribe.** Your school is planning an Olympic Day. Make a poster with the sports that you will play, the schedule of events, where each sport will take place, and the equipment needed.

▶ **Habla.** Present your poster to the class. Then talk with your classmates about what you will do at their events. Whose event sounds like the most fun?

Modelo *¡Bienvenidos a nuestro día de deportes! Hoy vamos a…*

Final del desafío

Vamos, Janet, tú juegas bien al béisbol. ¡Tú puedes hacerlo!

¡Vamos, vamos, vamos! ¡Sal del campo!

¡Siiiiii! Voy a jugar al béisbol mañana también.

80 ¿Qué pasa en la historia?

▶ **Lee y dibuja.** Janet is up to bat. Using the speech bubbles, draw pictures to represent the end of the story. Then present your pictures to the class.

 **→ TU DESAFÍO** Earn points for your own challenge! Listen to the questions for your *Minientrevista Desafío 4* on the website and write your answers.

ESCRIBIR Y HABLAR

81 **La semana de los deportes**

▶ **Escribe.** Your school is celebrating an Olympic Week. Write a list of what the people are doing according to the picture.

Modelo *Orlando está jugando al fútbol. Kate está grabando el partido.*

▶ **Habla.** Now in a small group, take turns announcing the sports while your classmates say who is playing them.

Está jugando al fútbol.

¡Es Orlando!

ESCRIBIR

82 **Una visita**

▶ **Escribe.** It's Olympic Week, and Mr. Goldberg is visiting your school for two days. Write what you think he is going to do during his visit.

Modelo Hoy a las 10 a. m.

→ *Hoy a las diez de la mañana el señor Goldberg va a hablar con el director.*

1. Hoy a las 12 p. m.
2. Hoy a las 3 p. m.
3. Hoy a las 5 p. m.
4. Mañana a las 11 a. m.
5. Mañana a la 1 p. m.
6. Mañana a las 4 p. m.

ESCUCHAR, ESCRIBIR Y HABLAR

83 ¿Qué ves?

▶ **Escucha y escribe.** Mack has taken some photos while in the United States. Listen and check whether Mack's descriptions match up with the photos. Write the differences.

Modelo 1. *Rita no está hablando por teléfono. Ella está leyendo un libro.*

 ▶ **Habla.** Compare what you have written with your partner's answers.

LEER, HABLAR Y ESCRIBIR

84 Un cuadro de Sorolla

Joaquín Sorolla es un famoso pintor español. Su pintura representa la luz y la vitalidad de su tierra, Valencia, junto al mar Mediterráneo. La Hispanic Society de Nueva York conserva muchas de sus obras.

▶ **Habla.** Talk about the painting with a partner. Answer the following questions:

1. ¿Dónde están las personas del cuadro?
2. ¿Qué están haciendo?
3. ¿Qué van a hacer después?

▶ **Escribe.** Write a conversation between the people in the painting.

Joaquín Sorolla. *Bajo el toldo, playa de Zarauz*, 1910.

El encuentro

En Grant Park

The four pairs meet in Chicago after their individual tasks. Did all of them complete their tasks successfully? Who will win the challenge in the United States?

Este dominó es de Miami. ¡Ven a jugar con nosotros!

En el museo de la Sociedad Hispánica hay cuadros muy interesantes... ¡Voy a ir a clase de pintura!

Hum, la foto de Juanes no está muy clara... ¡Tess está cantando sus canciones todo el día!

Janet juega muy bien al béisbol. ¡Es una campeona!

> ¿Vamos al Festival de Música Latina? ¡Están tocando jazz latino!

85 Al llegar

▶ **Escribe.** Write an e-mail to your classmates summarizing each pair's performance. Be sure to include the following information:

• Where they go and the task they have to complete.

> Modelo Diana y Rita van a Nueva York. Tienen que pasar una noche en el museo de la Sociedad Hispánica de América.

• What they do to complete the task.

> Modelo Diana y Rita no pueden usar la computadora ni el teléfono en el museo. Durante la noche van a mirar los cuadros, van a leer libros y van a escuchar música.

• What each character is going to do in his or her leisure time while in the United States.

> Modelo Rita va a jugar al baloncesto con Andy y Tim.

86 Las votaciones

▶ **Decide.** Which pair has done the most multicultural challenge? Take a vote to decide!

Multicultural

Canadá

Chicago

Nueva York

Washington

Los Ángeles

San Diego

San Antonio

Miami

OCÉANO ATLÁNTICO

OCÉANO PACÍFICO

México

0   200   400 millas
         kilómetros

ALASKA

0 200 400 millas
         kilómetros
0 200 400

Golfo de Alaska

ISLAS HAWÁI

OCÉANO PACÍFICO

0 200 400 millas
         kilómetros
0 200 400

Estados Unidos tiene una importante herencia hispana presente en la historia, en la arquitectura, en la gastronomía, en el arte y en los nombres de personas y lugares.

Según los datos de la Oficina del Censo para 2009, en los Estados Unidos hay 48 millones de personas de origen hispano. La presencia hispana es más importante en Florida, Texas, Nuevo México y California, y en las grandes ciudades como Nueva York o Chicago.

Algunos estados de la Unión tienen nombre español. Por ejemplo, Nevada, Florida y Colorado.

Y también muchos pueblos y ciudades.

87 **Los hispanos y los Estados Unidos**

▶ **Escribe.** Answer these questions.

- What contributions from Hispanics to the United States do you know?
- How many famous Hispanic people do you know? What are their professions?

La presencia hispana en los Estados Unidos

1. Huellas hispanas en los Estados Unidos

Los nombres de algunos lugares, la arquitectura colonial, la gastronomía, ciertos movimientos culturales y los medios de comunicación en español son testimonios de la herencia hispana de los Estados Unidos.

2. Estados con historia hispana

Algunos territorios de los Estados Unidos tienen un pasado hispano. Florida y Texas fueron colonizados por españoles, y las regiones que ahora son California, Nevada, Arizona, Utah, Nuevo México y parte de Colorado fueron territorios de España y, más tarde, de México.

Misión de San José y San Miguel de Aguayo (San Antonio, Texas).

Espectadores en el Desfile del Día de Puerto Rico (Nueva York).

3. Concentración hispana en las ciudades

Los Ángeles, Nueva York, Miami y Chicago son ciudades con mucha población hispana. En estas ciudades y en todo el país se festeja, entre septiembre y octubre, el Mes de la Herencia Hispana, una celebración de las aportaciones de la comunidad hispana a los Estados Unidos.

---

88 **¿Es de origen hispano?**

▶ **Completa.** Complete the chart with the information from the text.

 ▶ **Habla.** Should your state and/or your city be included in the chart? Why?

Presencia hispana en los Estados Unidos	
Estados de origen hispano	
Ciudades con mayor población hispana	
Huellas hispanas en los Estados Unidos	

1. Judy Baca y el muralismo de Los Ángeles

En Los Ángeles, los chicanos pintan murales para expresar su identidad. El mural más importante es *La Gran Pared de Los Ángeles*, de la artista chicana Judy Baca. Este mural mide casi un kilómetro y representa la historia de California. Es un monumento a la armonía interracial.

(1) La Gran Pared de Los Ángeles.

2. La comida tex-mex

La expresión tex-mex originalmente procede de una compañía ferroviaria llamada *Texas-Mexican Railway*. Después se usó para describir un tipo de comida.

La comida tex-mex es una mezcla de las recetas de México y de Texas.

Los ingredientes básicos de esta cocina son la carne picada, la salsa de chile y el queso amarillo. Nachos, tacos crujientes, chili con carne y fajitas son algunas recetas tex-mex.

(2) Un restaurante de comida tex-mex.

3. La Pequeña Habana

La Pequeña Habana es un área de Miami habitada principalmente por cubanos. En este barrio hay muchas actividades culturales: galerías de arte, teatros, espectáculos musicales y pasatiempos. En la Calle Ocho se celebra un famoso carnaval. Más de un millón de personas se reúnen para disfrutar de la música y el baile en la calle.

(3) Vista aérea del Festival de la Calle Ocho.

89 **Nombres y nombres**

▶ **Lee y clasifica.** Read the text and classify the names below by the graphic organizer provided.

> ## Nombres de origen hispano
>
> Muchos lugares de los Estados Unidos tienen un nombre de origen hispano. Algunos tienen nombres de santos, como San Diego; otros tienen nombres de ciudades españolas, como Toledo; hay nombres de animales o plantas de la zona, como Fresno, y otros describen el lugar que nombran, como Florida o Nevada.

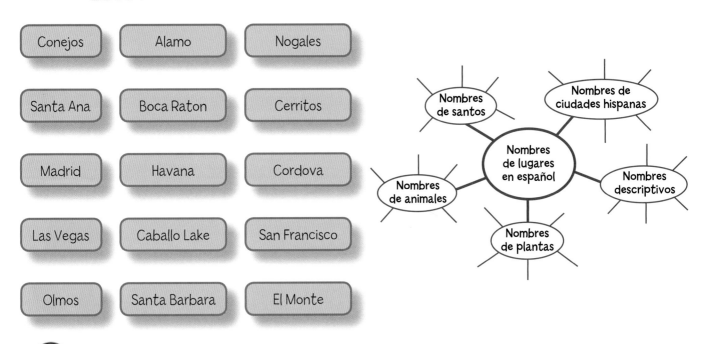

Conejos · Alamo · Nogales · Santa Ana · Boca Raton · Cerritos · Madrid · Havana · Cordova · Las Vegas · Caballo Lake · San Francisco · Olmos · Santa Barbara · El Monte

Nombres de lugares en español:
- Nombres de santos
- Nombres de ciudades hispanas
- Nombres de animales
- Nombres descriptivos
- Nombres de plantas

▶ **Habla.** Play a guessing game with your partner. Ask him or her where the places you added to your graphic organizer are and let him or her ask you back.

Celebramos la Herencia Hispana

La cultura hispana está transformando los Estados Unidos. Su influencia está presente en la moda, en la comida, en la música, en el baile, en la forma de hablar de la gente y en el arte.

Del 15 de septiembre al 15 de octubre muchas ciudades celebran el Mes de la Herencia Hispana. En ese tiempo los Estados Unidos reconocen la contribución de la comunidad hispana al progreso de la nación.

Coloridos desfiles, música y danzas tradicionales, exposiciones, comida y mucha alegría muestran la riqueza y la diversidad de la cultura hispana. Es una fiesta para todos. ¡No te la pierdas![1]

Nuestra propuesta

En Chicago
DESFILE DEL DÍA DE INDEPENDENCIA DE MÉXICO
FECHA: 16 de septiembre
HORA: 7 p. m.
LUGAR: Chicago Cultural Center

En Los Ángeles
FESTIVAL DE CINE LATINO DE LOS ÁNGELES
FECHA: del 12 de septiembre al 19 de octubre
LUGAR: UCLA North Campus

En Nueva York
FIESTA DE LA JUVENTUD CARIBEÑA DE BROOKLYN
FECHA: 13 de septiembre
HORA: de 10 a. m. a 5 p. m.
LUGAR: 4th Street, Brooklyn

1. Don't miss it!

ESTRATEGIA Utilizar el conocimiento previo

90 **Hacer conexiones**

▶ **Escribe.** Write connections between topics, images, or details in the text and the things or experiences they remind you of.

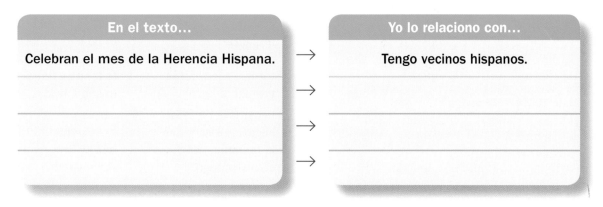

En el texto...		Yo lo relaciono con...
Celebran el mes de la Herencia Hispana.	→	Tengo vecinos hispanos.
	→	
	→	
	→	

COMPRENSIÓN

91 **Los hispanos y los Estados Unidos**

▶ **Corrige.** Correct the sentences so that they agree with the text.

1. El Mes de la Herencia Hispana es una celebración hispana en los Estados Unidos.
2. La influencia hispana en la vida de los Estados Unidos no es muy importante.
3. Los estadounidenses no hispanos no pueden participar en los festejos del Mes de la Herencia Hispana.
4. El Mes de la Herencia Hispana es una fiesta de la diversidad.

92 **Hispanos unidos**

▶ **Haz un cartel.** In a small group, make an eye-catching poster about Hispanic Heritage.

 **TU DESAFÍO** Use the website to learn more about Hispanic Heritage.

El trabajo

Lugares de trabajo

la escuela	*school*
la fábrica	*factory*
el hospital	*hospital*
la obra	*construction site*
la oficina	*office*

Las profesiones

el/la abogado(a)	*lawyer*
el/la director(a)	*director, principal*
el/la entrenador(a)	*coach*
el/la ingeniero(a)	*engineer*
el/la maestro(a)	*teacher*
el/la médico(a)	*doctor*
el/la secretario(a)	*secretary*

Tiempo libre

escribir correos	*to write e-mails*
escuchar la radio	*to listen to the radio*
grabar	*to tape, to record*
ir al cine	*to go to the movies*
jugar a los videojuegos	*to play video games*
tomar/sacar fotos	*to take pictures*
ver películas	*to see movies*
la cámara de fotos	*camera*
la cámara de video	*camcorder*
la película	*movie, film*
el videojuego	*video game*

Los pasatiempos

actuar	*to act*
bailar	*to dance*
caminar	*to walk*
cantar	*to sing*
escribir mensajes	*to send a text message*
escuchar música	*to listen to music*
hacer deporte, practicar deportes	*to play sports*
leer un libro	*to read a book*
montar en bicicleta	*to ride a bike*
nadar	*to swim*
pintar	*to paint*
tocar el piano	*to play the piano*
viajar	*to travel*

Los deportes

Los deportes

el baloncesto	*basketball*
el béisbol	*baseball*
el boliche	*bowling*
el fútbol	*soccer*
el fútbol americano	*football*
el golf	*golf*
la natación	*swimming*
el tenis	*tennis*
el voleibol	*volleyball*
jugar (a), practicar	*to play*

El equipamiento

el balón	*ball*
el bate	*bat*
la bola	*ball*
el casco	*helmet*
el guante	*glove*
la pelota	*ball*
la raqueta	*racket*
la red	*net*

La competición deportiva

el partido	*game*
el estadio	*stadium*
el/la jugador(a)	*player*
el equipo	*team*
ganar	*to win*
perder	*to lose*

DESAFÍO 1

1 **Profesiones.** Read the statements below and determine which person is talking from the people in the word bank.

> maestro   director   ingeniero   abogada   secretaria

1. Tengo que organizar el horario de la escuela y las reuniones con los padres.
2. Trabajo en una fábrica de coches. Hago muchos cálculos matemáticos y físicos.
3. Tengo muchas tareas en mi oficina: escribir cartas, hablar por teléfono…
4. Trabajo en una escuela. Tengo cinco clases cada día. Pongo notas.
5. Represento a mis clientes en asuntos legales.

DESAFÍO 2

2 **Preferencias.** Say what the first person likes to do and what the second person prefers.

Modelo *A ellos les gusta bailar. Yo prefiero cantar.*

1. Ángel / yo
2. nosotros / ella
3. Rosa / usted

DESAFÍO 3

3 **Buenos consejos.** Solve the problems with the appropriate advice.

1. Quiero ver a Juanes en directo.
2. Tengo que tomar fotos.
3. No me gusta ver películas en la tele.
4. Tengo que contactar con mi maestro.
5. Esta noche no puedo ver la película.

a. Usa mi cámara.
b. Escríbele un correo electrónico.
c. Pues grábala.
d. Asiste a su concierto en el teatro.
e. Entonces ve al cine.

DESAFÍO 4

4 **Deportes.** Answer the following questions in complete sentences.

1. ¿Dónde juega al fútbol o al béisbol un equipo profesional?
2. ¿Qué necesitas para jugar al béisbol?
3. ¿Cuántos jugadores necesita un equipo de baloncesto?
4. ¿Dónde practicas la natación?
5. ¿Qué deporte practicas con una raqueta y una pelota?

Imperativo afirmativo. Verbos irregulares (pág. 98)

Decir *(to say)*	di
Hacer *(to do)*	haz
Ir *(to go)*	ve
Poner *(to put)*	pon
Salir *(to leave)*	sal
Ser *(to be)*	sé
Tener *(to have)*	ten
Venir *(to come)*	ven

El presente continuo (pág. 114)

In Spanish the present progressive is formed as follows: **estar + gerundio.**

Estoy estudiando español.

El gerundio (pág. 116)

The present participle is formed this way:

▶ Add **-ando** to the stem of verbs ending in -ar.

▶ Add **-iendo** to the stem of verbs ending in -er and -ir.

VERBOS IRREGULARES EN GERUNDIO

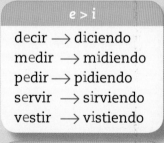

e > i
decir → diciendo
medir → midiendo
pedir → pidiendo
servir → sirviendo
vestir → vistiendo

o > u
dormir → durmiendo
morir → muriendo
poder → pudiendo

Ir *a* + infinitivo (pág. 106)

To express the intention to do something, use this structure: **ir a + infinitive.**

Vamos a viajar a Miami.

Expresiones temporales de futuro (pág. 106)

ahora	*now*
luego, después	*later*
hoy	*today*
esta mañana	*this morning*
esta tarde	*this afternoon*
esta noche	*tonight*
mañana	*tomorrow*
mañana por la mañana	*tomorrow morning*
mañana por la tarde	*tomorrow afternoon/ evening*
mañana por la noche	*tomorrow night*
la próxima semana, la semana que viene	*next week*
el próximo año, el año que viene	*next year*

Verbos con raíz irregular (*u > ue*) (pág. 124)

JUGAR

yo	juego	nosotros nosotras	jugamos
tú	juegas	vosotros vosotras	jugáis
usted él ella	juega	ustedes ellos ellas	juegan

DESAFÍO 1

5 **Órdenes.** Change the following obligations into commands.

Modelo Tienes que salir de casa. ⟶ *Sal de casa.*

1. Tienes que poner la mesa.
2. Tienes que ser prudente.
3. Tienes que hacer la tarea.

4. Tienes que venir a la fiesta.
5. Tienes que ir a la oficina.
6. Tienes que decir la verdad.

DESAFÍO 2

6 **Planes.** Ask and answer questions with a partner according to the model.

Modelo tú - esta tarde - jugar al fútbol ⟶ A. *¿Qué vas a hacer tú esta tarde?*
                                            B. *Esta tarde voy a jugar al fútbol.*

1. Rosa - esta noche - ver una película
2. ustedes - mañana - montar en bicicleta

3. María y Ana - el sábado - bailar
4. usted - ahora - tocar el piano

DESAFÍO 3

7 **¿Qué están haciendo?** Rewrite the sentences changing the present tense into the present progressive and the direct object into a direct object pronoun.

Modelo Ella *escribe un mensaje.* ⟶ *Ella está escribiéndolo* o *Ella lo está escribiendo.*

1. Yo compro un casco.
2. Tú ordenas tu dormitorio.
3. Nosotros oímos las canciones.

4. Ella pide la carta.
5. Ellos graban una película.
6. Ustedes ven la televisión.

DESAFÍO 4

8 **¿Jugamos?** Say what sport the people play according the pictures. Use the verb *jugar*.

 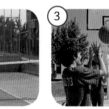 

nosotros   yo   ellos   tú   Pilar

CULTURA

9 **Estados Unidos hispano.** Answer the questions.

1. What is the Maximo Gomez Park in Miami better known as?
2. Which Hispanic artist has won the most Latin Grammy Awards?
3. Where does the Fiesta Noche del Río take place?
4. In what Hispanic countries is baseball the most popular?

Un cartel sobre

un hispano famoso

In this project you will create a poster about a well-known person of Hispanic origin in the United States.

– First, you will research well-known native Spanish speakers.

– Secondly, in groups, decide on the person that interests you the most. Then prepare an illustrated poster to introduce the person selected.

– Thirdly, you will announce and then make your presentation to your classmates.

PASO 1 Investiga

• Find out about well-known people of Hispanic origin who are distinguished in fields such as medicine, sport, entertainment, and business. Look for information to answer these questions:

   – ¿De qué país es?   – ¿Qué profesión tiene?

   – ¿Dónde vive o trabaja ahora?   – ¿Por qué es famoso(a)?

Aquí tienes algunas ideas:

Pedro Duque, astronauta.

Sonia Sotomayor, jueza.

Gloria Estefan, cantante.

Carolina Herrera, diseñadora.

Isabel Allende, escritora.

PASO 2 Prepara tu cartel

• In a group, select the person that interests you the most.

• Write the answers to the questions in Step 1 in complete sentences and creatively copy them onto your poster.

• Find photos to illustrate the information.

• Write captions to describe what is happening in each photo.

El español Pau Gasol es un jugador de baloncesto muy conocido en los Estados Unidos.

PASO 3 Anuncia tu presentación

- Prepare an advertisement for your presentation. Include the following information:
  - The name of the person you are going to present.
  - The time and place you will make your presentation.
  - Whom your presentation will appeal to.

¡El baloncesto con un experto!

Fecha:
el 10 de octubre

Hora:
a las 3 de la tarde

Lugar:
en el gimnasio

Tema:
el jugador Pau Gasol

¿Te gusta el baloncesto?
¡Ven a mi presentación!

PASO 4 Presenta el cartel

- Present your poster to the class.
- Invite your classmates to ask you questions at the end.

¿Hay preguntas?
¿Quieren saber más?

Unidad 6

Autoevaluación

¿Qué has aprendido en esta unidad?

Use these questions to evaluate how well you have understood this unit's concepts.

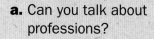

Evaluate your skills. For each activity, say Very well, Well, or I need more practice.

a. Can you talk about professions?

▶ Talk to your partner about which profession you would prefer to have and why.

b. Can you tell someone what to do using verbs like *decir*, *salir*, *venir*, and *poner*?

▶ Write four *tú* commands using the verbs *decir*, *salir*, *venir*, and *poner*. Ask your partner to act them out.

c. Can you say what you are going to do in the future?

▶ Ask your partner what are his or her plans for next week.

d. Can you describe what someone is doing now?

▶ Say what three classmates are doing now.

e. Can you talk about sports?

▶ Ask two classmates what sports they like to watch or play.

Unidad 7
Argentina
En tierra de gauchos

DESAFÍO **1**

DESAFÍO **2**

Los gauchos

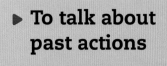

▶ **To talk about past actions**

Vocabulario
De viaje. Medios de transporte

Gramática
Verbos regulares en *-ar*. Pretérito

▶ **To express actions related to travel**

Vocabulario
Los viajes

Gramática
Verbos regulares en *-er* y en *-ir*. Pretérito

El tren a las nubes

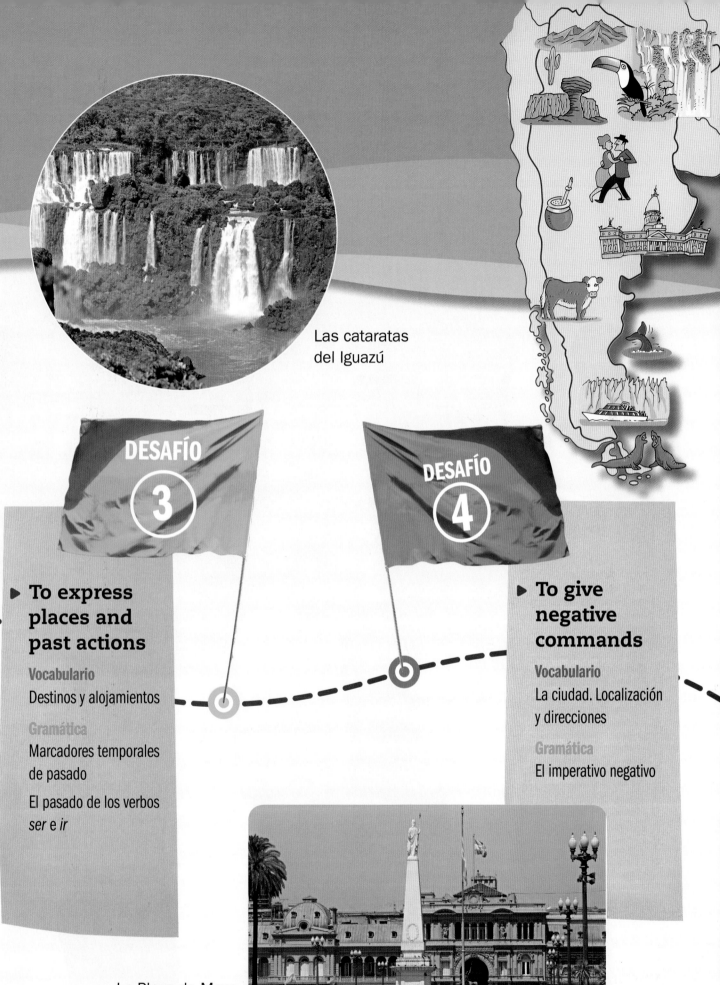

Las cataratas del Iguazú

DESAFÍO 3

▶ **To express places and past actions**

Vocabulario
Destinos y alojamientos

Gramática
Marcadores temporales de pasado

El pasado de los verbos *ser* e *ir*

DESAFÍO 4

▶ **To give negative commands**

Vocabulario
La ciudad. Localización y direcciones

Gramática
El imperativo negativo

La Plaza de Mayo

En Buenos Aires

In Argentina, the four pairs gather in Buenos Aires, the capital. They come together at the *Plaza de Mayo*, in downtown Buenos Aires. There they meet Alina Aguilar, a tango dancer. She welcomes them and assigns each pair their task.

Hola, soy Alina Aguilar. ¡Bienvenidos a Argentina, un país interesante y moderno!

¿Tienen sus pasaportes, sus maletas...? ¡Van a viajar mucho! En tren, en avión, en autobús...

¡Qué bien!

¿Están listos? ¡Buen viaje a todos!

Ushuaia

Vamos a San Antonio de los Cobres en tren. Salimos de la estación de Salta.

¿Vamos a Salta en autobús? ¿Compramos billetes de ida y vuelta?

¡Tenemos que caminar mucho! Hay que encontrar un parque, una iglesia...

No olvides el plano, Tess.

Sí, y el pasaporte. Tenemos que enseñarlo en el aeropuerto.

¿Tienes a mano los billetes, tía?

Llamé al hotel. No hay habitaciones libres...

No importa. ¿Preguntaste en el cámping?

1 ¿Comprendes?

▶ **Une.** Match each question (column A) with the corresponding answer (column B).

(A)

1. ¿Están preparados los personajes para el viaje?
2. ¿Viajan Tim y Mack en avión?
3. ¿Van Tess y Patricia en taxi a su destino?
4. ¿Reservó Andy una habitación en el hotel?
5. ¿Tienen Diana y Rita el pasaporte a mano?

(B)

a. No, no hay habitaciones libres.
b. No, van caminando.
c. Sí, lo necesitan para viajar.
d. Sí, están listos.
e. No, viajan en tren.

EXPRESIONES ÚTILES

Sí, tengo el pasaporte a mano.

To ask if someone is ready:

Estar listo(a). / Estar preparado(a).

To express having something handy:

Tener... a mano.

To talk about a round-trip ticket:

Comprar un billete de ida y vuelta.

To say that something does not matter:

No importa. / No pasa nada.

To wish someone a good trip:

¡Buen viaje!

2 Expresiones

▶ **Relaciona.** The expressions below don't correspond to the pictures under them. Match them appropriately.

a. ¿Tiene usted los documentos a mano?

b. ¡Buen viaje, Carmen!

c. Dos billetes de ida y vuelta, por favor.

d. ¡Estamos listos!

3 Preguntas y respuestas

▶ **Escucha y relaciona.** Listen to the statements. Match each one with a logical response.

a. Sí, tranquilo. Lo tengo a mano.

b. Sí, estamos listos.

c. No pasa nada.

d. ¡Buen viaje!

e. Sí. Compra dos billetes de ida y vuelta.

¿Quién ganará?

4 **Los desafíos**

▶ **Habla.** What will be the challenge for each team? Think about this question and discuss it with your classmates.

DESAFÍO ①

El tren a las nubes

Tim y Mack

DESAFÍO ②

Un gaucho de la Pampa

Diana y Rita

DESAFÍO ③

Las cataratas del Iguazú

Andy y Janet

DESAFÍO ④

Sobres en la calle

Tess y Patricia

5 **Las votaciones**

▶ **Decide.** You decide. You will vote to choose the most amazing challenge. Who do you think will win?

Sorprendente

El tren a las nubes

 Tim and Mack are traveling on the Train to the Clouds. This train is the third highest railway in the world. Tim and Mack must take a picture of each town they pass while the train is still moving.

> ¿Te gusta viajar en tren, Tim? A mí me gusta mucho.

> ¡Qué bien, abuelo, vamos de excursión en tren!

> Sí. El tren a las nubes pasa por el norte de Argentina. Vamos a ver paisajes fantásticos.

> Yo solo viajé en tren una vez y me gustó. Pero me gusta más viajar en avión.

> ¡Ay, abuelo, tomé una foto muy fea!

> Abuelo, ¿cuántas fotos tenemos que tomar?

> No sé... Necesitamos una foto de cada ciudad. ¡Y tenemos que tomar todas las fotos desde el tren!

> No importa, Tim. Toma otra foto, rápido. Estamos saliendo de esta ciudad...

Continuará...

---

6 **¿Comprendes?**

▶ **Completa.** Which verb or verb phrase from the dialogue matches these expressions?

I traveled	I liked it	I took a photo
1.	2.	3.

▶ **Habla.** Ask a partner about somewhere he or she has traveled.

Modelo A. ¿Viajaste a Miami?
        B. No, no viajé a Miami. Viajé a Orlando.

7 ¿Quién viajó?

▶ **Decide.** Read these statements. Are they referring to Mack or to Tim?

1. Él viajó en tren una vez.

2. A él le gustó viajar en tren.

3. Él tomó una foto muy fea.

8 Preparativos para la excursión

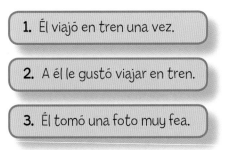 ▶ **Escucha y decide.** Listen and decide which of these activities Tim and Mack did.

1. visitar la agencia de viajes
2. desayunar en un café
3. hablar por teléfono con la abuela
4. comprar comida en un supermercado
5. preparar unos sándwiches
6. tomar un taxi
7. jugar un partido de dominó
8. pasear por el parque
9. descansar

▶ **Escucha y escribe.** Listen again and write the verb forms that correspond to the infinitives you chose above.

Modelo 1. *visitamos*

CULTURA

El tren a las nubes

El tren a las nubes sale de la ciudad de Salta y va hasta el viaducto La Polvorilla. La excursión comienza a las 7 de la mañana y termina después de la medianoche. El tren pasa por veintinueve puentes (*bridges*), veintiún túneles y dos zigzags. Se llama tren a las nubes porque sube a 4.200 metros sobre el nivel del mar.

9 Piensa.
Have you ever taken a trip by train? What are the advantages and disadvantages of travelling by train versus other means of transportation?

Vocabulario

De viaje

el avión

el barco

el tren

Me gusta **ir a pie.**

el metro

el autobús

el taxi

el coche

Nos **vamos de vacaciones.** ¡Nos gusta mucho **viajar en avión!**

el aeropuerto

Nos **vamos de excursión.** Vamos en tren.

la estación

10 El transporte ideal

▶ **Habla.** Mack and Tim are looking at the signs along the way. Read their notes and decide which would be the appropriate form(s) of transportation to take to each place.

Modelo A. ¿Cómo pueden ir al Parque don Tomás?
B. Pueden ir a pie.

Distancias

Parque don Tomás	1 km
Buenos Aires	577 km
Las Mercedes	45 km
San Carlos	7 km
Córdoba	580 km

11 ¡Cuántos viajeros!

▶ **Completa.** In the airport the four pairs heard many travelers talking around them. Complete their statements with a term from the boxes.

Modelo Normalmente voy a la escuela en **autobús**.

| metro | coche | a pie | avión | barco |

1. ¡Mi _____ sale inmediatamente! ¿Dónde está la terminal internacional?
2. Voy al puerto de Miami. Voy a tomar un _____ para viajar por el Caribe.
3. Para moverme por Washington DC uso el _____. Es más rápido y barato que un taxi.
4. Tengo licencia para conducir. Podemos rentar un _____ para viajar por la región.
5. El hotel está muy cerca del centro de la ciudad. Podemos ir _____.

12 ¿Qué haces durante las vacaciones?

▶ **Habla.** Talk with a classmate about the things you do during your summer break. Use the prompts below.

1. Me gusta ir de vacaciones a…
2. A mi familia y a mí nos gusta viajar a/por…
3. Vamos de excursión a/por…

CONEXIONES: CIENCIAS SOCIALES

El transporte público: el metro

Buenos Aires, igual que Nueva York, Madrid, la Ciudad de México y otras ciudades, tiene un servicio de transporte público muy popular: el metro o subte (de subterráneo). El metro argentino fue (*was*) el primero de Latinoamérica. Fue inaugurado en 1913.

13 Piensa. What are the public transportation services in your city or town? Are they efficient? What are the advantages of a public transportation system?

Gramática

Verbos regulares en *-ar*. Pretérito

- To talk about completed actions in the past, we use the preterite tense.

PRESENTE	PRETÉRITO
Yo **compro** una blusa. →	Yo **compré** una camisa.
Yo **viajo** en barco. →	Yo **viajé** en metro.

- These are the preterite tense endings of -ar verbs.

VERBO COMPRAR (TO BUY). PRETÉRITO

Singular		Plural	
yo	**compré**	nosotros nosotras	**compramos**
tú	**compraste**	vosotros vosotras	**comprasteis**
usted él ella	**compró**	ustedes ellos ellas	**compraron**

Note: The nosotros form is the same in the preterite as in the present. Context will clarify the tense.

PRESENTE

Todos los días **viajamos** en tren.

PRETÉRITO

En marzo **viajamos** en autobús.

14 **Compara.** How do we form the past tense in English? Are there any cases where the present and past tenses of a verb look the same?

15 **¿Qué pasó?**

▶ **Escucha y escribe.** Andy and Diana are talking about what they and two other characters did over the weekend. Listen and write a sentence about what each person did. You may find clues in the pictures.

Modelo 1. *Andy viajó a una isla en barco.*

16 ¿Compraste algo?

▶ **Habla.** Find out what a classmate did on a recent vacation. Ask whether he or she did each of the following things.

Modelo viajar a Argentina → A. *¿Viajaste a Argentina?*
B. *Sí, viajé a Argentina.*

1. tomar el metro
2. hablar con la gente
3. escuchar música tradicional
4. bailar salsa
5. pintar un paisaje
6. cantar en un karaoke
7. cenar muy tarde
8. tomar platos típicos
9. comprar recuerdos

17 Las compras

▶ **Escribe.** The characters went shopping yesterday. Write what each person bought, according to the photos.

Modelo 1. *Yo compré una bandera de Argentina.*

(1) yo   (2) tú   (3) Mack   (4) nosotras

(5) ustedes   (6) Rita   (7) Tim y Tess

▶ **Habla y presenta.** Imagine you bought one of the items above. Tell a partner which one you chose. Then, as a pair, report your purchases to the class.

Modelo

Yo compré una chaqueta de cuero. ¿Qué compraste tú?

Yo compré una bandera argentina.

Marta y yo compramos una chaqueta de cuero y una bandera de Argentina.

Comunicación

18 **¡Qué día!**

▶ **Lee e identifica.** Tim wrote an e-mail about his trip on the Train to the Clouds. As you read it, identify the verbs in the past tense and create a list.

Querida abuela:

El viaje en el tren a las nubes es sensacional. Es un viaje largo, pero lo pasé muy bien. Yo compré unos sándwiches de jamón y el abuelo y yo los disfrutamos mucho. Después de muchas horas de viaje, llegamos a la última estación en la frontera con Chile.

¿Qué tal la fiesta de la semana pasada? ¿Tomaste muchas fotos?

Descansa y escríbeme, abuela. Te quiero.

Tim

▶ **Escucha y escribe.** Listen to the message Tim's grandmother left for him and take notes about what she did each day.

lunes	Ella tomó fotos.
martes	
miércoles	
...	

19 **Una historia**

▶ **Escribe.** Create a short story using the people and verb phrases below.

Modelo *Tomás y Carolina viajaron en tren...*

Tomás Carolina Daniela	hablar por teléfono pasear desayunar cantar	tomar un refresco grabar viajar bailar

▶ **Lee y compara.** Now read your story to a classmate. Compare stories.

20 Tu semana

▶ **Completa.** Fill in a chart like the one below using the preterite *yo* form of the verbs.

estudiar	comprar un regalo
escuchar música	ver la televisión
usar la computadora	llamar a un(a) amigo(a)

lunes	
martes	
miércoles	
...	

▶ **Habla.** Ask your partner what he or she did last week and take notes. Did you both do some of the same things?

Modelo A. *¿Estudiaste el domingo?*
          B. *No. Estudié el sábado. ¿Compraste un regalo el lunes?*
          A. *Sí.*
          B. *¡Yo también!*

Final del desafío

① ② ③ ④

21 ¿Qué pasa en la historia?

▶ **Escribe.** Mack and Tim took the photos above during their trip. Write captions for each photo telling what they did. Use the verbs in the word bank.

hablar
comprar
viajar
mirar

▶→ TU DESAFÍO   Earn points for your own challenge! Listen to the questions for your *Minientrevista Desafío 1* on the website and write your answers.

Un gaucho de la Pampa

Diana and Rita have to travel to Santa Rosa, the capital of La Pampa, an Argentine province. There they must make their way to the Marathon A *Pampa Traviesa*. They must find a man running in gaucho attire. He will give them proof of their completed task. Will they find him?

> Diana, ¿vamos a Santa Rosa en avión o en coche?

> Depende... ¿Tu licencia es válida en Argentina, tía?

> Sí, pero ¿no prefieres viajar en avión?

> Sí, prefiero ir en avión. ¿Compramos los billetes en la agencia de viajes?

> ¿Llevas a mano el pasaporte, Diana?

> Sí, y llevo también la guía turística. Mira, habla del maratón...

> Por favor, dos billetes de avión de Buenos Aires a Santa Rosa.

> ¿Ida y vuelta? ¿Clase turista? ¿Prefieren el vuelo por la mañana o por la tarde?

Continuará...

22   Detective de palabras

▶ **Relaciona.** What term from the dialogue corresponds to each image?

1. PASSPORT — United States of America

2.

3. Buenos Aires y lo mejor de Argentina

¿Comprendes?

▶ **Decide.** Use the dialogue on page 158 to tell whether the statements below are true *(cierto)* or false *(falso)*. If they are false, revise them to express a true statement.

1. Diana y Rita van a Santa Rosa en autobús.
2. La licencia de conducir de Rita es válida en Argentina.
3. Van a comprar los billetes a la oficina de información y turismo.
4. Una agencia de viajes vende billetes de avión.
5. Rita y Diana pueden comprar billetes de ida y vuelta.

24 **En el avión**

▶ **Escucha y elige.** On the flight to Santa Rosa, Diana talks to Sabrina, a flight attendant. Listen and choose the correct option.

1. Sabrina es de _____
   a. Chile   **b.** Argentina   **c.** Perú

2. Su esposo es _____
   a. chileno   **b.** argentino   **c.** mexicano

3. Le gusta _____
   a. caminar   **b.** viajar   **c.** dormir

4. Ella viajó mucho por _____
   a. Australia   **b.** Asia   **c.** Europa

5. Ella tiene una casa en _____
   a. Santa Rosa   **b.** Buenos Aires   **c.** Santa Fe

COMPARACIONES
Los gauchos

Los gauchos son como los *cowboys* americanos. Viven en la Pampa argentina y en algunas regiones de Uruguay, Paraguay, Bolivia, Chile y Brasil. En Santa Rosa, la capital de la provincia de La Pampa, hay una Fiesta de la Tradición Gaucha durante el mes de noviembre.

25 **Piensa.** What do you think are some similarities between cowboys and gauchos?

▶ **TU DESAFÍO**   Visit the website to learn more about the Pampa and about the gaucho lifestyle.

Vocabulario

Los viajes

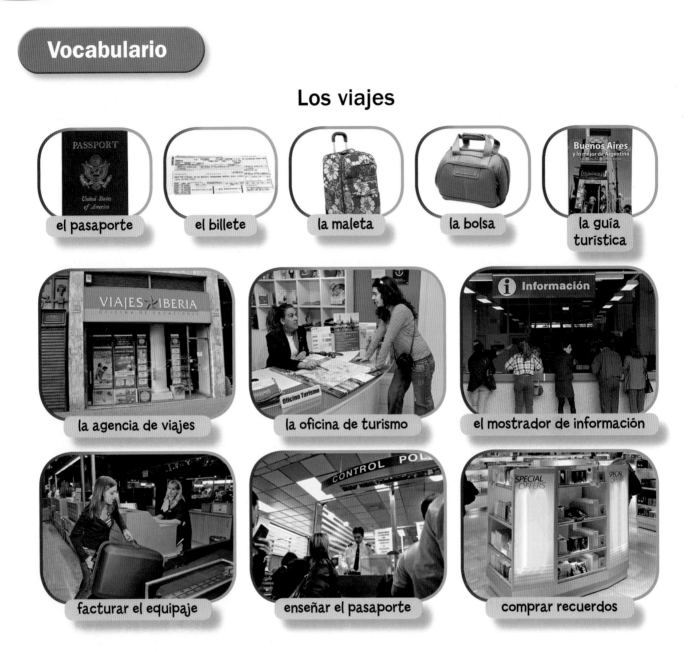

el pasaporte

el billete

la maleta

la bolsa

la guía turística

la agencia de viajes

la oficina de turismo

el mostrador de información

facturar el equipaje

enseñar el pasaporte

comprar recuerdos

26 Viajeros con experiencia

▶ **Escribe.** Rita gave Diana a lot of travel advice, which Diana has written in her notebook. Use her notes to report what Rita told her to do.

Modelo salir del metro con cuidado → *Sal del metro con cuidado.*

leer la guía turística	facturar pronto el equipaje
cerrar bien la maleta	ir a la oficina de turismo
mirar la hora del vuelo	visitar museos grandes y pequeños
llegar al aeropuerto temprano	comprar muchos recuerdos

27 ¿Estás lista para el viaje?

▶ **Escucha y ordena.** Listen to what Diana's mother says and decide in which order these items should be prepared for travel.

(A)　(B)　(C) PASSPORT United States of America　(D)　(E) ARGENTINA

▶ **Escribe.** Write a note to yourself telling why you need to bring or buy each of the things shown above.

Modelo 1. *Tengo que llevar una chaqueta para no tener frío en el avión.*

entrar en otro país
no tener frío en el avión
llevar toda la ropa
tomar el avión
saber más sobre Argentina

28 El itinerario del día

▶ **Escribe y habla.** You went on a fabulous vacation to Argentina! Write a list of the steps you took to prepare for the trip. Then tell your partner what you did before and during your vacation.

Modelo *Primero compré una guía turística…*

Mi viaje a Argentina

1. Compré una guía turística.
2. …

CULTURA

La Pampa

La Pampa es una provincia argentina importante por su agricultura y su industria. Está en el centro del país. A 30 kilómetros de Santa Rosa está la Reserva Natural Parque Luro. Allí puedes hacer cámping y practicar todo tipo de deportes.

29 Compara.
Considering the presence of gauchos and the information above, what region of the U.S. would be most like La Pampa? Why? What differences might there be?

Gramática

Verbos regulares en -er y en -ir. Pretérito

- Regular -er and -ir verbs have the same endings in the preterite tense. Here is how they are conjugated:

VERBO COMER (TO EAT). PRETÉRITO

Singular		Plural	
yo	comí	nosotros nosotras	comimos
tú	comiste	vosotros vosotras	comisteis
usted él ella	comió	ustedes ellos ellas	comieron

VERBO ESCRIBIR (TO WRITE). PRETÉRITO

Singular		Plural	
yo	escribí	nosotros nosotras	escribimos
tú	escribiste	vosotros vosotras	escribisteis
usted él ella	escribió	ustedes ellos ellas	escribieron

Note: Just as with -ar verbs, the nosotros form of -ir verbs is the same in the preterite and the present tense. The context helps to determine the tense of the verb.

30 **Piensa.** What other clues would make you think that a sentence was in the past tense or the present tense?

31 **¿Presente o pasado?**

▶ **Escucha y decide.** Diana and Rita overheard conversations on the plane. Listen and decide whether the people are talking about something that happened in the past or something that normally happens.

A. Pasó en el pasado.   **B.** Normalmente pasa.

▶ **Escribe y habla.** Write three sentences using the preterite or present tense. Say them aloud to a partner. He or she will indicate whether you are talking about something that happened in the past or something that normally happens.

Modelo

Yo viajé a Argentina.   Pasó en el pasado.

32 **¿Qué hicieron?**

▶ **Escribe.** What did these people do before and during their flight? Write a sentence describing each action.

Modelo *El hombre prendió la luz.*

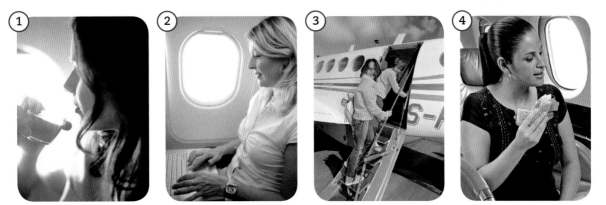

| ① | ② | ③ | ④ |
| la niña | la mujer | los chicos | Rita |

33 **Hoy y antes**

▶ **Escribe y habla.** Write ten sentences to talk about the day's events. Write five sentences in the *nosotros* form of the present tense and five sentences in the *nosotros* form of the preterite. Share your sentences with a partner.

Modelo Presente ⟶ *Todos los días escribimos en la clase de Ciencias.*
         Pretérito ⟶ *Esta mañana escribimos en la clase de Inglés.*

CULTURA

A Pampa Traviesa

A Pampa Traviesa es un maratón. Se celebra cada año en Santa Rosa, la capital de La Pampa. Los participantes corren veintiséis millas por la ciudad. No pueden correr más de mil personas.

Los atletas se reúnen delante del Edificio Mundial a las ocho de la mañana. Allí está la salida y también la llegada.

34 **Piensa.** What kind of training do you think it takes to run a marathon? What are the distances of the marathons and other races in your city or town?

Comunicación

35 **Pasó en Argentina...**

▶ **Completa.** Diana's e-mail to her best friend is incomplete—some verbs are missing. Complete her message by filling in the blanks with the appropriate preterite forms.

De:

▾ Para: 🔤

Asunto:

| Cuerpo del texto ▾ | Anchura variable ▾ | ■ | A+ A↑ | **B** *I* <u>U</u> | ⋮≡ ≔ ⇥ ⇤ | ■▾ ▯▾ ☺▾ |

Hola, Jaime:

Rita y yo estamos en Argentina. Hay muchas cosas interesantes y lugares fantásticos.

Ayer las dos ___1___ por Santa Rosa y ___2___ una empanada deliciosa. Rita ___3___
         salir   comer   perder

su guía turística, ¡qué pena! Por la noche, yo ___4___ para buscar un cibercafé,
                                                salir

pero no lo ___5___. Esta mañana mi tía ___6___ a correr y yo ___7___ en el hotel porque
         encontrar   salir   quedarse

a mí no me gusta correr. Ahora vamos a visitar la ciudad.

Hasta pronto.

Diana

36 **Un viaje de estudios**

▶ **Lee y escribe.** Read the memo sent to parents about a student trip to Argentina and write two interesting facts about the excursion.

▶ **Crea un póster.** Now find pictures about Argentina in a magazine and create a poster to try to convince your classmates to go there this year.

Viaje de estudios a Argentina

Estimados padres y madres:

El verano pasado, la organización Gauchos Argentinos invitó a varias escuelas americanas a conocer Buenos Aires y otras ciudades de Argentina. Los estudiantes conocieron a muchas personas y aprendieron mucho sobre la vida de los gauchos.

El próximo verano nuestra escuela va a pasar dos semanas en Argentina con el mismo programa. Este viernes ustedes pueden asistir a una reunión informativa sobre el viaje. Todos son bienvenidos.

Atentamente,

El Departamento de Español

37 **¡Tú también participas!**

▶ **Escribe.** You and a friend went to Santa Rosa, like Diana and Rita.
Write about your trip using some the verbs below, in the preterite tense.

Modelo *En marzo viajamos a Santa Rosa. Comimos en todos los restaurantes famosos.*

comer   comprar   visitar

viajar   conocer   perder

correr   competir   ver

Final del desafío

Aquí hay mucha gente, tía.
El gaucho ya ___1___ por aquí.

Sí, Diana, el gaucho ya
___2___ a la meta.

Aquel hombre nos está
___3___. Es el gaucho,
¿verdad?

¡Qué bien, tía! ¡El gaucho
nos ___4___ su sombrero!

38 **¿Qué pasa en la historia?**

▶ **Completa y representa.** Complete the dialogue with the correct forms of the verbs below.
Then, in a group, act out the ending of the *Desafío*.

saludar   regalar   llegar   pasar

Las cataratas del Iguazú

Andy and Janet are taking a trip to Iguazu Falls, one of the most spectacular waterfalls in South America. Their task is to make a video guide of the *Garganta del Diablo* (Devil's Throat), a waterfall that lies between Argentina and Brazil.

No veo la Garganta del Diablo en el mapa. ¿Y tú?

Sí, está aquí, al sur de la montaña.

¿Llamaste ayer al hotel para reservar una habitación?

No, finalmente reservé en el cámping.

Perdimos la ruta... ¿Fuimos en la dirección correcta?

No sé... Ayer miré la ruta en Internet. La Garganta del Diablo está al norte...

¡Oh, no, Janet! ¡Miramos mal el mapa!

Continuará...

39 Detective de palabras

▶ **Completa.** Complete the sentences using the dialogue above.

1. _____ en el cámping.
2. _____ la ruta...
3. _____ en la dirección correcta?
4. _____ mal el mapa.

▶ **Piensa.** Are the verbs above in the present or in the past tense?

¿Comprendes?

▶ **Decide y escribe.** Decide whether these statements are true *(cierto)* or false *(falso)* and correct the false statements.

Modelo Janet reservó habitación en un hotel.
  → *Falso. Janet reservó habitación en un cámping.*

1. Andy y Janet perdieron la ruta.
2. Ayer Janet miró la ruta en una guía turística.
3. La Garganta del Diablo está al sur.
4. Andy y Janet miraron mal el mapa.

41 **Buscando la Garganta del Diablo**

▶ **Ordena.** Put these events in order according to the dialogue.

a. Andy buscó la Garganta del Diablo en el mapa.
b. Andy y Janet perdieron la ruta.
c. Andy y Janet se sentaron para pensar.
d. Janet encontró la Garganta del Diablo en el mapa.
e. Andy descubrió el error.
f. Andy y Janet caminaron mucho tiempo.
g. Andy miró bien el mapa.

▶ **Escribe.** Now write Andy and Janet's adventure in search of the Devil's Throat. Use the sentences you ordered and the following words to connect them.

primero   después   luego   y   más tarde

CULTURA

Las cataratas del Iguazú

Las cataratas *(waterfalls)* del río Iguazú son unas de las cataratas más impresionantes del mundo. Están entre Paraguay, Argentina y Brasil. En esa zona está el Parque Nacional Iguazú, formado por más de 275 cataratas.

42 **Piensa.** Have you ever seen a waterfall? Can you name some waterfalls in North America? Are they located in a national park like Iguazu Falls?

→ TU DESAFÍO Visit the website to learn more about the *Parque Nacional Iguazú*.

Vocabulario

Destinos y alojamientos

el campo

la ciudad

Me gusta **hacer turismo** y conocer ciudades.

la playa

la costa

la montaña

¿Tienen una habitación para dos personas?

el hotel

el cámping

reservar habitación

43 **¿Adónde viajaron?**

▶ **Habla.** The characters visited different places during their vacations. According to what each one is wearing, where do you think they traveled?

Modelo

¿Adónde viajó Tim?

Tim viajó a la ciudad.

1

2

3

44 **¿Adónde vamos?**

▶ **Escucha y escribe.** The characters are going to many places in Argentina. Listen to Andy coordinate their destinations and write a sentence to say where everyone goes, and how they will get there.

Modelo 1. *Mack y Tim van al norte, a la montaña, en autobús.*

A	B	C	D
1. Mack y Tim	al norte	a la costa	en coche
2. Andy y Janet	al sur	a la montaña	en avión
3. Diana y Rita	al este	a la playa	en taxi
4. Tess y Patricia	al oeste	a la ciudad	en autobús

▶ **Habla.** Now tell a partner where and how the characters traveled.

Modelo A. *¿Adónde viajaron Mack y Tim?*
　　　　 B. *Ellos viajaron al norte, a la montaña, en autobús.*

45 **Una propuesta de viaje**

▶ **Escribe.** Your family cannot decide where to go on vacation this year. Write a proposal that includes answers to the following questions.

1. ¿Adónde van a ir tu familia y tú?
2. ¿Qué van a hacer allí?
3. ¿Cómo van a viajar?
4. ¿Por qué quieres ir tú allí?

▶ **Lee.** In a small group, read your proposal. Then vote for the most convincing plan.

CONEXIONES: GEOGRAFÍA

La rosa de los vientos

La rosa de los vientos representa los cuatro puntos cardinales (Norte, Sur, Este y Oeste). Puede mostrar también otras direcciones, como Noreste, Sureste, Noroeste y Suroeste. La rosa de los vientos se utiliza en muchos mapas.

46 **Piensa.** Why do you think that the compass rose is often highly decorative? If you were a mapmaker, what would your compass rose look like?

Gramática

Marcadores temporales de pasado

- The adverbs antes, ayer, and anoche refer to the past tense:

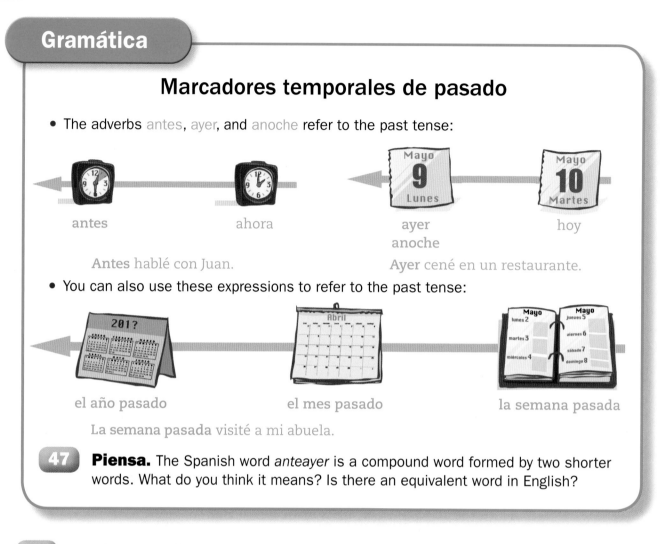

antes   ahora   ayer   hoy
                                                  anoche

Antes hablé con Juan.   Ayer cené en un restaurante.

- You can also use these expressions to refer to the past tense:

el año pasado   el mes pasado   la semana pasada

La semana pasada visité a mi abuela.

47 **Piensa.** The Spanish word *anteayer* is a compound word formed by two shorter words. What do you think it means? Is there an equivalent word in English?

48 **¿Cuándo pasó?**

▶ **Escribe.** Write sentences using this information.

Modelo 1. *Diana vio una película ayer.*

Actividades		
Quién	**Qué**	**Cuándo**
1. Diana	ver una película	ayer
2. Tim	hablar por teléfono	anoche
3. Janet	aprender una receta nueva	la semana pasada
4. Diana y Rita	comer en un restaurante	el mes pasado
5. Patricia y Tess	viajar en metro	el jueves pasado

▶ **Habla.** Now tell a partner when you last did these activities.

Modelo A. *¿Cuándo viste una película?*

B. *Vi una película la semana pasada.*

¿Qué hicieron?

▶ **Escucha y une.** Listen to Andy and Janet talk about what they did recently and match the elements in columns A and B.

Ⓐ

1. el mes pasado
2. el martes pasado
3. el miércoles
4. el jueves
5. el sábado
6. ayer
7. anoche
8. esta mañana

Ⓑ

a. visitar una playa
b. usar la computadora
c. cenar con Tim y Mack
d. comprar una guía turística
e. levantarse temprano
f. pasear y visitar museos
g. pasar la noche en un cámping
h. hablar con sus padres

▶ **Escribe.** Now write sentences about Andy and Janet's schedule.

Modelo 1. *El mes pasado compraron una guía turística.*

50 **Una agenda llena**

▶ **Escribe.** You are organizing your mom's birthday party. Write who did each thing and when they did it. (Note today's date on the agenda!)

Modelo *Esta mañana limpié mi habitación.*

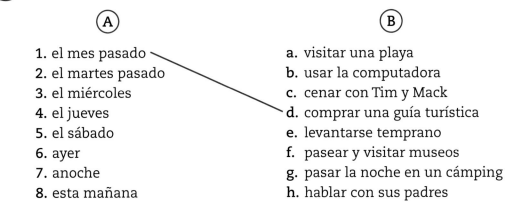

JULIO

1
Lunes
Organizar las invitaciones (los tíos).

2
Martes

3
Miércoles
Preparar la comida (papá y yo).

JULIO

4
Jueves
Escribir a los abuelos (Juliana).

5
Viernes
Por la mañana, comprar un regalo para mamá (yo). Por la tarde, llamar a la florería (Manuel).

6
Sábado
Limpiar mi habitación (yo).

7
Domingo

Gramática

Los verbos *ser* e *ir*. Pretérito

- The verbs ser and ir are irregular in the preterite and share the same forms.

VERBOS SER (TO BE) E IR (TO GO). PRETÉRITO

Singular		Plural	
yo	fui	nosotros nosotras	fuimos
tú	fuiste	vosotros vosotras	fuisteis
usted él ella	fue	ustedes ellos ellas	fueron

Prepositions of place

The verb ir can be used with prepositions to express various ideas.

- Remember, you can use ir a to say that you went to a certain place.

ir a + place

Fui **a** Buenos Aires en marzo.

- To express direction or destination, use these structures:

ir desde (from) + place + *hasta* (to) + place

Él fue **desde** México **hasta** Buenos Aires.

ir de (from) + place + *a* (to) + place

Yo fui **de** México **a** Buenos Aires.

---

51 **Viajes por Argentina**

▶ **Escucha y escribe.** The characters have traveled around Argentina. Listen and match each pair with their destination and transportation. Then write sentences.

Modelo 1. 2-C. *Diana y Rita fueron a la costa en taxi.*

Diana y Rita   Mack y Tim   Janet y Andy   Patricia y Tess

52 Una nota incompleta

▶ **Completa.** Andy left Janet a note about his activities. Fill in the missing parts using the words from the word bank.

(al) (fuimos) (a) (desde) (al) (fui) (al) (a)

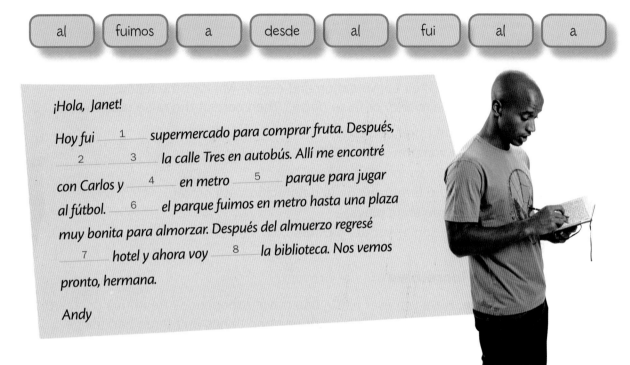

¡Hola, Janet!

Hoy fui ___1___ supermercado para comprar fruta. Después, ___2___ ___3___ la calle Tres en autobús. Allí me encontré con Carlos y ___4___ en metro ___5___ parque para jugar al fútbol. ___6___ el parque fuimos en metro hasta una plaza muy bonita para almorzar. Después del almuerzo regresé ___7___ hotel y ahora voy ___8___ la biblioteca. Nos vemos pronto, hermana.

Andy

53 Nuestros viajes

▶ **Habla y escribe.** Where is the most interesting place you have gone? Interview your classmates to find out each person's answer. Then write a summary of everyone's travels.

Modelo *Yo fui a Florida el año pasado. Catarina y Tommy fueron a Cancún.*

CONEXIONES: MATEMÁTICAS

Las distancias: ¿millas o kilómetros?

En los Estados Unidos y en Gran Bretaña utilizan las millas para medir las distancias. Pero en Latinoamérica y en muchos otros países usan el sistema métrico y los kilómetros.

Una milla equivale a 1,61 kilómetros. Un kilómetro es igual a 0,62 millas.

54 Piensa.
Some standard speed limits in Argentina are 40 km/hr, 60 km/hr, 80 km/hr, and 120 km/hr. If you were in a car going these speeds, how fast would you be going in miles per hour?

Comunicación

55 ## Habla Andy

▶ **Escucha y decide.** Andy has called Tess to see how she and Patricia are doing. Listen to their conversation and decide whether the following statements are true *(cierto)* or false *(falso)*. Then correct the false statements.

1. Andy reservó un hotel perfecto.
2. Tess y Patricia viajaron ayer.
3. Tess escribió un correo a su papá.
4. Ayer Patricia salió temprano de la habitación para correr.
5. Andy pasó tiempo en la playa.
6. Andy y Janet fueron al sur del parque.

56 ## Vacaciones increíbles

▶ **Lee y escribe.** Have you ever had a bad travel experience? Read this postcard from Andy to his friend Manuel. Write three good things and three bad things that happened.

> *Querido Manuel:*
>
> *¿Qué tal estás? Yo estoy muy contento, lo estamos pasando muy bien.*
>
> *La semana pasada fuimos a conocer las cataratas del Iguazú. Estuvimos en un cámping en el Parque Nacional. Allí conocimos a unos italianos muy simpáticos.*
>
> *El lunes comimos unas frutas deliciosas. Por la noche llovió mucho y por eso descansamos mal.*
>
> *El martes me desperté temprano para tomar fotos, pero no encontré mi cámara. ¡Qué horror! Pero tomé unas fotos maravillosas con la cámara de Janet.*
>
> *¡Son unas vacaciones increíbles!*
>
> *Hasta pronto.*
>
> *Andy*

Manuel Ortiz
1234 5th Street
Santa Fe, NM 87507

▶ **Escribe.** Write a postcard to a friend about a particularly wonderful or horrible vacation experience. Don't forget to use the preterite tense!

57 Encuestas

▶ **Habla y escribe.** What do you know about your classmates' activities? In a small group, conduct mini-interviews to find out who did the things below and when they did them. Then write a paragraph with your findings.

Modelo 1. A. *¿Cuándo viste una película en el cine?*

B. *La semana pasada.*

A. *Irene y John vieron una película en el cine la semana pasada.*

1. ¿Quién vio una película en el cine?
2. ¿Quién comió en un restaurante argentino?
3. ¿Quién compró algo en un centro comercial?
4. ¿Quién fue de vacaciones a otro país?
5. ¿Quién fue a un concierto?

Final del desafío

58 ¿Cuándo pasó?

▶ **Ordena y escribe.** Put the scenes in the most logical order and write the script. What did Andy and Janet tell their friends after they got back to camp for the night?

 **→ TU DESAFÍO** Earn points for your own challenge! Listen to the questions for your *Minientrevista Desafío 3* on the website and write your answers.

Sobres en la calle

Tess and Patricia are in Buenos Aires. Their task is to collect four envelopes with the pieces of a puzzle in the *Plaza de Mayo*, the main square in the city. Will they be able to find all the envelopes?

> Comenzamos en la calle Balcarce, ¿no?

> Sí, pero no vayas por esa calle. Es más rápido por aquí.

> ¡Aquí hay un sobre!

> No lo celebres todavía. Ahora hay que cruzar el parque.

> El segundo sobre está al lado de la iglesia... ¡Aquí está! Vamos a la calle Bolívar.

> ¡Aquí no hay nada!

> No seas tan pesimista, mamá. Mira, aquí está el tercer sobre. Solo uno más...

> No camines tan rápido, Tess.

Continuará...

59 ### Detective de palabras

▶ **Completa.** Fill in the blanks to complete each negative statement.

1. No _____ por esa calle.
2. No lo _____ todavía.
3. No _____ tan rápido.
4. No _____ tan pesimista.

60 ### ¿Comprendes?

▶ **Decide.** Decide if these statements about Tess and Patricia are true *(cierto)* or false *(falso)*. If they are false, correct them.

1. Comenzaron en la calle Rivadavia.
2. Encontraron cuatro sobres.
3. Cruzaron el parque.
4. No fueron a la calle Bolívar.
5. Tess caminó despacio.
6. No encontraron el tercer sobre.

61 La ruta más corta

▶ **Escucha e identifica.** Tess and Patricia are taking a tour of the *Plaza de Mayo* to help them find the envelopes with the clues. Listen to the tour guide and take notes.

▶ **Habla y escribe.** Now, with a partner, write a paragraph about the route they followed.

Modelo *Comenzaron aquí, en la calle Balcarce.*

CULTURA

La Plaza de Mayo

La Plaza de Mayo es la plaza principal de Buenos Aires y está en el centro de la ciudad. Esta plaza es el lugar donde comenzó la revolución por la independencia de Argentina, en mayo del año 1810.

La Casa Rosada, sede (*seat*) de la presidencia del gobierno, está delante de la plaza. Por eso, la Plaza de Mayo se considera el centro de la vida política de Buenos Aires.

62 Piensa. Where is the center of political power in the United States? If you could create your own political party, what would it be called and where would it be located? Why?

Vocabulario

La ciudad

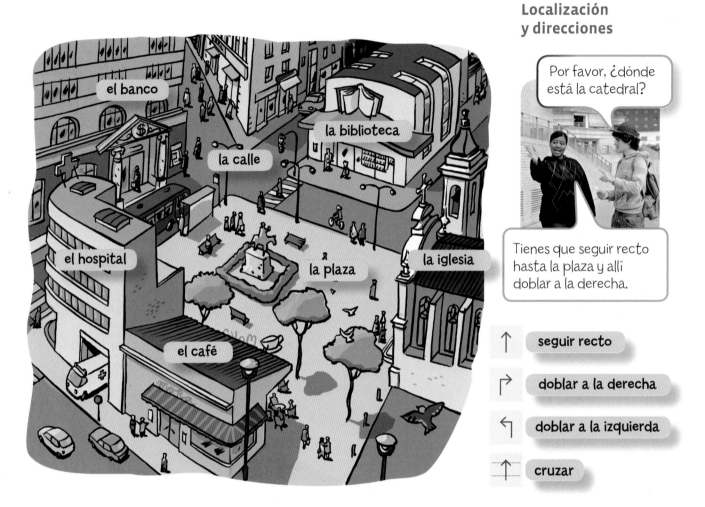

el banco

la biblioteca

la calle

el hospital

la plaza

la iglesia

el café

Localización y direcciones

Por favor, ¿dónde está la catedral?

Tienes que seguir recto hasta la plaza y allí doblar a la derecha.

↑ **seguir recto**

↱ **doblar a la derecha**

↰ **doblar a la izquierda**

↑ **cruzar**

63 **¿Adónde fueron?**

▶ **Escucha y escribe.** On the phone, Tess and Patricia describe where they went yesterday. Write sentences about the places each one visited.

Modelo 1. *Tess fue al cine y…*

64 Instrucciones para Tess

▶ **Completa y adivina.** Tess is lost. Look at the map and complete the note Patricia left her.

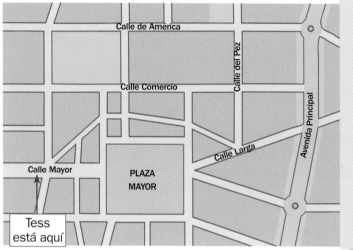

Hola, Tess.

Para llegar al museo tienes que ___1___ recto por la calle Mayor. Luego tienes que ___2___ la plaza y caminar por la calle Larga. Después tienes que ___3___ a la izquierda y ___4___ por la avenida Principal hasta la plaza.

Yo te espero allí.

Patricia

65 Direcciones

▶ **Escribe.** Write simple instructions telling how to get from your Spanish classroom to the following places in your school.

- la cafetería
- la biblioteca
- el gimnasio
- el salón de computación
- la oficina de la enfermera
- la oficina principal

▶ **Dibuja.** Now, with a partner, try out your instructions. As he or she reads each one, draw a map to that place.

CULTURA

La Casa Rosada

La Casa Rosada es el palacio presidencial. Está en el centro de Buenos Aires. Es de color rosado desde el siglo XIX. Una teoría es que el presidente escogió este color, mezcla de los colores rojo y blanco, para representar la unión de dos partidos políticos en tensión.

66 Piensa. If you were the president of Argentina, what color would you choose for your house? What would that color represent?

Gramática

El imperativo negativo

- To tell someone what not to do or to prohibit something, Spanish uses the negative command form preceded by the word no.

  No viajes sin el pasaporte.

- To give someone a friendly command, use the negative tú commands:

VERBOS REGULARES. IMPERATIVO NEGATIVO

Comprar	Comer	Escribir
no compres	no comas	no escribas

- Negative commands do not generally include a subject pronoun.

Forming the negative commands

- The negative command forms are based on the yo form of the present tense, substituting the -o for these endings:
  - -es for -ar verbs
  - -as for -er and -ir verbs

Verbo	Presente	Imperativo negativo
comprar	yo compro	no compres
comer	yo como	no comas
escribir	yo escribo	no escribas

- The verbs ser and ir are an exception:

VERBOS SER E IR. IMPERATIVO NEGATIVO

Ser	Ir
no seas	no vayas

No seas pesimista.
No vayas a ese hotel.

67 **Piensa.** How do we form negative commands in English? How is this different from the negative commands in Spanish? How is this similar?

68 **¿Lo hago o no lo hago?**

▶ **Habla.** With a partner, take turns acting out different actions. Tell your friend not to do whatever he or she is doing.

Modelo *No abras el libro.*

69 **Consejos para tu viaje**

▶ **Escribe.** Write sentences about what to do and what not to do according to the clues below. Use the *tú* commands.

Modelo 1. *No camines por el parque. Camina por la calle.*

	No	Sí
1. Caminar (por)		
2. Ir		
3. Estudiar		

▶ **Habla.** Now offer your partner a suggestion about when not to do each thing.

Modelo 1. A. *Voy al parque.*
B. *No vayas al parque ahora. Hace mucho frío.*

CULTURA

La Pirámide de Mayo

La Pirámide de Mayo es el monumento nacional más antiguo de Buenos Aires. Está situada en el centro de la Plaza de Mayo y fue construida en el año 1811 para celebrar el primer aniversario de la Revolución de Mayo. El 21 de mayo de 1942 la Pirámide de Mayo fue declarada monumento histórico.

70 **Piensa.** Can you think of any statues in the United States that represent a revolution or the liberation of people? Where are they located?

Comunicación

71 **¿Dónde está el hospital?**

▶ **Escribe.** Look at the map and write how to get to the places below. Use the *tú* commands.

Modelo el cine

⟶ *Para ir al cine, sigue recto, cruza la plaza y dobla a la derecha en la calle Libreros.*

1. la plaza　　2. el hospital　　3. la biblioteca　　4. el Banco Central

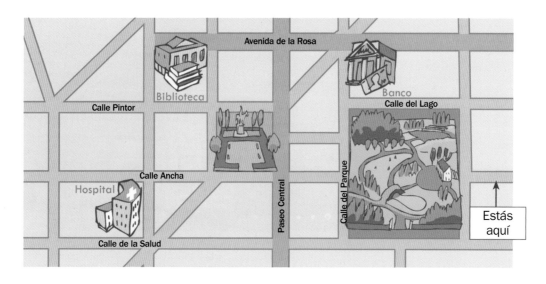

 ▶ **Habla.** Using the map, ask your partner how to get to other places in the city. Take turns.

Modelo A. *Por favor, ¿cómo puedo ir al teatro?*
　　　　 B. *Para ir al teatro, sigue recto...*

72 **Sugerencias**

▶ **Escucha y decide.** Tess wants to do many things this summer. Listen and decide whether Patricia agrees with Tess about each item on her list.

1. estudiar en una escuela de baile
2. pasar unas noches en un hotel
3. ir mucho al teatro
4. viajar por todo el país en autobús
5. visitar el parque
6. pasear por el centro de la ciudad
7. trabajar en el banco
8. cenar todas las noches en el café

▶ **Escribe.** For each activity that Patricia disapproves of, write her negative command and give a possible alternative.

Modelo *No estudies en una escuela de baile. Estudia en una escuela de música.*

73 Mi ciudad

▶ **Lee y contesta.** Read this description of Patricia's hometown and answer the questions.

Mi ciudad

Mi ciudad es grande y bonita.
Me gustan mucho las calles
anchas con árboles y flores.
En el centro, los edificios son
muy altos y elegantes.
Las calles están llenas de
cafés. Mi cine favorito está
en el centro, cerca del teatro.
¡Es divertido salir por la noche
en mi ciudad!

1. ¿Qué piensa Patricia de su ciudad?
2. ¿Cómo son los edificios del centro?
3. ¿Qué hay en las calles del centro?
4. ¿Dónde está el cine?

▶ **Escribe.** Now write a description of your city or town. Include landmarks and direction words.

Final del desafío

Mamá, estoy cansada. Caminamos todo el día buscando los sobres. ¿Podemos sentarnos?

No bebas tan rápido. Tenemos tiempo. La plaza está allí.

Sí. Mira, allí hay un café. Pero no comas todavía y comemos juntas después, ¿quieres?

¡Es cierto! ¿Ves la biblioteca?

74 ¿Qué pasó en la historia?

▶ **Escribe.** Look at the scenes above. Decide what happens in the next scene and write a summary of what happened in this *Desafío*.

Modelo *Tess y Patricia caminaron todo el día buscando los sobres…*

Todo junto

ESCUCHAR, ESCRIBIR Y HABLAR

75 **El viaje de tus sueños**

▶ **Escucha y elige.** Your local radio station is sponsoring a contest to win a fantasy trip. First listen to the advertisement that explains the rules of the contest. Then choose the answer that was NOT mentioned in the advertisement.

1. Necesitas...	a. el pasaporte	b. la maleta	c. el billete de ida y vuelta
2. Tú escoges ir a...	a. la montaña	b. la ciudad	c. la playa
3. Puedes ir en...	a. tren	b. taxi	c. avión
4. Te quedas en un...	a. hotel	b. hostal	c. cámping
5. Visitas...	a. museos	b. teatros	c. iglesias

▶ **Escribe.** Write the script for your contest entry, describing the "trip of your dreams." Be sure to include answers to the following questions:

1. ¿Adónde quieres ir?

2. ¿Qué vas a llevar?

3. ¿Cómo vas a viajar?

4. ¿Dónde te vas a quedar?

5. ¿Qué piensas visitar?

▶ **Presenta.** When you have written your script, record it on an MP3 player or onto a CD. Then play your contest entry for the class. As you listen to your classmates, fill in a chart like the one below to keep track of the most popular places.

¿Adónde quieres ir?

a la montaña	a la playa	a la ciudad
Karen y Bill		

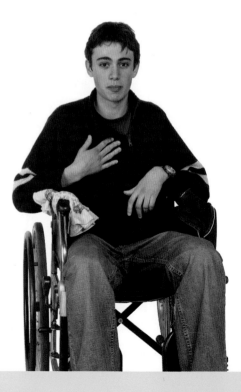

HABLAR

No viajes a la costa.

¡Viajé a la costa la semana pasada!

76 **¡Ya viajé a la costa!**

▶ **Habla.** With a partner, take turns telling each other what not to do and what you already did and when. Follow the model.

1. ir a la ciudad en tren
2. comer en ese restaurante
3. pasear de noche por ese parque
4. viajar a la playa

5. comprar recuerdos en la terminal
6. comprar un billete de ida y vuelta
7. beber agua del río
8. escribir en el libro

LEER

77 **¡Tocamos las nubes!**

▶ **Lee y contesta.** Read the following extract from Tim's diary about their trip on the Train to the Clouds, and answer the questions.

Lunes, 3 de marzo

¡Tocamos las nubes!

Primero mi abuelo y yo viajamos en autobús desde Buenos Aires hasta Salta. En Salta tomamos el tren a las nubes. El viaje duró casi doce horas.

Cuando el tren alcanza los 3.000 metros (9,000 feet) casi no se puede respirar.

San Antonio de los Cobres fue nuestra última estación. Está situada a 4.000 metros de altura (12,000 feet). ¡Allí puedes tocar las nubes!

1. ¿Cómo viajaron Tim y Mack desde Buenos Aires hasta Salta?
2. ¿Desde dónde sale el tren a las nubes?
3. ¿Cuánto tiempo duró el viaje en el tren a las nubes?
4. ¿Qué pasa cuando el tren alcanza los 3.000 metros?
5. ¿Por qué llaman a este tren el tren a las nubes?

En el Teatro Colón

The four pairs meet in Buenos Aires after attempting to complete their individual tasks. Did all the pairs successfully carry out their assignments?

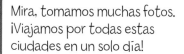

> Mira, tomamos muchas fotos. ¡Viajamos por todas estas ciudades en un solo día!

> ¡Encontramos al gaucho! ¡Él corrió rápido, pero nosotras corrimos más rápido que él!

> Ayer fuimos a Iguazú. ¡Qué impresionante! Nos perdimos, pero grabamos un video.

> Encontramos todos los sobres en la ciudad. ¡Cuidado, Tess, no los pierdas!

78 Al llegar

▶ **Habla.** In a small group, play charades by choosing one scene and acting it out for the rest of your classmates. See if they can guess which scene is being portrayed.

▶ **Escribe.** After reviewing the scenes and the task that each pair faced, choose a winning team and try to convince the other students why they deserve to win. Write a description answering the following questions:

- ¿De dónde salieron?
- ¿Adónde fueron?
- ¿Cómo llegaron?
- ¿Qué encontraron?
- ¿Qué lugares visitaron?

Modelo

> Andy y Janet fueron desde Buenos Aires hasta Iguazú en avión. Visitaron las cataratas del Iguazú, pero...

79 Las votaciones

▶ **Decide.** Which pair has done the most amazing challenge in Argentina? Take a vote to decide!

> ¡Qué lástima! Nuestros amigos no probaron nuestro postre más tradicional: el dulce de leche.

Sorprendente

Argentina

0   125   250 millas

0   125   250 kilómetros

Paraguay

Salta

Brasil

OCÉANO PACÍFICO

Aconcagua

Uruguay

Chile

Santa Rosa

Buenos Aires

Argentina es una república situada en el sur de América. La capital de la nación es Buenos Aires.

Argentina es el país hispanohablante más grande del mundo, aunque no es el más poblado: tiene aproximadamente 40 millones de habitantes. El 86% de la población desciende de europeos, especialmente de españoles e italianos.

¿Sabes que la montaña más alta de América está en Argentina?

Glaciar Perito Moreno

Río Gallegos

¡Claro! Se llama Aconcagua y mide 6.959 metros.

80 **¿Exactamente dónde?**

▶ **Elige.** Look at the map and choose the appropriate ending for each sentence.

1. Argentina está…
   - **a.** al sur de Paraguay
   - **b.** al norte de Paraguay

2. Buenos Aires está…
   - **a.** en el centro del país
   - **b.** en el este del país

3. Las cataratas del Iguazú están cerca de…
   - **a.** Chile
   - **b.** Paraguay

4. El glaciar Perito Moreno está lejos de…
   - **a.** Chile
   - **b.** Brasil

Los paisajes de Argentina

Argentina está atravesada de norte a sur por la cordillera de los Andes. Tiene tres regiones muy diferentes: el Chaco, la Pampa y la Patagonia.

1. El Chaco

El Chaco es una región cálida de bosques y selvas en el norte de Argentina. Es una de las zonas menos pobladas.

En el noroeste, en la frontera con Brasil, están las **cataratas del Iguazú**.

(1) Cataratas del Iguazú.

(2) Avenida 9 de Julio (Buenos Aires).

(3) Glaciar Perito Moreno.

2. La Pampa y Buenos Aires

En el centro de Argentina está **la Pampa**. Es una llanura muy extensa cubierta de hierba. En el este de esta región está **Buenos Aires**, la capital.

3. La Patagonia

La Patagonia ocupa el sur de Argentina. Es una región árida de glaciares. El glaciar más espectacular es el **Perito Moreno**, en la frontera con Chile.

81 **Así es Argentina**

▶ **Escribe.** What are the three regions like? Put the adjectives in the corresponding boxes.

¿Cómo es cada región?	
El Chaco	
La Pampa	
La Patagonia	

cálida   fría

extensa   llana

1. El tango

El **tango** es un tipo de música
y de baile conocido en todo el mundo. Su origen está
en los barrios populares de Buenos Aires y de otras
ciudades de Argentina y de Uruguay.

Los tangos hablan del amor, del paso del tiempo,
del barrio, etc.

El instrumento básico de los tangos es el bandoneón.

(1) Una orquesta tocando tangos.

Una pareja bailando
un tango.

2. Mafalda

Mafalda es el personaje principal
de la historieta gráfica más famosa
de Argentina. El autor de esas historietas
es Quino (Joaquín Salvador Lavado).

Durante años, las historietas de Mafalda
sirvieron para denunciar con humor
los problemas de los argentinos.

(2) Un dibujo de Mafalda.

Quino, el creador
de Mafalda.

3. Buenos Aires

Buenos Aires, la capital de Argentina, es una gran ciudad. Sus habitantes dicen que tienen la avenida más ancha del mundo (la avenida **9 de Julio**) y la más larga (la avenida **Rivadavia**).

Entre los barrios de Buenos Aires está el famoso barrio obrero de **La Boca**. En su calle Caminito, el pintor **Benito Quinquela** organizó un museo al aire libre.

(3) La Plaza de Mayo, en el centro de Buenos Aires.

(4) Una familia comiendo ñoquis.

4. Los ñoquis del 29 del mes

Tradicionalmente, los argentinos comen **ñoquis** el día **29** de cada mes. Ese día colocan dinero debajo del plato de ñoquis; los argentinos creen que así atraen a la suerte. Esta costumbre se llama «ñoquis del 29».

 82 **Mitos argentinos**

▶ **Investiga y escribe.**
Search for information about one of these people and write a brief summary of his or her life.

Include photos and biographical information such as main achievements and music, literature, or movie tributes.

Jorge Luis Borges.

Eva Perón (Evita).

La vuelta al mundo
de Cinthia Scoch

Cinthia Scoch es una chica muy obediente. Un día, su madre la mandó a comprar un kilo de azúcar.

–Anda al almacén[1] de la derecha –le indicó la señora Scoch.

Cinthia pensó: «En realidad, el almacén está a la izquierda», pero, para no contradecir a su madre, caminó hacia la derecha.

Oliendo el lindo aroma de los tilos[2] de su barrio, caminó una, dos, tres cuadras[3], pero no encontró el almacén.

A las tres horas llegó al puerto de Buenos Aires. Allí tomó un barco con ruta de navegación hacia la derecha.

El barco navegó días y días y al fin llegó a un puerto de Australia. Cinthia Scoch bajó a tierra. Continuó hacia la derecha. Cruzó toda Australia. En la ciudad de Sidney no encontró ningún almacén, así que tomó otro barco, también hacia la derecha.

Llegó al puerto de Valparaíso, en Chile. Continuó hacia la derecha. Cruzó los Andes. Llegó a Mendoza y cruzó las provincias de San Luis y Santa Fe.

Llegó a Buenos Aires, y siempre caminando hacia la derecha, finalmente se encontró[4] en su barrio. Así completó la vuelta al mundo y de nuevo olió el lindo aroma de los tilos de su barrio. Una cuadra antes de su casa, encontró el almacén. Es decir, a la izquierda de su casa. «Mamá está equivocada[5]», pensó.

Compró un kilo de azúcar.

Entró en casa y le entregó[6] el paquete a la señora Scoch.

La madre de Cinthia guardó el azúcar en un tarro[7].

–Hija –le dijo a Cinthia–, ¡cuánto tardaste[8]!

RICARDO MARIÑO, *Botella al mar* (texto adaptado).

---

1. grocer's shop	2. lime trees	3. blocks	4. was
5. wrong	6. gave	7. jar	8. it took you so long!

ESTRATEGIA Elementos de la narración

83 Una historia con muchos elementos

▶ **Escribe.** Complete the story map with the different elements of Cinthia Scoch's story.

Título y autor:		
Marco *(setting)*	**Tiempo** *(when):*	
	Lugar *(where):*	
Personajes *(characters)*		
Argumento *(plot)*		

COMPRENSIÓN

84 ¿Está claro?

▶ **Completa.** Complete these sentences.

a. Cinthia salió a la calle para…

b. Cinthia caminó hacia la derecha para…

c. Cinthia caminó por su barrio, pero…

d. En el puerto de Buenos Aires…

e. Cinthia cruzó…

f. Cinthia encontró el almacén…

g. En el almacén…

h. En su casa…

85 Un resumen

▶ **Escribe.** Write a summary of Cinthia's travels. Include the main elements of the story. If you wish, illustrate the story with a drawing.

 **TU DESAFÍO** Earn points for your own challenge! Visit the website to take a virtual tour around Argentina and describe your trip in a letter to a friend.

De viaje

Medios de transporte

(ir) a pie	*on foot, walking*
el autobús	*bus*
el avión	*plane*
el barco	*boat*
el coche	*car*
el metro	*subway*
el taxi	*taxi*
el tren	*train*

Acciones

ir de vacaciones	*to go on vacation*
ir de excursión	*to go on an excursion*
viajar	*to travel*

Lugares

el aeropuerto	*airport*
la estación	*station*

Los viajes

Objetos

el billete	*ticket*
la bolsa	*bag*
la guía turística	*travel guide, guidebook*
la maleta	*suitcase*
el pasaporte	*passport*

Acciones

comprar recuerdos	*to buy souvenirs*
enseñar el pasaporte	*to show your passport*
facturar el equipaje	*to check the baggage*

Lugares

la agencia de viajes	*travel agency*
la oficina de turismo	*tourist office*
el mostrador de información	*information desk*

Destinos y alojamientos

el campo	*countryside*
la ciudad	*city, town*
la costa	*coast*
la montaña	*mountain*
la playa	*beach*
el cámping	*campsite*
el hotel	*hotel*
reservar habitación	*to reserve a room*
hacer turismo	*to be a tourist*

La ciudad

Lugares

el banco	*bank*
la biblioteca	*library*
el café	*café*
la calle	*street*
el hospital	*hospital*
la iglesia	*church*
la plaza	*square, plaza*

Localización y direcciones

cruzar la calle	*to cross the street*
doblar a la derecha	*to turn right*
doblar a la izquierda	*to turn left*
seguir recto	*to go/walk straight ahead*

DESAFÍO 1

1 **Respuestas lógicas.** Complete each sentence with the most logical answer.

1. En Buenos Aires yo viajo casi siempre...
   a. en tren   **b.** en avión   **c.** en metro

2. Yo vivo lejos y casi nunca voy a la escuela...
   a. a pie   **b.** en tren   **c.** en avión

3. Para viajar desde Buenos Aires hasta Nueva York tengo que ir...
   a. en autobús   **b.** en metro   **c.** en avión

4. Cuando voy de excursión con mi clase, normalmente vamos...
   a. a pie   **b.** en autobús   **c.** en barco

DESAFÍO 2

2 **De viaje.** Match each place with the corresponding actions.

1. En una tienda

2. En una agencia de viajes

3. En una oficina de turismo

   a. compras los billetes de avión.
   b. pides un plano de la ciudad.
   c. compras recuerdos.
   d. pagas el viaje.
   e. pides información de la ciudad.
   f. compras una maleta.

DESAFÍO 3

3 **Las vacaciones.** Match each statement with the corresponding picture.

1. El año pasado nos alojamos en un cámping.
2. Este verano pasamos las vacaciones en la playa.
3. En Navidad fuimos a esquiar a la montaña.
4. La semana pasada reservamos habitación en un hotel.

DESAFÍO 4

4 **¿Adónde vas?** Answer the questions in complete sentences. Use the word bank.

1. ¿Adónde vas si necesitas dinero?
2. ¿Adónde vas si estás muy enfermo?
3. ¿Adónde vas si tienes mucha hambre?
4. ¿Adónde vas si quieres leer un libro?

restaurante   banco

hospital   biblioteca

Verbos regulares. Pretérito (págs. 154, 162)

	COMPRAR	COMER	ESCRIBIR
yo	compré	comí	escribí
tú	compraste	comiste	escribiste
usted él ella	compró	comió	escribió
nosotros nosotras	compramos	comimos	escribimos
vosotros vosotras	comprasteis	comisteis	escribisteis
ustedes ellos ellas	compraron	comieron	escribieron

Marcadores temporales de pasado (pág. 170)

anteayer	*the day before yesterday*
antes	*before*
ayer	*yesterday*
anoche	*last night*
la semana pasada	*last week*
el mes pasado	*last month*
el año pasado	*last year*

Los verbos *ser* e *ir*. Pretérito (pág. 172)

singular		plural	
yo	fui	nosotros nosotras	fuimos
tú	fuiste	vosotros vosotras	fuisteis
usted él ella	fue	ustedes ellos ellas	fueron

Preposiciones de lugar (pág. 172)

a	*to*
de… a…	*from … to …*
desde… hasta…	*from … to / until …*

El imperativo negativo (pág. 180)

Verbos regulares

Comprar	Comer	Escribir
no compres	no comas	no escribas

Verbos *ser* e *ir*

Ser	Ir
no seas	no vayas

DESAFÍO 1

5 **Nuestro fin de semana.** Write sentences about what everyone did last weekend.

Modelo 1. *Yo viajé en avión.*

yo   ellas   nosotros   usted   tú

DESAFÍO 2

6 **Experiencias.** Answer the questions in complete sentences.

Modelo ¿Escribiste el correo electrónico a tus abuelos?
→ *Sí, escribí el correo electrónico a mis abuelos.*

1. ¿Comiste en un restaurante argentino?   3. ¿Fuiste a otro país?
2. ¿Leíste el último libro de Harry Potter?   4. ¿Participaste en un maratón?

DESAFÍO 3

7 **Recuerda.** Write what you did at the times indicated below.

1. antes   3. ayer   5. el lunes pasado   7. el mes pasado
2. anoche   4. anteayer   6. la semana pasada   8. el año pasado

DESAFÍO 4

8 **Órdenes.** Write negative commands based on the information provided.

Modelo Si abres **la puerta**, hace frío. (abrir) → *No abras la puerta.*

1. **Esa carne** está mala. (comer)   3. Tus amigos no van **al cine** esta noche. (ir)
2. **Ese libro** es muy aburrido. (leer)   4. **Esa mochila** es muy cara. (comprar)

 **CULTURA**

9 **¡Descubre Argentina!** Answer the questions.

1. Why is *tren a las nubes* well named?
2. What do you know about the Pampa region?
3. Where is Iguazu Falls located?
4. What color is the Presidential Palace in Buenos Aires?
5. Describe the different geographical regions in Argentina.

Crónica de

un viaje

In this project you will prepare an illustrated travelogue. The traveler can be someone in your family, a person in your community, or a famous person. You will present your travelogue to your classmates, who will vote for the best trip in each of these categories: most interesting, most fun, and most dangerous.

PASO 1 Decide qué viaje vas a describir

- Decide what trip you are going to describe. For example:
  - El viaje de una persona de tu familia.
  - El viaje de una persona de tu comunidad.
  - Un viaje histórico.

> ### Viaje a la Patagonia
>
> En 1978 una expedición viajó a la Patagonia, en Argentina, para recordar los viajes de Francisco P. Moreno, cien años antes.

PASO 2 Busca información sobre el viaje

- Interview people or do research on the Internet to find information.

El viaje de...

¿Adónde viajó?
¿Cuándo viajó?
¿Cómo viajó? En tren, en avión, en coche...
¿Qué objetos llevó? Pasaporte, cámara...
¿Qué ocurrió en el viaje?
¿Qué vio?

- Gather documents to illustrate the trip:
  - Fotos de los viajeros.
  - Un mapa o un plano para dibujar el itinerario.
  - Postales, billetes, recuerdos...

PASO 3 Escribe la crónica

- Organize all your information in chronological order and write one or two sentences to describe the information.

En noviembre de 1979, la expedición visitó el glaciar Perito Moreno. El glaciar se llama así en honor al perito Francisco P. Moreno.

PASO 4 Presenta la crónica

- Present your report and answer your classmates' questions.

¿Qué ropa llevan?

Llevan chaquetas, gorros, guantes y botas.

PASO 5 Vota la mejor crónica

- Take a vote to decide which travelogue is the best in each category: *más interesante, más divertido, más peligroso.* Give reasons for your vote.

El viaje de la expedición al glaciar Perito Moreno es el más interesante: viajaron en coche y en barco a este glaciar del sur de Argentina.

Unidad 7

Autoevaluación

¿Qué has aprendido en esta unidad?

Do the following activities to evaluate how well you get along in Spanish.

Evaluate your skills. For each item, say Very well, Well, or I need more practice.

a. Can you talk about what you did yesterday?

▶ Tell your partner what you did before and after breakfast yesterday.

b. Can you talk about where you live?

▶ Ask your partner to name three important places where you live.

▶ Tell your partner the location of the same three places.

c. Can you say how people travel in your region?

▶ Ask your partner how his or her family goes shopping.

▶ Say how you get to school.

Chile

De vuelta a los Andes

DESAFÍO
1

DESAFÍO
2

▶ **To express cause**

Vocabulario
El universo

Gramática
Expresar causa:
- La conjunción *porque*
- La preposición *por*

La Isla de Pascua

▶ **To express quantity**

Vocabulario
Geografía

Gramática
Expresar cantidad.
Los indefinidos

El desierto de Atacama

Valparaíso

DESAFÍO
3

▶ **To express past actions**

Vocabulario
Divisiones políticas
Números del 101
al 1.000

Gramática
Verbos irregulares
en el pasado. *Decir*
y *hacer*

Verbos irregulares
en el pasado. *Estar*
y *tener*

DESAFÍO
4

Parque Nacional
Torres del Paine

▶ **To express permission and prohibition**

Vocabulario
La naturaleza
y el medio ambiente

Gramática
Expresar permiso
y prohibición

En Santiago de Chile

In this unit the four pairs are in Santiago, the capital of Chile. Héctor Basualdo, their Chilean host, welcomes them at *La Chascona*. This house was once owned by Pablo Neruda, a Nobel Prize-winning poet.

¿Esta es la casa del famoso poeta Pablo Neruda?

Sí, Andy. La Chascona es famosa porque fue la casa de Pablo Neruda. Ahora es un museo muy visitado.

¿Vieron el cuadro de la mujer en el salón? ¡Es fantástico!

Bien, aquí tienen sus desafíos. ¡Suerte!

Sí, Rita. Lo pintó otro gran artista, Diego Rivera. La mujer del cuadro es Matilde, la esposa de Pablo Neruda.

1 ¿Comprendes?

▶ **Responde.** Answer the questions according to what you read.

1. ¿Qué es La Chascona? ¿Por qué es famosa?
2. ¿Quién es Matilde?
3. ¿Cómo son las estatuas?
4. ¿Qué quiere botar Diana en el contenedor de basura?

EXPRESIONES ÚTILES

¡Cuántas estatuas!

To wish someone good luck:
  ¡Suerte!

To show admiration:
  ¡Qué impresionante!

To stress quantity:
  ¡Cuánto dinero!
  ¡Cuánta gente!
  ¡Cuántos moáis!
  ¡Cuántas estatuas!

2 **Expresiones**

▶ **Escribe.** Match each expression with the corresponding picture.

a. ¡Suerte!　　**b.** ¡Qué impresionante!　　**c.** ¡Cuánta gente!　　**d.** ¡Qué grande!

¿Quién ganará?

3 **Los desafíos**

▶ **Habla.** What will be the challenge for each pair? Think about this question and discuss it with your classmates.

DESAFÍO ①

Las estrellas de Atacama

Andy y Janet

DESAFÍO ②

Una estatua falsa

Tess y Patricia

DESAFÍO ③

El Maratón de las Escaleras

Tim y Mack

DESAFÍO ④

Diana y Rita

La famosa Ruta W

4 **Las votaciones**

▶ **Decide.** Who will win this unit's challenge? Vote to choose the most enriching task.

Enriquecedor

Las estrellas de Atacama

👁 Andy and Janet are in the *Valle de la Luna*, a moon-like landscape in the Atacama Desert. They will spend the night there searching for a rock formation in the shape of a howling dog.

> Estamos en el Valle de la Luna, Janet. ¡Vamos a explorarlo!

> ¡Allí hay gente... pero no se mueve!

> No se mueven porque no son personas, Janet. Son rocas.

> Estas rocas son interesantes...

> ¡Cuántas estrellas! El cielo está muy limpio.

> ¡Mira, aquello es el planeta Marte!

> Vamos, Janet, tenemos que buscar las rocas para resolver la prueba.

> Tengo la cámara lista para tomar fotos...

Continuará...

5 ### Detective de palabras

▶ **Relaciona.** What word from the dialogue relates to each of these images?

6 ¿Comprendes?

▶ **Escribe.** Use the dialogue in the *fotonovela* to answer these questions.

1. ¿Dónde están Andy y Janet?
2. ¿Qué van a hacer Andy y Janet?
3. ¿Qué ve Janet?
4. ¿Cómo está el cielo de Atacama?
5. ¿Qué tienen que hacer Andy y Janet?

7 Cada oveja con su pareja

▶ **Une.** Match each sentence in column A with the corresponding ending in column B according to the *fotonovela*.

(A)

1. Este lugar se llama Valle de la Luna
2. Las figuras no se mueven
3. Andy y Janet ven muchas estrellas
4. Janet va a tomar fotos
5. Andy y Janet tienen que buscar unas rocas

(B)

a. porque la cámara está lista.
b. porque quieren resolver la prueba.
c. porque su paisaje es similar al de la Luna.
d. porque no son personas. ¡Son rocas!
e. porque el cielo está muy limpio.

 CULTURA

El Valle de la Luna

El Valle de la Luna está cerca de San Pedro de Atacama. El valle tiene ese nombre porque su aspecto es muy similar al paisaje de la Luna. Este valle es considerado uno de los lugares más secos de la Tierra. ¡En algunas áreas no llueve nunca!

8 **Piensa.** Do you think there is life on the Moon or on other planets? If so, what kind of life forms would live there?

Vocabulario

El universo

el planeta Júpiter

la Tierra

el planeta Marte

el Sol

el sistema solar

la Luna

la estrella

el cometa

el eclipse

Me gusta mirar **el cielo** por la noche.

A mí me gusta **explorar** y **descubrir** cosas del universo.

la astronauta

9 **Tus conocimientos**

▶ **Completa.** Complete the sentences with the vocabulary above.

1. _____ es una estrella.

2. _____ brillan en el cielo por la noche.

3. _____ giran alrededor del Sol.

4. _____ es el satélite de la Tierra.

5. _____ pueden ser de sol o de luna.

10 Errores

 ▶ **Escucha y decide.** Janet has learned about space, but she seems to have confused some facts. Listen and decide whether her statements are true *(cierto)* or false *(falso)*.

▶ **Escribe.** Write facts that you know about each of the following topics.

Modelo el cielo ⟶ *El cielo es azul.*

1. la Tierra

2. las estrellas

3. la Luna

4. el Sol

11 Las actividades típicas

▶ **Escribe.** Use the prompts below to write four sentences about the things you like to do during the seasons of the year.

1. En primavera me gusta…
2. Me gusta el verano porque puedo…
3. El otoño es especial para…
4. Durante el invierno puedo…

 ▶ **Habla.** Compare your answers with a partner's. What activities do you have in common?

Modelo A. *A mí me gusta el invierno porque puedo esquiar. ¿Y a ti?*
B. *A mí también.*

CONEXIONES: CIENCIAS

San Pedro de Atacama

San Pedro de Atacama es un pueblo del norte de Chile famoso por su situación geográfica. Está a casi 8.000 pies sobre el nivel del mar (más alto que muchas montañas). El pueblo también es famoso por su cielo nocturno: ¡en el cielo de San Pedro de Atacama se pueden ver millones de estrellas!

12 **Piensa.** How do you think San Pedro's geographic situation influences its view of the night sky? How does the geographic situation in your city or town influence your view of the night sky?

Gramática

Expresar causa

La conjunción porque

- To express cause, use the conjunction porque followed by a sentence with a conjugated verb.

    Lily sabe muchas cosas **porque** lee mucho.

- To ask for a reason, use the question ¿Por qué…? To respond, use the word porque.

    –¿**Por qué** no puedes ir a la fiesta?
    –**Porque** estoy enfermo.

La preposición por

- The preposition por sometimes expresses cause or reason.

    No fuimos a la playa **por** el viento.

- The preposition por is usually followed by a noun.

    Le compré un regalo **por su cumpleaños**.

13 **Compara.** How do we state cause in English? Describe similarities and differences in the way we express this concept in English and in Spanish.

14 **Razones para todo**

▶ **Relaciona y escribe.** Match the actions below with the corresponding picture. Write sentences using *por*.

Modelo 1. ⟶ B. *Janet fue a ese café por los helados.*

1. Janet fue a ese café…
2. Janet bebió mucha agua…
3. Janet visitó Chile…
4. Janet vio las rocas de noche…
5. Janet compró unas gafas…

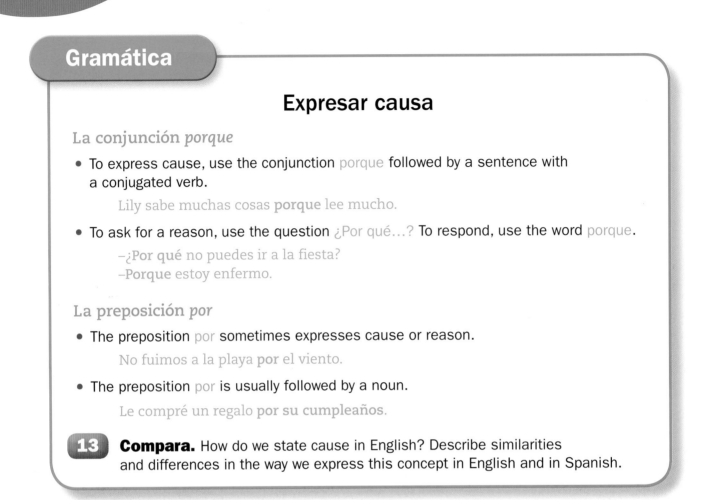

A

la luna llena

B

los helados

C

una oferta especial

D

el calor

E

sus paisajes

15 **Los motivos de Andy y Janet**

▶ **Completa.** Complete the sentences with *por* or *porque*.

1. Andy y Janet fueron al desierto _____ el desafío.

2. Janet tiene miedo _____ es de noche.

3. Andy lleva su cámara _____ le gusta tomar fotos.

4. El cielo está bonito _____ hay muchas estrellas.

5. Andy y Janet pasan mala noche _____ el frío del desierto.

16 **¡A conocernos!**

▶ **Escribe.** Read the following topics and choose five. Then write a sentence about yourself in relation to each topic.

Modelo 1. la familia ⟶ *Nunca estoy solo(a) porque mi familia es muy grande.*

1. la familia
2. los deportes
3. las películas
4. la escuela
5. el arte
6. el trabajo

7. los amigos
8. la música
9. la comunicación
10. las fiestas
11. las compras
12. la casa

CONEXIONES: CIENCIAS

El salar de Atacama

El salar de Atacama es el depósito de sal más grande de Chile. Está situado al sur de San Pedro de Atacama. Casi todo el depósito está permanentemente seco, pero hay lagunas. Gracias a ellas muchas aves y otros animales viven allí.

17 **Piensa.** Plant and animal life has adapted to live in this area, which, in some places, has never had rainfall recorded. What kinds of plants and animals would be able to survive? What adaptations would they have to make?

Comunicación

18 Nuestro universo

▶ **Escucha y decide.** Listen to a scientist talk about space.
Then decide whether the statements below are true *(cierto)* or false *(falso)*.

Prueba tus conocimientos sobre el espacio

1. El Sol es una estrella.
2. El planeta Tierra no está en el sistema solar.
3. Desde la Tierra no pueden verse otros planetas.
4. Saturno es un planeta con anillos.
5. Júpiter es el planeta más grande de nuestro sistema solar.
6. No hay cometas en nuestro sistema solar.
7. Los cometas están formados por hielo y otras sustancias.
8. Neil Armstrong fue el primer hombre en caminar por la Luna.

19 Una entrevista de radio

▶ **Escribe.** You are interviewing a space scientist for the school's Internet Radiocast.
Write five questions you would like to ask about his or her work.

Modelo

1. ¿Por qué estudias el universo?

▶ **Habla.** With your partner, role-play the interview. You ask the questions and he or she answers. Then switch roles.

¿Por qué estudias el universo?

Porque en el universo hay muchas cosas interesantes.

20 ¿Razones o excusas?

▶ **Habla.** What excuses do your classmates have for not doing
the chores below? Ask five friends.

| poner la mesa | barrer el suelo | ordenar el garaje | cocinar | limpiar el baño |

Modelo A. ¿Qué excusa tienes para no limpiar tu dormitorio?
            B. Yo no limpio mi dormitorio porque estoy cansado.

▶ **Escribe.** Using your classmates' answers, write a short essay
of five sentences about their excuses.

Modelo Jim no limpia su dormitorio porque está cansado…

Final del desafío

El blog de Andy

3 de marzo. San Pedro de Atacama

Observar el cielo de Atacama
fue fantástico. El cielo allí es muy claro
y puedes ver muchas estrellas.
También puedes ver Marte y otros
planetas.

En Chile estamos en verano, pero
las noches son frías. Anoche fue difícil
dormir en la tienda de campaña
por el frío.

Janet y yo hablamos mucho de la Luna,
de los eclipses y de los cometas,
y por la noche soñé con ser astronauta.
Quiero descubrir y explorar nuevos
mundos.

¡Ah! Janet tomó la foto de las rocas
en forma de perro porque queremos
ganar el desafío.

21 ¿Qué pasa en la historia?

▶ **Escribe.** Andy and Janet spent the night in the Atacama Desert. Read Andy's
blog and see if they accomplished their task. Then write your own blog entry
describing what you think happened to Andy and Janet the following day when
they woke up. Share your blog with the class.

Una estatua falsa

Tess and Patricia are on Easter Island, Chile. There they have to find and topple a fake moai. The native Rapanui people believed that the moai offered them protection.

La Isla de Pascua tiene unos paisajes extraordinarios.

¡Sí! Tiene volcanes, pero no están activos.

Sabemos muy poco sobre la cultura rapanui...

Mira, ahí hay algunos moáis. Todos parecen auténticos, ¿verdad?

Camina con cuidado, la costa es rocosa.

Ahí no está el moái falso. Tenemos que buscar un lago...

Continuará...

22 **Detective de palabras**

▶ **Identifica.** What nouns from the dialogue relate to these images?

(1) (2) (3) (4)

▶ **Escribe.** Write one sentence for each noun.

23 **¿Comprendes?**

▶ **Escribe.** Answer the questions in complete sentences.

1. ¿Cómo son los paisajes de la Isla de Pascua según Patricia?
2. ¿Cómo es la costa de la isla?
3. ¿De qué cultura son los moáis?
4. ¿Qué pista tienen Tess y Patricia para encontrar el moái falso?

En la isla no llueve con frecuencia.

24 **Una isla espectacular**

▶ **Escucha y contesta.** Before their trip, Tess and Patricia talked about Easter Island. Listen to the conversation and answer the questions.

1. ¿Qué tiene ganas de ver Tess?
2. ¿Cuántas lenguas hablan en la Isla de Pascua?
3. ¿Cuántos volcanes no activos hay en la isla?
4. ¿Cómo se llaman las islas que rodean a la isla principal?
5. ¿Por qué hay pocos árboles en la Isla de Pascua?

25 **Algunas cosas**

▶ **Habla.** Do you know the names of any of the following? Make a list, then ask a partner if he or she knows of any.

Modelo A. ¿Conoces algún lago?
B. Sí, conozco el lago Ontario.

1. ¿Conoces alguna isla?
2. ¿Conoces alguna estatua?
3. ¿Conoces algún volcán?
4. ¿Conoces algún bosque tropical?

CULTURA

La Isla de Pascua

La Isla de Pascua está en el océano Pacífico, en la Polinesia. Esta isla forma parte de Chile. Allí viven los descendientes de la civilización rapanui. Sabemos poco sobre esta antigua cultura. En 1877 quedaron en la isla poco más de cien personas. Hoy la población es de cuatro mil habitantes aproximadamente. Las imágenes de los moáis de la isla son famosas en todo el mundo.

26 **Piensa.** What would you like to find out about the Rapanui? Why?

DESAFÍO 2

Vocabulario

Geografía

¿Viajamos por **tierra** o por **mar**?

el continente

la isla

el océano

la montaña

el valle

el lago

el río

El desierto es seco.

El bosque es tropical.

27 **¿Dónde vivimos?**

▶ **Clasifica.** Classify the places by the geographic feature(s) that each represents. Then add one more place that you know to each column.

el Sahara   el Mississippi   el Amazonas   Hawái   Asia

el Mediterráneo   Yellowstone   el Atlántico   Bermudas   África

océanos	continentes	islas	ríos	desiertos	mares	bosques

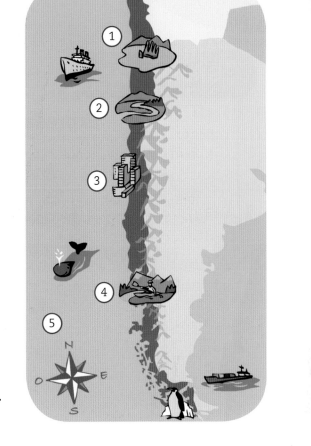

28 **La geografía chilena**

▶ **Escribe.** These are the places Tess and Patricia would like to visit in Chile.
What kind of geographic features are they?

Modelo los Andes ⟶ *Los Andes son montañas.*

1. Atacama
2. Loa
3. Viña del Mar
4. Rupanco
5. El Pacífico

29 **Una guía para turistas**

▶ **Escucha y decide.** Tess is describing geographic features of the United States to a friend in Chile. Listen and tell if the statements below are true *(cierto)* or false *(falso)*. If they are false, correct them.

1. Hay mar al este y al oeste.
2. California es un estado de la costa este.
3. Manhattan es una isla.
4. Los Estados Unidos forman parte del continente americano.
5. En los Estados Unidos no hay bosques tropicales.
6. En el este de los Estados Unidos hay un gran desierto.

CONEXIONES: GEOGRAFÍA

Un balneario en Chile

Viña del Mar es una ciudad balneario *(beach resort)* famosa en todo el mundo. Tiene un clima mediterráneo similar al de California: las estaciones lluviosas son el otoño y el invierno. Pero, recuerda, Chile está en el hemisferio sur de nuestro planeta. Por eso sus estaciones son opuestas a las nuestras.

30 **Piensa.** During which months would it be safe to visit Viña del Mar if you want to minimize your chances of rain?

Gramática

Expresar cantidad. Los indefinidos

- In many cases, nouns can be counted using specific numbers.

    Tengo **tres** libros de español.   Hay **veinte** estudiantes en la clase.

    It is possible, however, to refer to nouns using nonspecific terms of number. These terms are called *indefinites*.

    Hay **algunos** libros de español allí.   **Muchas** personas visitaron el museo ayer.

- These are the most common indefinites:

PRINCIPALES INDEFINIDOS

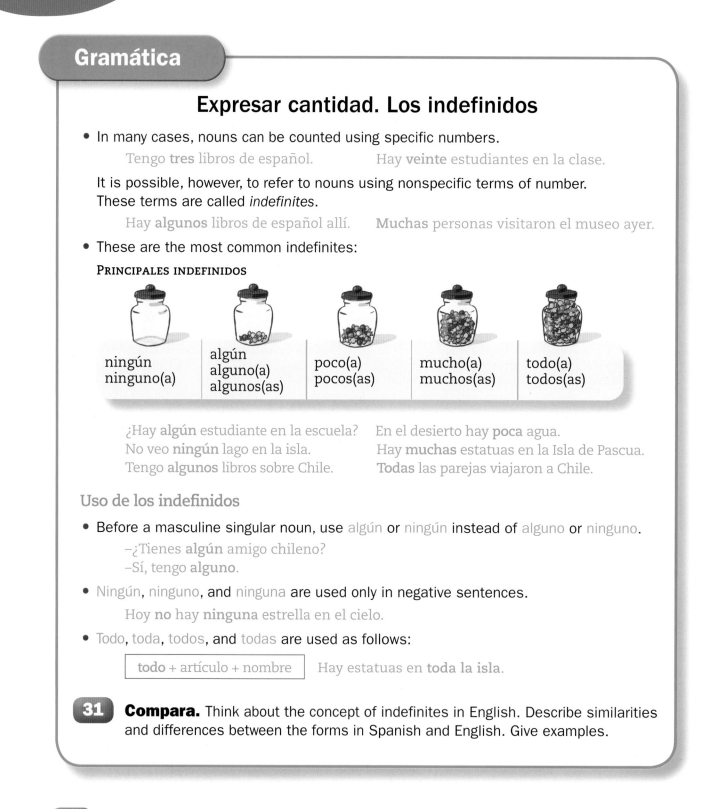

| ningún
ninguno(a) | algún
alguno(a)
algunos(as) | poco(a)
pocos(as) | mucho(a)
muchos(as) | todo(a)
todos(as) |

    ¿Hay **algún** estudiante en la escuela?   En el desierto hay **poca** agua.
    No veo **ningún** lago en la isla.   Hay **muchas** estatuas en la Isla de Pascua.
    Tengo **algunos** libros sobre Chile.   **Todas** las parejas viajaron a Chile.

Uso de los indefinidos

- Before a masculine singular noun, use algún or ningún instead of alguno or ninguno.

    –¿Tienes **algún** amigo chileno?
    –Sí, tengo **alguno**.

- Ningún, ninguno, and ninguna are used only in negative sentences.

    Hoy **no** hay **ninguna** estrella en el cielo.

- Todo, toda, todos, and todas are used as follows:

    | **todo** + artículo + nombre | Hay estatuas en **toda la isla**.

31 **Compara.** Think about the concept of indefinites in English. Describe similarities and differences between the forms in Spanish and English. Give examples.

32 **Tus compañeros**

▶ **Habla.** Talk with a partner about your classmates' characteristics.

1. Todos los compañeros…   3. Muchos compañeros…
2. Algunos compañeros…   4. Ningún compañero…

Durante el viaje a Chile

▶ **Completa.** Complete the statements with the appropriate word.

Modelo *No hay ninguna estación de trenes en la isla.*

(muchos)   (ningún)   (ninguno)   (todos)   (poca)   (algún)

1. No tengo _____ libro sobre Chile.
2. _____ los chilenos están orgullosos de su país.
3. En Chile descubrimos _____ lugares maravillosos.
4. ¿Ves _____ lago? En el centro de la isla no hay _____.
5. Hay _____ información sobre la cultura rapanui.

Impresiones y experiencias

▶ **Escucha y contesta.** Listen to the characters talk about their experience in Chile and answer the following questions in complete sentences.

1. ¿A algún personaje le gusta caminar por las montañas?
2. ¿Hay moáis en alguna tienda turística?
3. ¿Algún personaje está cansado de viajar?
4. ¿Alguno tiene muchas ganas de ver a su familia?
5. ¿A alguno le gusta viajar?

CONEXIONES: CIENCIAS

La deforestación

La deforestación de la Isla de Pascua es un fenómeno estudiado por los científicos. Algunos fósiles indican que existieron bosques tropicales en esta isla. Hoy no hay bosques. Llueve poco en la isla y esto contribuye a la deforestación.

Piensa. What other reasons can account for the disappearance of the rainforest on Easter Island, and in other parts of the world?

Comunicación

36 Un boletín escolar

▶ **Lee y escribe.** Read Tess's notes and write a list of the three facts that would be most interesting in a promotional poster for Chile.

 ▶ **Habla.** With a partner, ask thought-provoking questions about each fact to guide your research.

Modelo   Los Andes son unas montañas altas.
A. ¿Qué actividades puedes hacer en las montañas?
B. En las montañas puedes caminar y ver animales.

▶ **Crea un póster.** Create a poster with the facts you chose and some images and other information about Chile.

Chile, simplemente espectacular

- *Chile tiene 2.700 millas de costa.*
- *El desierto de Atacama es uno de los desiertos más secos del mundo.*
- *Los Andes son unas montañas altas.*
- *Viña del Mar es una ciudad balneario con playas sensacionales. Tiene un festival de música muy famoso.*
- *Los moáis están en la Isla de Pascua.*
- *Chile tiene al oeste el océano Pacífico.*
- *Tiene ríos para practicar deportes acuáticos.*

37 Similitudes y diferencias

 ▶ **Escucha y escribe.** Listen as Tess describes the major ecological problems on Easter Island. Write down the problems she discusses.

- La isla está casi deforestada.

 ▶ **Habla.** With a partner, compare the environmental problems of Easter Island with those of the United States. What are some possible solutions?

38 **Encuesta general**

▶ **Habla.** You want to find out your classmates' travel history. Ask each student if he or she has gone to the places below.

Modelo *¿Fuiste a algún río?*

1. una isla
2. un bosque
3. una montaña
4. un desierto
5. un mar
6. otro continente

▶ **Presenta.** Create a chart like this one to display your classmates' answers.

	una isla	un bosque	una montaña	...
todos	✔			
algunos		✔		
ninguno			✔	

Final del desafío

El diario de Tess

39 **¿Qué pasa en la historia?**

▶ **Escribe.** Tess forgot to write in her diary last night. Look at the images and write a short description of what happened.

 **→ TU DESAFÍO** Earn points for your own challenge! Listen to the questions for your *Minientrevista Desafío 2* on the website and write your answers.

El Maratón de las Escaleras

Tim and Mack are in Valparaiso, Chile, to participate in the *Maratón de las Escaleras* (the Stairs Marathon). Their task is to run this challenging race!

Tim, este maratón es muy difícil. ¿Viste las escaleras?

Héctor Basualdo dijo que Valparaíso es la capital de esta provincia y una de las ciudades más importantes del país.

Sí, abuelo, las vi. Hay escaleras porque la ciudad de Valparaíso está en la montaña.

Abuelo, ¿dónde estuviste?

Bueno, abuelo, ¿cómo vamos a correr el maratón?... ¿Abuelo?

Estuve con una señora. ¡Me dijo que hay más de quinientos escalones!

Vamos, abuelo. Tenemos que continuar.

Estoy cansado.

Continuará...

---

40 **Detective de palabras**

▶ **Completa.** Fill in each blank with the appropriate word, according to the dialogue above.

La ciudad de Valparaíso

1. La _____ de Valparaíso está en la montaña.
2. Valparaíso es la _____ de esta _____.
3. Es una de las ciudades más importantes del _____.

41 ¿Comprendiste?

▶ **Contesta.** Answer the questions in complete sentences.

1. ¿Dónde están Tim y Mack?
2. ¿Dónde está Valparaíso?
3. ¿Qué tienen que hacer allí?
4. ¿Por qué es difícil su tarea?
5. ¿Cuántos escalones hay?
6. ¿Por qué está cansado Mack?

42 ¿Qué viste?

▶ **Escucha y escribe.** Two spectators are commenting on the marathon. Listen and write whether or not they saw the following people and things.

1. un hombre muy alto
2. un gaucho
3. un niño corriendo
4. la Luna
5. una papelería
6. una montaña
7. una entrenadora de fútbol

43 ¿Dónde estuviste?

▶ **Habla.** Find out where five classmates were on a significant date in the past year.

Modelo   A. *¿Dónde estuviste el 1 de enero?*
         B. *Estuve en Nueva York, en Times Square.*

CULTURA

El Maratón de las Escaleras de Valparaíso

El Maratón de las Escaleras es un evento especial. Tiene lugar en Valparaíso, una ciudad en la costa de Chile. En el maratón, la gente corre por la ciudad. Los corredores suben y bajan más de quinientos escalones. Hay muchas personas y la carrera se divide en varios grupos por el peligro de accidentes. Las camisetas tienen códigos para identificar a cada corredor.

44   Piensa. Have you ever run a race? Why or why not?

⚑→ TU DESAFÍO   Use the website to learn more about the *Maratón de las Escaleras*.

Vocabulario

Divisiones políticas

Números del 101 al 1.000

101 ciento uno	**200** doscientos	**500** quinientos	**800** ochocientos
110 ciento diez	**300** trescientos	**600** seiscientos	**900** novecientos
132 ciento treinta y dos	**400** cuatrocientos	**700** setecientos	**1.000** mil

45 **Yo soy de...**

▶ **Piensa y escribe.** What are the geographic divisions where you were born? Write this information in your notebook.

Mi país: _____

La capital de mi país: _____

Mi estado: _____

Mi ciudad o pueblo: _____

▶ **Presenta.** Now share this information with the class. Does everyone have the same information?

46 Lluvia de ideas

▶ **Escribe.** Can you give examples of each part of our world? Take two minutes and write as many examples of each term as you can brainstorm.

país	capital	ciudad	pueblo
Chile Los Estados Unidos			

montaña	océano	isla	río
	Atlántico		

47 A sumar y restar

▶ **Escucha y escribe.** Listen to the characters and write the things they want to buy in the supermarket, and how much they cost.

Modelo Tim - 540 pesos

→ *Quiere comprar un jugo en el supermercado. El jugo cuesta 600 pesos.*

1. Tess - 175 pesos
2. Patricia - 980 pesos
3. Andy - 460 pesos

4. Rita - 715 pesos
5. Mack - 625 pesos
6. Diana - 860 pesos

▶ **Habla.** Now look at the amount of pesos each person brought and talk with a partner about whether that person can purchase the items he or she wants, and why or why not.

Modelo A. *¿Tim puede comprar el jugo?*

B. *No, porque solo tiene quinientos cuarenta pesos.*

CONEXIONES: MATEMÁTICAS

El dinero chileno

La moneda de Chile es el peso. Hay monedas de 10, 50 y 100 pesos. Los billetes son de 500, 1.000, 5.000 y 10.000 pesos. Un dólar americano tiene un valor aproximado de 500 pesos chilenos.

48 Piensa. Do the math to convert your school's lunch menu prices into Chilean pesos. Can you find a pattern in order to estimate the conversion without using a calculator?

Gramática

Verbos irregulares en el pasado. *Decir* y *hacer*

- The verbs decir *(to say)* y hacer *(to do, to make)* are irregular in the preterite. Here are their conjugations:

VERBO DECIR (TO SAY). PRETÉRITO

Singular		Plural	
yo	dije	nosotros nosotras	dijimos
tú	dijiste	vosotros vosotras	dijisteis
usted él ella	dijo	ustedes ellos ellas	dijeron

VERBO HACER (TO DO, TO MAKE). PRETÉRITO

Singular		Plural	
yo	hice	nosotros nosotras	hicimos
tú	hiciste	vosotros vosotras	hicisteis
usted él ella	hizo	ustedes ellos ellas	hicieron

Héctor **dijo** que Valparaíso es la capital.

Ayer **hice** una comida chilena.

49 **Piensa.** Why does the *c* change to a *z* in the form hizo? How would that form be pronounced if it kept the letter *c*?

50 ## Tim dijo que...

▶ **Escucha y escribe.** Tim and Mack are talking at a water stand. Listen and note who makes each statement. Then write a sentence about each.

Modelo Valparaíso es muy grande.

→ *Tim y Mack dijeron que Valparaíso es muy grande.*

1. La ciudad es muy bonita.
2. Le gusta mucho Valparaíso.
3. Hay mucha gente.
4. El maratón es emocionante.
5. Las escaleras son altas.

51 ## Cinco estudiantes dijeron

▶ **Habla y escribe.** The game show *Cien mexicanos dijeron* has asked you to poll your class for their next show. Create three questions to ask your classmates, then compile their answers in writing.

Modelo A. *¿Cuál es tu bebida favorita?*

B. *Mi bebida favorita es el jugo de naranja.*

A. *Dos estudiantes dijeron que el jugo de naranja es su bebida favorita.*

52 ¿Qué hicieron?

▶ **Escucha y une.** Listen to the characters talk about what they did last weekend. Match the participants with their activities.

Ⓐ

1. Tim y Mack
2. Diana
3. Rita
4. Andy y Janet
5. Tess y Patricia

Ⓑ

a. una cena deliciosa
b. una nueva amiga
c. unas figuras de cerámica
d. un viaje a la costa
e. planes para el verano

▶ **Escribe.** Now write a complete sentence telling what the character(s) did.

Modelo *Tim y Mack hicieron...*

53 Mensaje perdido

▶ **Escribe.** Mack took a phone message from Martin, Tim's friend from home. Read the note and fill in the missing forms of the verbs *ver* and *decir*.

> ¡Hola, Tim! Soy Mack.
>
> Tu amigo Martin llamó desde San Francisco. Él ___1___ que anoche te ___2___
>   decir   ver
> en las noticias. ¡Qué emoción! Yo le ___3___ que tu mamá me llamó ayer
>   decir
> para decirme lo mismo. Martin ___4___ que ustedes ___5___ planes para
>   decir   hacer
> el verano. ¿ ___6___ todas tus tareas? Nos vemos luego.
>   hacer, tú

COMUNIDADES

EL LAPISLÁZULI

El lapislázuli es una piedra (*stone*) semipreciosa usada en trabajos de artesanía y en joyas (*jewelry*). Su color azul simboliza la pureza, la salud, la suerte y la nobleza. La producción de lapislázuli es muy importante en Chile.

54 Relaciona. Is there a place in your city or town where people make jewelry by hand? If there is, where is this jewelry sold?

Gramática

Verbos irregulares en el pasado. *Estar* y *tener*

- Two more commonly used irregular verbs in the preterite tense are estar *(to be)* and tener *(to have)*. Here are their conjugations:

VERBO ESTAR (TO BE). PRETÉRITO

Singular		Plural	
yo	estuve	nosotros nosotras	estuvimos
tú	estuviste	vosotros vosotras	estuvisteis
usted él ella	estuvo	ustedes ellos ellas	estuvieron

VERBO TENER (TO HAVE). PRETÉRITO

Singular		Plural	
yo	tuve	nosotros nosotras	tuvimos
tú	tuviste	vosotros vosotras	tuvisteis
usted él ella	tuvo	ustedes ellos ellas	tuvieron

Estuvimos en la costa con nuestros amigos.   Andy y Janet **tuvieron** un resfriado en Chile.

55 **Piensa.** What differences do you notice between the endings of the regular preterite verbs and the endings of these irregular preterite verbs?

56 **¡Inclúyame!**

▶ **Escribe.** Your teacher has asked your class to digitally paste yourselves into pictures with the characters in Chile. Using the pictures below, describe where each person was.

Modelo 1. *Mi amigo Pepe estuvo con Tess en la playa.*

1. Pepe   2. Julia y yo   3. yo   4. ellos

57 ¿Qué tuviste?

▶ **Une y escribe.** Match the columns and write sentences with the preterite of the verb *tener*.

(A)

1. Liliana
2. Mi papá y yo
3. Tú
4. Mi mamá
5. Mis hermanos
6. Yo

(B)

a. ganas de viajar a Chile.
b. un buen viaje.
c. dos perros y un pájaro.
d. hambre esta mañana.
e. una amiga chilena en la escuela.
f. sed después de hacer deporte.

Modelo 1. *Liliana tuvo un buen viaje.*

58 Viajes

▶ **Escribe.** Write where the people below were, or what they had, using the appropriate forms of *estar* or *tener*.

Modelo *Juan estuvo en la capital.*

1. Mi abuela _____ en una playa muy bonita.
2. Nosotros _____ en las montañas.
3. Tú _____ una fiesta fantástica en el hotel.
4. Yo _____ en otro país.
5. Ellas _____ buen tiempo durante el viaje.
6. Carlos y Marta _____ en una isla tropical.
7. Mi familia y yo _____ algún problema en el viaje.

CONEXIONES: MÚSICA

El Festival Internacional de la Canción de Viña del Mar

El Festival Internacional de la Canción de Viña del Mar se celebra anualmente desde 1959. Incluye conciertos y un concurso de música popular y folclórica. Este festival es muy importante y en él participan artistas de todo el mundo. Los jueces del concurso son cantantes y músicos famosos.

59 Piensa. Can you think of any music competitions in the United States or around the world? How do they help aspiring artists?

Comunicación

60 ¿Qué hizo Mark ayer?

▶ **Escribe.** Write about Mark's day according to the pictures and the clues below.

Modelo 1. *Ayer hizo sol.*

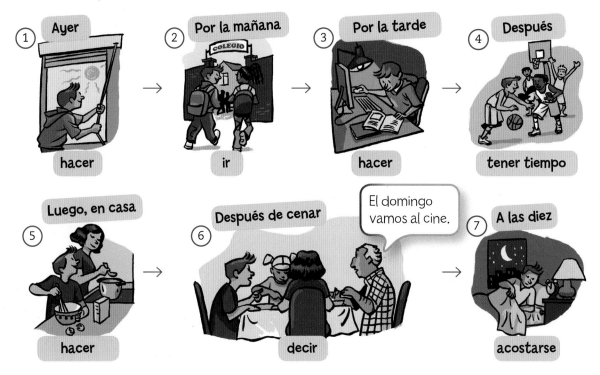

① Ayer — hacer

② Por la mañana — COLEGIO — ir

③ Por la tarde — hacer

④ Después — tener tiempo

⑤ Luego, en casa — hacer

⑥ Después de cenar — decir

El domingo vamos al cine.

⑦ A las diez — acostarse

61 ¿Qué distancia hay?

▶ **Lee y habla.** With a partner, take turns asking and answering questions about the distance between these cities in Chile.

Modelo A. *¿Qué distancia hay de Iquique a Arica?*
B. *Hay trescientos dos kilómetros.*

Ciudades	Distancias
Santiago de Chile - Valparaíso	120 km
Chillán - Temuco	270 km
Iquique - Arica	302 km
Chillán - Santiago de Chile	407 km
Villarica - Castro	527 km
Calama - Arica	600 km
Viña del Mar - Temuco	796 km
Santiago de Chile - Valdivia	841 km

▶ **Piensa y escribe.** A kilometer is roughly 0.6 miles (*millas*). Convert the distances above into miles.

Modelo 1. *De Santiago de Chile a Valparaíso = 120 km*
→ 120 × 0.6 = 72
→ *De Santiago a Valparaíso hay setenta y dos millas.*

62 **Tú, el detective**

▶ **Habla.** Imagine you are a detective in charge of solving a mystery. Interview five witnesses about where they were, what they did there, and what they saw.

Modelo A. ¿Dónde estuviste el martes?
 B. Estuve en el parque.
 A. ¿Qué hiciste allí?
 B. Hice mi tarea y hablé con Manuel.
 A. ¿Qué viste?
 B. Vi a mucha gente corriendo.

▶ **Escribe.** Now fill in a detective notebook with a chart of information like the one below.

Nombre(s)	¿Dónde estuvo / estuvieron?	¿Qué hizo / hicieron?	¿Qué vio / vieron?
Paola	Estuvo en el parque.	Hizo su tarea. Habló con Manuel.	Vio a mucha gente corriendo.

Final del desafío

63 **¿Dónde estuvieron?**

▶ **Escribe.** Describe what is happening in each scene. Write about where the characters were, what they did, what they saw, and what they said.

La famosa Ruta W

Diana and Rita are visiting the Torres del Paine National Park in Patagonia, Chile. They are going to hike the W Route, the most popular route in the park. They must collect five pounds of litter from the trail ... and hike back with it!

> El guía dijo que tenemos que tomar la Ruta W.

> ¿Por qué se llama así?

> Hola, chicas. Aquí tienen sus bolsas para la basura.

> Porque tiene forma de W.

> Hay flores y pájaros muy bonitos. ¿Podemos tomar fotos de los animales y las plantas durante la ruta?

> Mira, tía, esos chicos están dejando mucha basura.

> Sí, pero no podemos tocarlos.

> ¡Oigan, se puede comer en el parque, pero no se puede dejar la basura!

Continuará...

64 **Detective de palabras**

▶ **Relaciona.** Using the dialogue, match the images below with words from the box.

flor
planta
pájaro
basura

1

2

3

4

65 ¿Comprendes?

▶ **Elige.** Decide which things can and cannot be done while walking along the W Route. Choose the correct option to complete each sentence.

1. En la ruta _____ tomar fotos de los animales.
   se pueden/no se pueden

2. En la ruta _____ tocar a los animales.
   se puede/no se puede

3. _____ comer en el parque.
   Se puede/No se puede

4. _____ dejar la basura en el parque.
   Se puede/No se puede

66 Fotos del parque

▶ **Escucha y ordena.** Diana sent some picture messages to her mom. Listen to the voice mail she left and put the photos in the order you hear about them.

Ⓐ

Ⓑ

Ⓒ

CULTURA

Parque Nacional Torres del Paine

El Parque Nacional Torres del Paine está en la cordillera del Paine, en la Patagonia chilena. El pico (*peak*) más alto, Cerro Paine Grande, mide casi 3.000 metros de altura. Hay tres picos famosos, llamados las Torres del Paine. El parque tiene una gran variedad de paisajes: montañas, valles, ríos, lagos y glaciares. La flora y la fauna del parque son muy ricas.

67 Piensa.
Have you ever hiked up a tall mountain? If so, how did it feel? If not, would you like to one day?

Vocabulario

La naturaleza y el medio ambiente

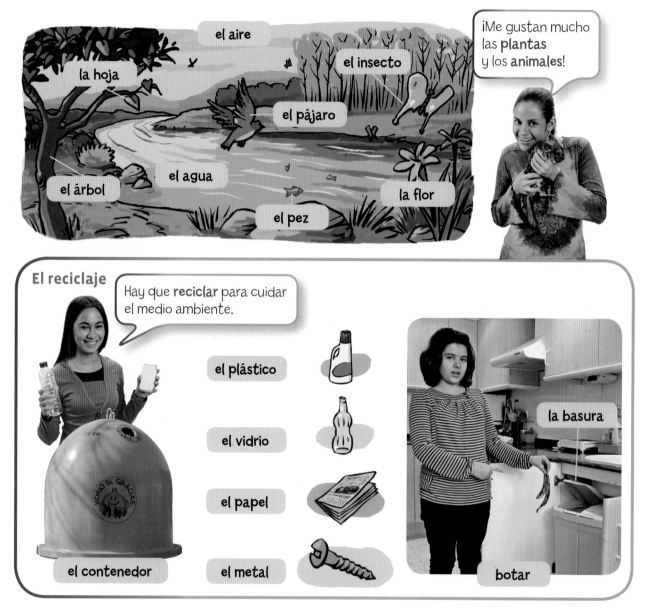

el aire

la hoja

el insecto

el pájaro

¡Me gustan mucho las **plantas** y los **animales**!

el agua

el árbol

la flor

el pez

El reciclaje

Hay que **reciclar** para cuidar el medio ambiente.

el plástico

el vidrio

la basura

el papel

el contenedor

el metal

botar

68 Flora y fauna

▶ **Completa.** Complete the sentences with the correct option.

1. ¡Qué bien huelen estas _____!   a. animales   b. flores
2. Ese río tiene el _____ muy limpia.   a. agua   b. aire
3. Muchos _____ viven en los árboles.   a. peces   b. pájaros
4. Los mosquitos son un tipo de _____.   a. insectos   b. peces
5. Ese contenedor es para reciclar el _____.   a. medio ambiente   b. vidrio

69 **¿Oíste algo?**

 ▶ **Escucha y dibuja.** Diana and Rita could not see well in the forest. Copy the chart below and fill it in with drawings of what they heard and felt.

Modelo

Sentido		
Elemento del bosque		

 ▶ **Habla.** Now tell a partner what Diana and Rita experienced.

Modelo A. *¿Qué oyó Diana?*
B. *Diana oyó el sonido del aire.*

70 **¿Botar o reciclar?**

▶ **Escribe.** Decide whether these materials are recyclable or not and write complete sentences.

Modelo *Las botellas de vidrio son para reciclar.*

para reciclar   para botar a la basura

①

②

③

④

CONEXIONES: ECOLOGÍA

¡A reciclar!

Para salvar nuestro planeta, es muy importante reducir la cantidad de basura y reciclar. En nuestras casas podemos reciclar el plástico, el metal, el vidrio y el papel. Si reciclamos estos materiales, podemos ayudar a conservar nuestros recursos naturales.

71 **Compara.** What items do you recycle in your home? Do you help separate your trash at home? What other ways can you think of to keep trash from ending up in our landfills?

Gramática

Expresar permiso y prohibición

Expresar permiso

- Use the verb poder to ask for and to give permission.

  –¿**Puedo** salir este fin de semana?

  –Sí, **puedes** salir después de hacer tus tareas.

- When you want to express permission in general terms, use these formulas:

  | se puede + infinitivo *(with singular object)* | **Se puede** dar comida a los peces. |

  | se puede(n) + infinitivo *(with plural object)* | ¿**Se puede(n)** tomar fotos en el museo? |

- The verb poder means *can* or *to be able to*.

  Puedes reciclar el plástico aquí.   **Podemos** hacer la excursión en bicicleta.

Expresar prohibición

- The negative form of poder can be used to deny permission or express prohibition.

  No puedes usar la computadora aquí.   **No puedes** volver tarde a casa.

- When you want to express prohibition in general terms, use these formulas:

  | no se puede + infinitivo | **No se puede** botar basura en el suelo. |

  | no se puede(n) + infinitivo | **No se puede(n)** botar las botellas de vidrio a la basura. |

72 **Piensa.** Poder is also the Spanish word for *power*. How are the two definitions —*to be able to* and *power*— related?

73 **Reglas para la casa**

▶ **Escribe.** The notes below were brainstormed during a family meeting prior to drawing up some house rules. Write the rules of what is allowed or prohibited.

Modelo *No se puede correr por la casa.*

Se puede

Se pueden

No se puede

No se pueden

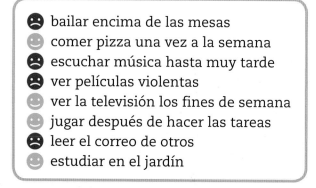

🙁 bailar encima de las mesas
🙂 comer pizza una vez a la semana
🙁 escuchar música hasta muy tarde
🙁 ver películas violentas
🙂 ver la televisión los fines de semana
🙂 jugar después de hacer las tareas
🙁 leer el correo de otros
🙂 estudiar en el jardín

74 Empacando para el viaje

▶ **Escucha y decide.** Diana wants to know what items she can bring with her to Torres del Paine National Park. Listen to her conversation with Rita and decide if these things are allowed or not allowed in the park.

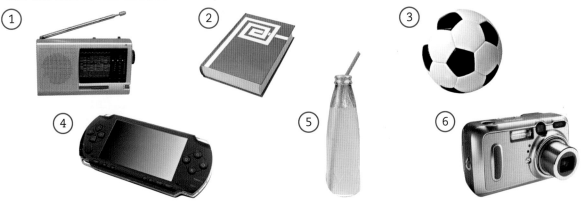

① ② ③
④ ⑤ ⑥

▶ **Escribe.** Write sentences to tell if each of the items above is permitted or not.

75 ¿Lo hago o no lo hago?

▶ **Escribe.** Using a chart like the one below, list five things that you are allowed to do and five things that you are not allowed to do in a national park.

En el parque se puede...	En el parque no se puede...
leer un libro	jugar al hockey

▶ **Habla.** Now tell a partner the park rules that you came up with.

Modelo *En el parque se puede leer un libro, pero no se puede jugar al hockey.*

CONEXIONES: CIENCIAS

Animales en peligro de extinción

Muchos animales están en peligro de extinción por factores como el desarrollo humano y la contaminación. En Chile están en peligro aves como el pájaro carpintero y el ñandú; mamíferos, como la vicuña y la chinchilla cordillera; y mamíferos marinos, como algunas ballenas y delfines.

76 Piensa y busca. What other reasons might account for these animals' status on the endangered-species list? Find out what animals are in danger where you live.

Comunicación

77 **¿Qué podemos hacer?**

▶ **Elige.** There are many ways we can help save our environment. Choose the correct word to complete each sentence.

1. Es importante reciclar las latas de _____   **a.** papel   **b.** metal
2. Hay que plantar más _____   **a.** animales   **b.** árboles
3. Debemos escribir en los dos lados de una hoja de _____   **a.** planta   **b.** papel
4. Hay que mantener limpio el aire para proteger a los _____   **a.** pájaros   **b.** peces
5. Siempre hay que apagar la luz para no gastar _____   **a.** metal   **b.** electricidad

78 **¿Se puede reciclar?**

▶ **Habla.** Look at the items below. Talk with your partner about what they are made of and ask if they can be recycled or not.

Modelo   A. *¿De qué es esta botella?*   A. *¿Se puede reciclar?*
            B. *Es de plástico.*   B. *Sí, se puede.*

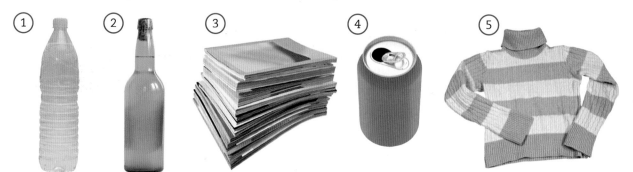

①   ②   ③   ④   ⑤

79 **¿Qué puede hacer ella?**

▶ **Escucha y dibuja.** Diana was inspired by the Torres del Paine National Park. Listen to her plans and draw pictures of four things she will do to help the environment.

▶ **Escribe.** Now reflect on Diana's plans and write what you too can do at home.

Modelo

> En casa yo puedo reciclar el papel.
> También puedo plantar un árbol.

¿Qué puedo hacer yo?

▶ **Escribe.** Everyone can do something to help conserve our natural resources. Write a short statement about what you can do to help.

> **Todos podemos conservar los recursos naturales del mundo. Por ejemplo, se puede(n)...**
>
> **Pero no se puede(n)...**
>
> **Por eso, yo puedo...**

Final del desafío

a. Sí, tía. Tenemos que reciclarlas.

b. Vamos, Diana. Ya tenemos nuestras cinco libras de basura. Si caminamos más rápido, podemos llegar a tiempo.

c. ¡Qué horror! ¡Mira cuántas latas y cuántas botellas de plástico! No podemos dejarlas aquí.

81 **¿Qué pasó?**

▶ **Habla y escribe.** Look at the scenes above and decide which caption corresponds to each. Do you think Diana and Rita made it to the park entrance to turn in their five pounds of trash? Write a final caption to tell what you think happened.

 Earn points for your own challenge! Listen to the questions for your *Minientrevista Desafío 4* on the website and write your answers.

Todo junto

LEER Y ESCRIBIR

82 **Las aventuras de Bill y de Ted**

▶ **Lee y elige.** Bill and Ted are on separate cross-country trips. Read their conversation and fill in the blanks, choosing the correct option for each.

> BILL: Yo ayer _____ en Chicago, en el estado de Illinois.
> <u>1</u>
> estuvieron / estuve
>
> TED: ¿Sí? Yo fui al sur del país. _____ tiempo de ver ciudades y zonas naturales
> <u>2</u>
> Tuvo / Tuve
> muy interesantes.
>
> BILL: ¡Qué bien! ¿ _____ calor?
> <u>3</u>
> Hicieron / Hizo
>
> TED: No, pero mi papá me _____ que en el sur normalmente hace mucho calor.
> <u>4</u>
> dijo / dije
> ¡Casi parece un bosque tropical!
>
> BILL: Estoy muy cansado porque _____ cuatrocientas millas ayer.
> <u>5</u>
> viajó / viajé
>
> TED: ¡Cuatrocientas millas! ¿Y adónde _____ antes de ir a Chicago?
> <u>6</u>
> viajamos / viajaste
>
> BILL: Viajé por tres estados. La semana pasada _____ algunos parques nacionales.
> <u>7</u>
> visitasteis / visité
>
> TED: ¿Sabes si _____ entrar en los parques nacionales por la noche?
> <u>8</u>
> se puede / se pueden
> Quiero ver las estrellas desde Yellowstone.

▶ **Escribe.** How does the conversation between Bill and Ted continue? Write it.

ESCUCHAR Y ESCRIBIR

83 **Un programa especial**

▶ **Escucha y escribe.** There is a special show on television tonight about life on other planets. Listen to the preview and take notes.

▶ **Diseña un cartel.** Design the promotional poster that will be used for advertising. Include images, words, phrases, and sentences to show the program's content.

¿HAY VIDA EN OTROS PLANETAS?

Hoy a las 9:00 p. m., programa especial

LEER, ESCRIBIR Y HABLAR

84 **Un libro de texto chileno**

▶ **Lee e identifica.** Tim borrowed a social studies textbook from a friend in Chile. Read the pages and identify the most important facts and issues about Chile.

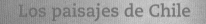

Los paisajes de Chile

Chile es un país con diferentes paisajes: costas, montañas, desiertos, valles y volcanes.

La capital de Chile es Santiago de Chile, que fue fundada por los españoles en el año 1541.

Santiago de Chile

La ciudad de Santiago de Chile tiene problemas de contaminación del aire, especialmente en invierno (junio, julio y agosto). También hay contaminación del agua a causa de la industria y la agricultura. Es muy importante reciclar para ayudar a limpiar el aire y el agua.

▶ **Escribe.** Write a five-question quiz to give a partner. You should test whether your partner learned the key information from the textbook pages.

Modelo

> ¿Por qué hay contaminación del agua en Santiago de Chile?

▶ **Habla.** Ask a partner your quiz questions. He or she should point out where the answers can be found on the textbook pages.

El encuentro

En la Plaza de Armas

The four pairs meet in Santiago de Chile after completing their individual tasks.
Did they all carry out their challenges successfully?

¡Fue fantástico observar el cielo en el desierto!

¡Y encontramos las rocas en forma de perro!

Caminamos por toda la isla hasta llegar a un lago. ¡Allí encontramos el moái falso!

Corrimos como unos campeones, ¿verdad?

¡Sí, hicimos el circuito completo y llegamos a la meta!

Después de caminar mucho llenamos las bolsas de basura.

¡Sí, cuánta basura para reciclar!

¿Aprendieron a bailar la cueca? Es la danza nacional de Chile.

85 **Al llegar**

▶ **Escribe.** Together with three classmates, complete a graphic organizer for each pair. Then each student turns one of the webs into a story summarizing the adventures of that pair in Chile.

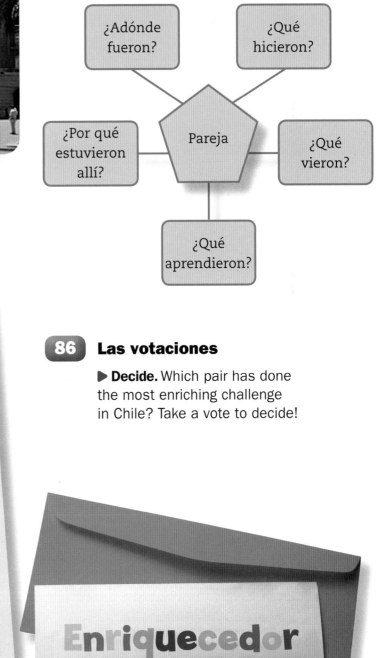

¿Adónde fueron?

¿Qué hicieron?

¿Por qué estuvieron allí?

Pareja

¿Qué vieron?

¿Qué aprendieron?

86 **Las votaciones**

▶ **Decide.** Which pair has done the most enriching challenge in Chile? Take a vote to decide!

Enriquecedor

Chile es una república situada en el suroeste de América del Sur. Su capital es Santiago de Chile.

Chile se extiende a lo largo de la costa del océano Pacífico. Es un país muy estrecho y muy largo, y está atravesado por dos cordilleras: los Andes y la cordillera de la Costa. También forman parte de Chile algunos archipiélagos y la Isla de Pascua (*Easter Island*), situada en la Polinesia.

Chile tiene casi 17 millones de habitantes. El 90% vive en las ciudades.

¡Chile es un país muuuuy largo!

Sí, tiene más de 4.300 kilómetros de norte a sur. Es el país más largo del mundo.

87 **¿Cuál es la ruta?**

▶ **Decide.** Look at the map and decide if the statements are true (*cierto*) or false (*falso*).

1. Para ir de Atacama a la Patagonia chilena tengo que pasar por Valparaíso.
2. Para ir desde Santiago de Chile hasta la Isla de Pascua debo cruzar el océano Atlántico.
3. Para ir de Valparaíso a Punta Arenas hay que cruzar el desierto.
4. Para conocer el norte de Chile, puedo pasar por el desierto de Atacama.

Los paisajes de Chile

De norte a sur, Chile tiene tres regiones muy distintas: el árido norte, el fértil Valle Central y el sur.

1. El árido norte

En el norte de Chile está el **desierto de Atacama**, el lugar del mundo donde menos llueve.

(1) El desierto de Atacama.

(2) Santiago de Chile.

(3) Lago Rupanco y volcán Osorno.

2. El fértil Valle Central y Santiago de Chile

El centro es la zona más activa del país. Allí están las ciudades más importantes: **Valparaíso**, **Viña del Mar** y **Santiago de Chile**.

Santiago de Chile, la capital, está en un valle entre los Andes y la cordillera de la Costa.

3. El sur

El sur de Chile se divide en dos zonas: la **Araucanía**, llena de volcanes, lagos y bosques, y la **Patagonia**, un laberinto de canales, montañas, islas y glaciares.

88 Con lupa

▶ **Completa.** Fill in the chart according to the text.

▶ **Habla.** Are there any regions in Chile that are similar to regions in other Spanish-speaking countries? Think of Argentina and Mexico and discuss similarities with a partner.

| bosques | glaciares | desierto |
| ciudades | lagos |

El norte	El centro	El sur

1. La Isla de Pascua

La **Isla de Pascua** es la isla más grande de Chile. Está en la Polinesia, en el océano Pacífico.

En la Isla de Pascua hay unas estatuas gigantescas de piedra llamadas **moáis**. Los moáis fueron construidos por los primeros pobladores de la Isla de Pascua.

(1) Playa de Anakena (Isla de Pascua).

(2) Casa de Pablo Neruda en Valparaíso.

2. Pablo Neruda

Pablo Neruda (1904–1973) es el poeta más conocido de Chile. A los veinte años publicó su obra *Veinte poemas de amor y una canción desesperada*. Ganó el **Premio Nobel de Literatura** en 1971.

Pablo Neruda.

(3) Escenario del Festival de Viña del Mar.

(3) Viña del Mar.

3. El Festival Internacional de la Canción de Viña del Mar

Viña del Mar es una localidad costera muy turística situada en el centro de Chile. Desde 1959, allí se celebra anualmente el *Festival Internacional de la Canción de Viña del Mar*, el evento musical más importante de Hispanoamérica. Los países compiten en dos categorías: música popular y música folclórica.

89 ## Los moáis de la Isla de Pascua

▶ **Investiga y explica.** Search for information and explain the following:

1. Who built the moai? Why?
2. How did they build them?
3. Why have the moai intrigued scientists?

90 ## Un concierto de música chilena

▶ **Investiga y escribe.** Search for information about Chilean music and make an advertisement. You may follow these steps:

1. Search for information about Chilean music and about current Chilean bands.
2. Write down the genre and the groups you like.
3. Organize the information in a poster or ad. Include images and other elements to promote the concert.
4. As a class, organize a Chilean music festival featuring each concert.

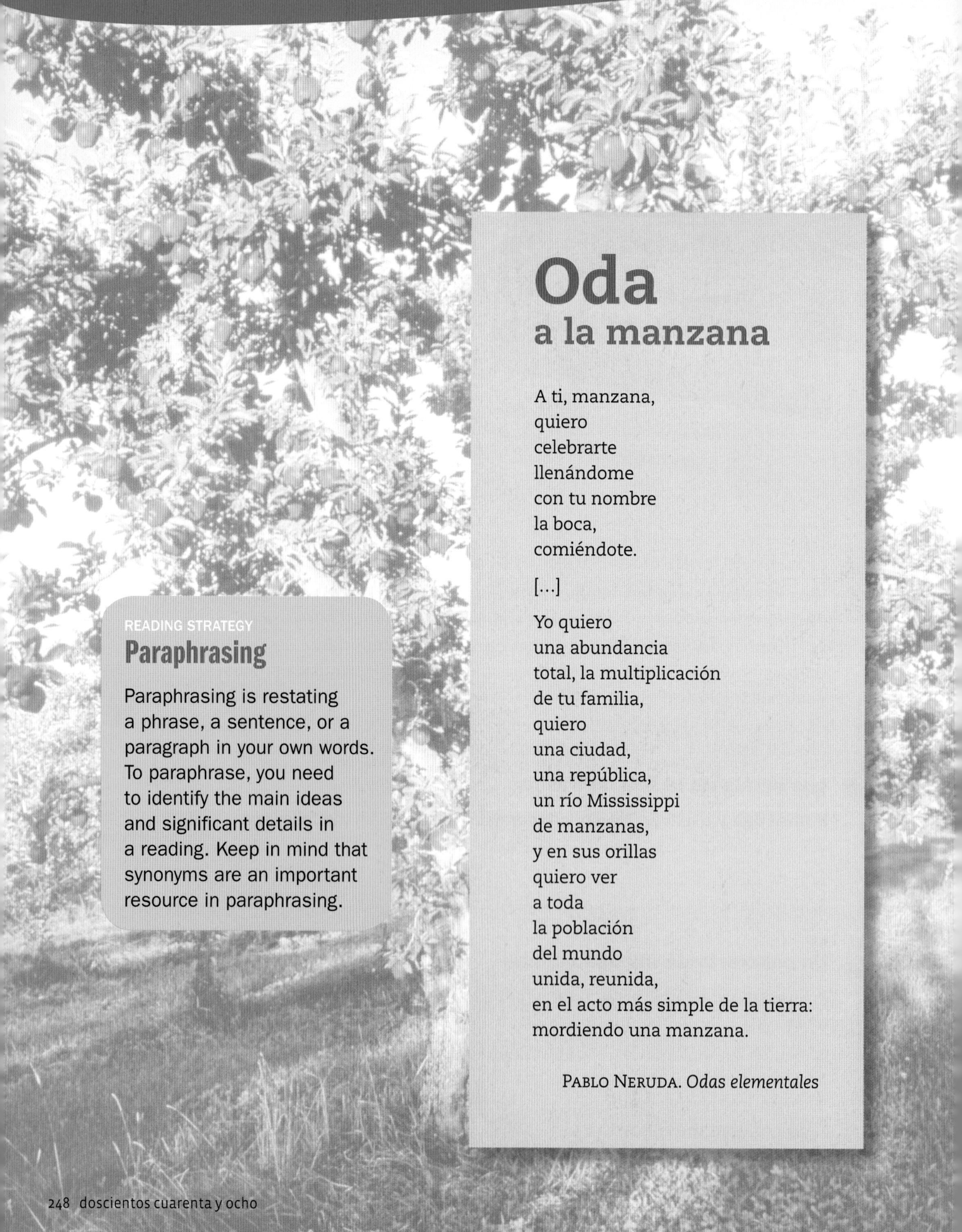

Oda
a la manzana

A ti, manzana,
quiero
celebrarte
llenándome
con tu nombre
la boca,
comiéndote.

[…]

Yo quiero
una abundancia
total, la multiplicación
de tu familia,
quiero
una ciudad,
una república,
un río Mississippi
de manzanas,
y en sus orillas
quiero ver
a toda
la población
del mundo
unida, reunida,
en el acto más simple de la tierra:
mordiendo una manzana.

PABLO NERUDA. *Odas elementales*

READING STRATEGY
Paraphrasing

Paraphrasing is restating a phrase, a sentence, or a paragraph in your own words. To paraphrase, you need to identify the main ideas and significant details in a reading. Keep in mind that synonyms are an important resource in paraphrasing.

91 **Con mis palabras**

▶ **Escribe.** State the meaning of the poem *Oda a la manzana* using your own words. You may write more than one sentence.

92 **Tu investigación**

▶ **Escribe.** Find information about Pablo Neruda and fill in a chart like the one below.

Nombre: Pablo Neruda
Fecha y lugar de nacimiento:
Algunos datos de su biografía:

Algunos títulos de sus obras:

COMPRENSIÓN

93 **La manzana y la vida**

▶ **Relaciona y escribe.** Relate each picture to a main idea expressed in the poem. Then put them in order and write a sentence summarizing each idea.

94 **El mensaje del poema**

▶ **Escribe.** Write another title for the poem. Then compare it with your partner's.

 Earn points for your own challenge! Visit the website to learn more about Pablo Neruda.

El universo

el universo	universe
el sistema solar	solar system
el cielo	sky
el cometa	comet
el eclipse	eclipse
la estrella	star
el planeta	planet
el Sol	Sun
la Luna	Moon
la Tierra	Earth
el/la astronauta	astronaut
descubrir	to discover
explorar	to explore

Geografía

Geografía	Geography
el bosque	forest
el continente	continent
el desierto	desert
la isla	island
el lago	lake
el mar	sea
la montaña	mountain
el océano	ocean
el río	river
la roca	rock
la tierra	land
el valle	valley
seco	dry
tropical	tropical

Divisiones políticas

la capital	capital
la ciudad	city
la frontera	border
el país	country
la provincia	province
el pueblo	town
la región	region

Los números

cien	one hundred
doscientos	two hundred
trescientos	three hundred
cuatrocientos	four hundred
quinientos	five hundred
seiscientos	six hundred
setecientos	seven hundred
ochocientos	eight hundred
novecientos	nine hundred
mil	one thousand

La naturaleza y el medio ambiente

la naturaleza	nature
el medio ambiente	environment
el agua	water
el aire	air
el animal	animal
el insecto	insect
el pájaro	bird
el pez	fish
el árbol	tree
la flor	flower
la hoja	leaf
la planta	plant

El reciclaje

el reciclaje	recycling
la basura	trash
el contenedor	container
la electricidad	electricity
el metal	metal
el papel	paper
el plástico	plastic
el vidrio	glass
botar	to throw away
reciclar	to recycle

DESAFÍO 1

1 **El sistema solar.** Use the clues to identify each part of the solar system.

1. El _____ es la persona que explora y observa el universo.
2. Hay ocho _____ y uno de ellos se llama Júpiter.
3. En una noche clara se pueden ver las _____
4. Si la Luna pasa frente al _____ se produce un eclipse.
5. La _____ es el nombre de nuestro planeta.

DESAFÍO 2

2 **Paisajes.** Which geographic features do the photos represent? Identify the features by writing a sentence and a short description of each.

Modelo 1. *Es un bosque tropical. En él hay árboles y animales.*

DESAFÍO 3

3 **Distancias.** Write the distance from Washington DC to the following places in the U.S.

Modelo el condado de Fairfax (16 millas)
→ *El condado de Fairfax está a dieciséis millas de Washington.*

1. la capital de Pennsylvania (123 millas)
2. la ciudad de Chicago (699 millas)
3. la frontera con Canadá (560 millas)
4. la ciudad de Nueva York (204 millas)
5. el país de Canadá (624 millas)
6. el pueblo de Ashland, KY (428 millas)

DESAFÍO 4

4 **Ecología.** Classify these items according to whether they are natural or unnatural in a park.

una botella de plástico	un río
una botella de plástico	un río
un árbol	un insecto
una lata de metal	un pájaro
una flor	una botella de vidrio
una hoja	una planta

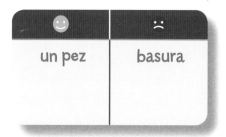

🙂	🙁
un pez	basura

Expresar causa (pág. 210)

- Conjunción porque + oración con verbo conjugado

  ¿Por qué no puedes ir?

  No puedo ir porque estoy enferma.

- Conjunción por + sustantivo

  No fuimos por el mal tiempo.

Expresar cantidad. Los indefinidos (pág. 218)

ningún, ninguno(a)	*no, (not) any*
algún, alguno(a), algunos(as)	*one, some, any, a few*
poco(a), pocos(as)	*some, few*
mucho(a), muchos(as)	*many, a lot of*
todo(a), todos(as)	*all, every, throughout*

Verbos irregulares en el pasado (págs. 226, 228)

DECIR

yo	dije	nosotros nosotras	dijimos
tú	dijiste	vosotros vosotras	dijisteis
usted él ella	dijo	ustedes ellos ellas	dijeron

HACER

yo	hice	nosotros nosotras	hicimos
tú	hiciste	vosotros vosotras	hicisteis
usted él ella	hizo	ustedes ellos ellas	hicieron

ESTAR

yo	estuve	nosotros nosotras	estuvimos
tú	estuviste	vosotros vosotras	estuvisteis
usted él ella	estuvo	ustedes ellos ellas	estuvieron

TENER

yo	tuve	nosotros nosotras	tuvimos
tú	tuviste	vosotros vosotras	tuvisteis
usted él ella	tuvo	ustedes ellos ellas	tuvieron

Expresar permiso y prohibición (pág. 236)

Expresar permiso

se puede + infinitivo   Se puede dar comida a los animales.

se puede(n) + infinitivo   Se puede(n) tomar fotos en el museo.

Expresar prohibición

no se puede + infinitivo   No se puede botar la basura en el suelo.

no se puede(n) + infinitivo   No se puede(n) botar las botellas de vidrio a la basura.

DESAFÍO 1

5 **Causas.** Match the columns and write five sentences. Use *por* or *porque*.

Modelo *No quiero ir a la fiesta porque tengo que estudiar.*

1. ir a la fiesta
2. hacer ejercicio
3. leer
4. comer
5. salir a pasear

a. estar cansado
b. el dolor de estómago
c. tener que estudiar
d. la lluvia
e. doler la cabeza

DESAFÍO 2

6 **¿Qué comemos?** Choose the words that logically complete the dialogue.

CARMEN: ¡Mira cuánta comida! Hay (pocos / muchos) tipos de carnes, verduras y postres.

SARAH: Sí. Y (poco / algún) postre tiene chocolate blanco, mi favorito.

CARMEN: No me gusta el chocolate blanco. ¿Hay (alguno / ninguno) sin chocolate?

SARAH: ¡Claro que sí! Creo que hay (ninguno / algunos) con fruta.

CARMEN: ¡Perfecto! (Muchos / Todos) los postres con fruta me gustan mucho.

DESAFÍO 3

7 **¿Qué hicieron?** Create sentences about what each person did and when.

Modelo Miguel - estar - ciudad - sábado → *El sábado Miguel estuvo en la ciudad.*

1. Yo - hacer la tarea - biblioteca - miércoles
2. Nosotros - tener que hacer - examen - lunes
3. Vosotros - estar - centro de la ciudad - sábado
4. Ella - decir la verdad - escuela - viernes

DESAFÍO 4

8 **Reglas.** Write a memorandum about what is allowed and what is not allowed in your rental cabin in Yellowstone National Park.

Modelo *En mi cabaña se puede cocinar, pero no se puede hacer fuego...*

CULTURA

9 **Está en Chile.** Answer the questions.

1. What is the land of the *Valle de la Luna* compared to? Why?
2. Who constructed the moai on Easter Island?
3. Compare the Torres del Paine National Park with a national park in the United States.
4. Who was Pablo Neruda? Why is he significant?

Un póster sobre

animales en peligro

There are endangered animals throughout the world. In Chile alone, there are more than forty endangered species.

In this project you are going to do research on an endangered animal. Your research involves learning about the animal and its habitat, discovering why it is endangered, and indicating what people can do to protect it. Your final goal is to display all your work on a poster.

Nutria de río.

Vicuña.

PASO 1 Investiga sobre los animales en peligro de extinción en Chile y selecciona un animal

- Research the endangered mammals, fish, and birds in Chile.
- Choose one animal to research. These criteria may help you decide:
  - you like its appearance;
  - it is also an endangered animal where you live;
  - it lives in extreme climatic conditions: desert, mountain, tiny island.
- Select several photos and find out the animal's name in Spanish.

Albatros ojeroso.

PASO 2 Busca información para una ficha y un mapa

- Organize your information on a file card, and make a map to show the animal's habitat.

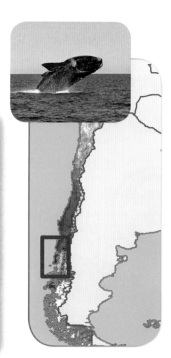

Nombre	Ballena azul
Descripción física Color Peso Tamaño	Negro, azul 181.500 kg (400,000 lb.) 24-27 m (80-100')
Población	3.000-5.000
Hábitat	Océano Pacífico
Alimentación	Pequeños crustáceos, krill
Dato curioso	Come 3.600 kg (8,000 lb.) de krill al día. Es más grande que 25 elefantes.

PASO 3 Explica por qué ese animal está en peligro y prepara sugerencias para protegerlo

- Why is the animal endangered? Summarize two or three of the most important causes. Some of the most common causes are:

  – Los cambios en el hábitat. Por ejemplo, la temperatura.
  – La intervención de los seres humanos. Por ejemplo, la contaminación o la caza (hunting).
  – Causas naturales. Por ejemplo, las enfermedades.

  > – Cazaron muchas ballenas por su carne.
  > – Ahora hay menos krill porque la temperatura del agua está cambiando.

- Suggest some ways to protect this endangered animal. For example:

  – Prohibir la caza de ballenas.
  – Controlar los cambios del clima.

PASO 4 Organiza toda la información en tu póster y preséntala a la clase

- Arrange all your information in a logical way on your poster.

- Practice presenting your information aloud. Then present it to your classmates. Answer their questions.

¿A las ballenas azules les gusta el agua fría?

Sí. Prefieren el agua fría.

Unidad 8

Autoevaluación

¿Qué has aprendido en esta unidad?

Do the following activities to evaluate how well you can manage in Spanish.

Evaluate your skills. For each item, say Very well, Well, or I need more practice.

a. Can you talk about the seasons and the solar system?
  ▶ Draw three items in space and ask your partner to identify them.
  ▶ Say what season your birthday falls in.

b. Can you express cause or reason?
  ▶ Write three reasons to visit Chile. Use *por* or *porque*.

c. Can you describe the geography of Chile?
  ▶ Describe land and water features. Use words like *alguno*, *todo*, *mucho*, and *poco*.

d. Can you talk about where you live?
  ▶ Choose three cities in your country and guess how far they are from you.

e. Can you narrate past events?
  ▶ Ask your partner what living things he or she saw yesterday.

f. Can you explain how to protect the environment?
  ▶ Tell three things that are allowed or prohibited with regard to the environment.

Nouns and articles

Gender of nouns

In Spanish all nouns are **masculine** or **feminine**. Most nouns that end in -o are masculine, and most nouns that end in -a are feminine. Nouns that end in -e or in a **consonant** can be either masculine or feminine.

Nouns that refer to people have a masculine and a feminine form. The feminine is usually formed by changing the -o of the masculine form to an -a, or by adding an -a.

Masculine form	Feminine form	Examples
Ends in -o.	Changes -o to -a.	el niño → la niña
Ends in a consonant.	Adds -a.	el profesor → la profesora

Plural of nouns

Nouns can be **singular** (one person or thing) or **plural** (more than one person or thing). To form the plural, add -s to the singular form if the noun ends in a vowel. If it ends in a consonant, add -es.

Singular form	Plural form	Examples
Ends in a vowel.	Adds -s.	el edificio → los edificios
Ends in a consonant.	Adds -es.	el ascensor → los ascensores

Articles

Definite articles refer to a specific noun. In English the definite article has only one form: the. In Spanish there are four forms: el, la, los, and las.

Indefinite articles refer to a nonspecific noun. In Spanish, the indefinite article has four forms: un, una (*a* or *an*) and unos, unas (*some* or *a few*).

DEFINITE ARTICLES

	Masculine	Feminine
Singular	el	la
Plural	los	las

INDEFINITE ARTICLES

	Masculine	Feminine
Singular	un	una
Plural	unos	unas

Contractions

The combination of the prepositions **a** and **de** with the definite article **el** results in a contraction.

a + el → al	de + el → del

Adjectives

Agreement with nouns

Adjectives describe nouns. Spanish adjectives can be masculine or feminine, singular or plural. They must agree with the noun both in gender and in number.

GENDER

Masculine form	Feminine form	Examples
Ends in -o.	Changes -o to -a.	niño simpático → niña simpática
Ends in -e or in a consonant.	Does not change.	niño inteligente → niña inteligente

NUMBER

Singular form	Plural form	Examples
Ends in a vowel.	Adds -s.	amigo simpático → amigos simpáticos
Ends in a consonant.	Adds -es.	amigo joven → amigos jóvenes

Demonstrative adjectives

Demonstrative adjectives indicate where something or someone is located in relation to the person speaking.

Distance from speaker	Singular		Plural	
	Masculine	Feminine	Masculine	Feminine
Near	este	esta	estos	estas
At a distance	ese	esa	esos	esas
Far away	aquel	aquella	aquellos	aquellas

Possessive adjectives

Possessive adjectives express ownership. They agree with the noun they accompany. They agree with the thing (or person) possessed, not with the owner.

mi mis	my	nuestro, nuestra nuestros, nuestras	our
tu tus	your (informal)	vuestro, vuestra vuestros, vuestras	your (informal)
su sus	his, her, your	su sus	their, your

Indefinite adjectives

Indefinite adjectives express number of nouns in nonspecific terms.

ningún, ninguno(a)	no, (not) any
algún, alguno(a), algunos(as)	one, some, any, a few
poco(a), pocos(as)	some, few
mucho(a), muchos(as)	many, a lot of
todo(a), todos(as)	all, every, throughout

Comparatives

Comparisons of inequality and equality

To express a difference regarding one characteristic, use **más... que** (*more … than*) or **menos... que** (*less … than*). To express equality, use **tan... como** (*as … as*).

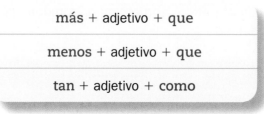

más + adjetivo + que
menos + adjetivo + que
tan + adjetivo + como

Comparative adjectives

Mejor and **peor** are used just like the English words *better* and *worse* to indicate a comparative degree.

bueno *good*	→	mejor, mejores *better*	malo *bad*	→	peor, peores *worse*

Pronouns

Subject pronouns

Subject pronouns identify the person who is performing an action.

	Singular			Plural	
yo	I		nosotros nosotras	we	
tú	you (informal)		vosotros vosotras	you (informal)	
usted él ella	you (formal) he she		ustedes ellos ellas	you they they	

Direct object pronouns

To avoid repeating words that have already been mentioned, you can replace the direct object with a pronoun.

Singular				Plural			
Masculine		Feminine		Masculine		Feminine	
lo	him, it	la	her, it	los	them	las	them

Indirect object pronouns

To avoid repeating words that have already been mentioned, you can replace the indirect object with a pronoun.

Indirect object pronouns are the same as those used with the verb gustar.

	Singular		Plural
me	to me	nos	to us
te	to you (informal)	os	to you (informal)
le	to him, to her, to you (formal)	les	to them, to you

Adverbs and prepositions

Adverbs of frequency

These adverbs and adverbial phrases express how often something is done:

nunca	*never*	muchas veces	*usually, normally*
casi nunca	*almost never*	casi siempre	*many times, often*
rara vez	*seldom, rarely*	siempre	*always*
a veces	*sometimes*	todos los días	*every day*

Adverbs of quantity

These adverbs express a quantity:

nada	poco	bastante	mucho
not at all	*little, not much*	*quite, enough*	*a lot, much*

Adverbs and phrases of location

aquí	*here*	encima de	*on, on top of*
ahí	*there*	debajo de	*under*
allí	*over there*	delante de	*in front of*
al lado de	*next to*	detrás de	*behind*
a la derecha de	*to the right of*	cerca de	*near, close to*
a la izquierda de	*to the left of*	lejos de	*far from*

Adverbs and phrases about the future

When you express intention or future plans you can use these adverbs or expressions:

		mañana	*tomorrow*
ahora	*now*	mañana por la mañana	*tomorrow morning*
luego, después	*later*	mañana por la tarde	*tomorrow afternoon/evening*
		mañana por la noche	*tomorrow night*
hoy	*today*	la próxima semana, la semana que viene	*next week*
esta mañana	*this morning*		
esta tarde	*this afternoon*	el próximo año, el año que viene	*next year*
esta noche	*tonight*		

Adverbs and phrases about the past

These adverbs and time expressions refer to the past tense:

antes	*before*	la semana pasada	*last week*
anoche	*last night*	el mes pasado	*last month*
ayer	*yesterday*	el año pasado	*last year*
anteayer	*the day before yesterday*		

Prepositions of place

en	*at, in, on, inside* (to express location)
a	*to* (after the verb *ir* indicating destination) *(not translated in English before direct and indirect objects)*
de	*from* (to express origin)
desde... hasta de... a	*from ... to* (to express direction or destination)

Conjunctions

Sentences with *si*

In order to express what you do if something happens, use this formula:

Si + condition...

The conjunction *porque*

To express cause, use the conjunction **porque** or the preposition **por**:

porque + sentence

por + noun

Interrogatives

Interrogative words

Interrogatives are question words.

¿Qué?	¿Quién?	¿Cómo?	¿Cuándo?	¿Dónde?	¿Cuánto(a)? ¿Cuántos(as)?	¿Por qué?
What?	*Who?*	*How?* *What?*	*When?*	*Where?*	*How much?* *How many?*	*Why?*

Verbs: present tense

Regular verbs: *lavar, prender, abrir*

Lavar *(to wash)*			
Singular		**Plural**	
yo	**lav**o	nosotros nosotras	**lav**amos
tú	**lav**as	vosotros vosotras	**lav**áis
usted él ella	**lav**a	ustedes ellos ellas	**lav**an

Prender *(to switch on)*			
Singular		**Plural**	
yo	**prend**o	nosotros nosotras	**prend**emos
tú	**prend**es	vosotros vosotras	**prend**éis
usted él ella	**prend**e	ustedes ellos ellas	**prend**en

Abrir *(to open)*			
Singular		**Plural**	
yo	**abr**o	nosotros nosotras	**abr**imos
tú	**abr**es	vosotros vosotras	**abr**ís
usted él ella	**abr**e	ustedes ellos ellas	**abr**en

Irregular verbs: *ser, estar, tener, ir*

Ser *(to be)*			
Singular		**Plural**	
yo	soy	nosotros nosotras	somos
tú	eres	vosotros vosotras	sois
usted él ella	es	ustedes ellos ellas	son

Estar *(to be)*			
Singular		**Plural**	
yo	estoy	nosotros nosotras	estamos
tú	estás	vosotros vosotras	estáis
usted él ella	está	ustedes ellos ellas	están

Tener (to have)

Singular		Plural	
yo	tengo	nosotros nosotras	tenemos
tú	tienes	vosotros vosotras	tenéis
usted él ella	tiene	ustedes ellos ellas	tienen

Ir (to go)

Singular		Plural	
yo	voy	nosotros nosotras	vamos
tú	vas	vosotros vosotras	vais
usted él ella	va	ustedes ellos ellas	van

Ir a + infinitive

To express the intention to do something, use this structure:

ir a + infinitive

The verb *gustar*

Gustar (to like)

	Singular	Plural
(A mí)	me **gusta**	me **gustan**
(A ti)	te **gusta**	te **gustan**
(A usted) (A él) (A ella)	le **gusta**	le **gustan**
(A nosotros) (A nosotras)	nos **gusta**	nos **gustan**
(A vosotros) (A vosotras)	os **gusta**	os **gustan**
(A ustedes) (A ellos) (A ellas)	les **gusta**	les **gustan**

The verb *doler*

Doler (to hurt, to ache)

	Singular	Plural
(A mí)	me **duele**	me **duelen**
(A ti)	te **duele**	te **duelen**
(A usted) (A él) (A ella)	le **duele**	le **duelen**
(A nosotros) (A nosotras)	nos **duele**	nos **duelen**
(A vosotros) (A vosotras)	os **duele**	os **duelen**
(A ustedes) (A ellos) (A ellas)	les **duele**	les **duelen**

Stem-changing verbs

Cerrar *(e > ie)* *(to close)*

Singular		Plural	
yo	cierro	nosotros nosotras	cerramos
tú	cierras	vosotros vosotras	cerráis
usted él ella	cierra	ustedes ellos ellas	cierran

Poder *(o > ue)* *(to be able to)*

Singular		Plural	
yo	puedo	nosotros nosotras	podemos
tú	puedes	vosotros vosotras	podéis
usted él ella	puede	ustedes ellos ellas	pueden

Pedir *(e > i)* *(to ask)*

Singular		Plural	
yo	pido	nosotros nosotras	pedimos
tú	pides	vosotros vosotras	pedís
usted él ella	pide	ustedes ellos ellas	piden

Jugar *(u > ue)* *(to play)*

Singular		Plural	
yo	juego	nosotros nosotras	jugamos
tú	juegas	vosotros vosotras	jugáis
usted él ella	juega	ustedes ellos ellas	juegan

The verb *sentirse*

Sentirse *(to feel)*

Singular		Plural	
yo	me siento	nosotros nosotras	nos sentimos
tú	te sientes	vosotros vosotras	os sentís
usted él ella	se siente	ustedes ellos ellas	se sienten

Verbs with irregular yo forms

Hacer (to do, to make)

Singular		Plural	
yo	hago	nosotros nosotras	hacemos
tú	haces	vosotros vosotras	hacéis
usted él ella	hace	ustedes ellos ellas	hacen

Poner (to put)

Singular		Plural	
yo	pongo	nosotros nosotras	ponemos
tú	pones	vosotros vosotras	ponéis
usted él ella	pone	ustedes ellos ellas	ponen

Traer (to bring)

Singular		Plural	
yo	traigo	nosotros nosotras	traemos
tú	traes	vosotros vosotras	traéis
usted él ella	trae	ustedes ellos ellas	traen

Salir (to leave)

Singular		Plural	
yo	salgo	nosotros nosotras	salimos
tú	sales	vosotros vosotras	salís
usted él ella	sale	ustedes ellos ellas	salen

Irregular verbs: *ver*, *oír*, *oler*, and *decir*

Ver (to see)

Singular		Plural	
yo	veo	nosotros nosotras	vemos
tú	ves	vosotros vosotras	veis
usted él ella	ve	ustedes ellos ellas	ven

Oír (to hear)

Singular		Plural	
yo	oigo	nosotros nosotras	oímos
tú	oyes	vosotros vosotras	oís
usted él ella	oye	ustedes ellos ellas	oyen

Oler *(to smell)*			
Singular		**Plural**	
yo	huelo	nosotros nosotras	**olemos**
tú	hueles	vosotros vosotras	**oléis**
usted él ella	huele	ustedes ellos ellas	huelen

Decir *(to say)*			
Singular		**Plural**	
yo	digo	nosotros nosotras	**decimos**
tú	dices	vosotros vosotras	**decís**
usted él ella	dice	ustedes ellos ellas	dicen

Reflexive verbs

Lavarse *(to wash oneself)*			
Singular		**Plural**	
yo	me lavo	nosotros nosotras	nos lavamos
tú	te lavas	vosotros vosotras	os laváis
usted él ella	se lava	ustedes ellos ellas	se lavan

Other reflexive verbs are:

acostarse (ue) *(to go to bed)* → yo me acuesto

despertarse (ie) *(to wake up)* → yo me despierto

dormirse (ue) *(to fall asleep)* → yo me duermo

levantarse *(to get up)* → yo me levanto

Expressions of obligation

hay que + infinitive	tener que + infinitive
a general obligation; rules or norms	*a personal obligation*

Expressions of permission and prohibition

Expressing permission:

se puede + infinitive (with singular object)
se puede(n) + infinitive (with plural object)

Expressing prohibition:

no se puede + infinitive
no se puede(n) + infinitive

Verbs: the present participle

Regular present participle forms

The *gerundio* (present participle) is formed by adding the following endings to the verb stem:

-ando	for *-ar* verbs	escuchar	→	escuchando
-iendo	for *-er*, *-ir* verbs	hacer escribir	→ →	haciendo escribiendo

Irregular present participle forms

e > ie				o > u		
decir → diciendo	servir → sirviendo	dormir → durmiendo
medir → midiendo	vestir → vistiendo	morir → muriendo
pedir → pidiendo		poder → pudiendo

When the stem of an *-er* or *-ir* verb ends in a vowel (*leer*, *creer*, *oír*), the ending *-iendo* becomes *-yendo*.

leer → leyendo	creer → creyendo	oír → oyendo

Verbs: the present progressive

The present progressive is formed with *estar* + *gerundio* (present participle):

Trabajar *(to work)*			
Singular		**Plural**	
yo	estoy trabajando	nosotros nosotras	estamos trabajando
tú	estás trabajando	vosotros vosotras	estáis trabajando
usted él ella	está trabajando	ustedes ellos ellas	están trabajando

Verbs: commands

Affirmative *tú* commands

REGULAR VERBS

Caminar *(to walk)*	Comer *(to eat)*	Escribir *(to write)*
camina	come	escribe

IRREGULAR VERBS

Tener *(to have)*	Hacer *(to do)*	Poner *(to put)*	Venir *(to come)*	Salir *(to leave)*		Ser *(to be)*	Decir *(to say)*	Ir *(to go)*
ten	haz	pon	ven	sal		sé	di	ve

Negative *tú* commands

REGULAR VERBS

Comprar *(to buy)*	Comer *(to eat)*	Escribir *(to write)*
no compres	no comas	no escribas

IRREGULAR VERBS *SER* AND *IR*

Ser *(to be)*	Ir *(to go)*
no seas	no vayas

Verbs: the preterite tense

Regular verbs (*-ar, -er, -ir*)

	Comprar *(to buy)*	Comer *(to eat)*	Escribir *(to write)*
yo	compré	comí	escribí
tú	compraste	comiste	escribiste
usted él ella	compró	comió	escribió
nosotros nosotras	compramos	comimos	escribimos
vosotros vosotras	comprasteis	comisteis	escribisteis
ustedes ellos ellas	compraron	comieron	escribieron

Irregular verbs

Ser (to be) e ir (to go)

Singular		Plural	
yo	fui	nosotros nosotras	fuimos
tú	fuiste	vosotros vosotras	fuisteis
usted él ella	fue	ustedes ellos ellas	fueron

Decir (to say)

Singular		Plural	
yo	dije	nosotros nosotras	dijimos
tú	dijiste	vosotros vosotras	dijisteis
usted él ella	dijo	ustedes ellos ellas	dijeron

Hacer (to do, to make)

Singular		Plural	
yo	hice	nosotros nosotras	hicimos
tú	hiciste	vosotros vosotras	hicisteis
usted él ella	hizo	ustedes ellos ellas	hicieron

Estar (to be)

Singular		Plural	
yo	estuve	nosotros nosotras	estuvimos
tú	estuviste	vosotros vosotras	estuvisteis
usted él ella	estuvo	ustedes ellos ellas	estuvieron

Tener (to have)

Singular		Plural	
yo	tuve	nosotros nosotras	tuvimos
tú	tuviste	vosotros vosotras	tuvisteis
usted él ella	tuvo	ustedes ellos ellas	tuvieron

GLOSARIO ESPAÑOL-INGLÉS

A

a *to* 16
a causa de *because of* 241
a diario *daily* 73
A la(s)... *At ... (time)* 22
a la derecha de *to the right of* 16
a la izquierda de *to the left of* 16
a la vez *at the same time* 117
a lo largo de *along* 113
¿A qué hora abre...? *What time does ... open?* 22
¿A qué hora cierra...? *What time does ... close?* 22
¿A qué te dedicas? *What do you do for living?* 92
a veces *sometimes* 18
abajo *down* 80
abierto(a) *open* 22
el/la **abogado(a)** *lawyer* 96
abrir *to open* 18
la **abuela** *grandmother* 2
el **abuelo** *grandfather* 2
los **abuelos** *grandparents, grandfathers* 2
la **abundancia** *abundance* 77
aburrido(a) *boring* 69
el **accidente** *accident* 38
la **acción** *action* 12
el **aceite** *oil* 67
el **acento** *accent* 99
el **acordeón** *accordion* 115
acostarse (o > ue) *to go to bed* 50
la **actividad** *activity* 14
las **actividades de ocio** *leisure activities* 14
activo(a) *active* 214
el **acto** *act* 248
el **actor** *actor* 113
actuar *to act* 104
acuático(a) *aquatic* 109
además *what's more* 43
la **adivinanza** *riddle* 45
adivinar *to guess* 119
el **adjetivo** *adjective* 6
los **adjetivos posesivos** *possessive adjectives* 8
la **adolescencia** *adolescence* 51
¿Adónde? *Where to?* 43
los **adverbios de cantidad** *adverbs of quantity* 26
los **adverbios de frecuencia** *adverbs of frequency* 18
los **adverbios de lugar** *adverbs of location* 16

el **aeropuerto** *airport* 152
afeitarse *to shave* 48
afirmativo(a) *affirmative* 68
la **agencia de viajes** *travel agency* 160
la **agenda** *agenda* 97
agosto *August* 241
la **agricultura** *agriculture* 161
agrio(a) *sour* 24
el **agua** *water* 24
las **aguas termales** *hot springs* 52
ahí *there* 16
ahora *now* 17
el **aire** *air* 234
al *to the* 16
al aire libre *outdoors, in the open air* 191
al fin *finally* 192
al lado de *next to* 16
al llegar *upon arriving* 75
el **albatros** *albatross* 254
alcanzar *to reach* 185
la **alegría** *joy* 136
algo *something* 54
el **algodón** *cotton* 23
algún, alguno(a)(os)(as) *a few, any, one, some* 218
la **alimentación** *feeding* 254
los **alimentos** *food* 61
allí *there (far)* 16
el **almacén** *grocery store* 192
almorzar (o > ue) *to have lunch* 69
el **almuerzo** *lunch* 108
el **alojamiento** *accomodations* 168
alojarse *to stay* 195
alrededor de *around* 208
alto(a) *tall* 4 *loud* 43
la **altura** *height* 185
amargo(a) *bitter* 24
amarillo(a) *yellow* 22
americano(a) *American* 159
el/la **amigo(a)** *friend* 2
los **amigos** *friends (males, males and females)* 8
el **amor** *love* 35
anaranjado(a) *orange* 22
ancho(a) *wide* 183
andar *to go, to walk* 192
el **anillo** *ring* 212
el **animal** *animal* 234
el **aniversario** *anniversary* 181
anoche *last night* 170
anteayer *the day before yesterday* 170
antes (de) *before* 48

antiguo(a) *old* 37
anualmente *annually* 229
el **anuncio** *ad* 73
el **año** *year* 8
apagar *to turn off* 43
el **apellido** *last name* 85
la **aportación** *contribution* 133
aprender *to learn* 44
aprovechar *to take advantage* 100
aproximadamente *approximately* 188
aproximado(a) *rough* 225
aquel, aquella *that (far away)* 30
aquello *that (neutral)* 206
aquí *here* 16
árabe *Arab* 47
el **árbol** *tree* 234
el **archipiélago** *archipelago* 76
el **área** *area* 135
argentino(a) *Argentinian* 153
el **argumento** *plot* 193
árido(a) *arid, dry* 189
el **arma** *weapon* 242
el **armario** *closet* 12
la **armonía** *harmony* 134
el **aroma** *scent* 192
la **arquitectura** *architecture* 65
el **arroz** *rice* 24
el **arte** *art* 103
la **artesanía** *handicraft* 227
el **artículo** *article* 10
el/la **artista** *artist* 103
artístico(a) *artistic* 43
el **ascensor** *elevator* 12
así que *so that* 192
asistir *to attend* 100
el/la **astronauta** *astronaut* 208
el **asunto** *matter* 139
atado(a) *tied* 125
Atentamente. *Sincerely yours,* 52
atlántico(a) *Atlantic* 76
el/la **atleta** *athlete* 97
atlético(a) *athletic* 4
atraer *to attract* 191
atravesado(a) *crossed* 189
atrevido(a) *daring* 4
aunque *although* 188
los **auriculares** *headphones* 96
auténtico(a) *authentic* 214
el **autobús** *bus* 152
la **autoevaluación** *self-evaluation* 87

el/la **autor(a)** *author* 190

el **autorretrato** *self-portrait* 41

el **ave** *bird* 211

la **avenida** *avenue* 79

la **aventura** *adventure* 78

el **avión** *plane* 152

¡Ay! *Ouch!* 58

ayer *yesterday* 170

ayudar *to help* 51

el **azúcar** *sugar* 24

azul *blue* 22

el **azulejo** *tile* 37

B

bailar *to dance* 104

el **baile** *dance* 114

bajar *to get off* 192 *to go down* 223

bajo(a) *short* 4

la **ballena** *whale* 237

el **balneario** *beach resort* 217

el **balón** *ball* 122

el **baloncesto** *basketball* 122

la **banana** *banana* 27

el **banco** *bank* 178

la **banda** *band* 115

la **bandera** *flag* 155

el **bandoneón** *Argentinian large accordion* 190

bañar *to bathe* 77

bañarse *to take a bath* 48

la **bañera** *bathtub* 12

el **baño** *bathroom* 12

barato(a) *cheap* 153

el **barco** *ship* 152

barrer *to sweep* 14

el **barrio** *neighborhood* 95

básico(a) *basic* 66

bastante *quite, enough* 26

la **basura** *garbage* 14

el **bate** *bat* 122

beber *to drink* 25

la **bebida** *drink* 24

el **béisbol** *baseball* 122

la **belleza** *beauty* 69

bello(a) *beautiful* 79

el **beso** *kiss* 17

la **biblioteca** *library* 178

bien *well* 2 *properly* 160 *correctly* 167

Bienvenido(a). *Welcome.* 57

bilingüe *bilingual* 97

el **billete** *ticket* 160 *bill* 225

blanco(a) *white* 22

la **blusa** *blouse* 22

la **boca** *mouth* 40

la **bola** *ball* 122

el **boletín** *bulletin* 220

el **boleto** *ticket* 108

el **boliche** *bowling* 122

el **bolígrafo** *ballpoint* 17

la **bolsa** *bag* 160

bonito(a) *pretty* 11

el **bosque** *forest* 216

botar *to throw away* 234

la **botella** *bottle* 24

el **brazo** *arm* 40

brillar *to shine* 208

la **broma** *joke* 46

la **brutalidad** *brutality* 80

buen, bueno(a) *good* 10

¡Buen fin de semana! *Have a nice weekend!* 19

¡Buen viaje! *Have a good trip!* 148

Bueno, … *Well …* 17

buscar *to find, to look for* 13

C

el **caballo** *horse* 80

la **cabaña** *cabin* 253

la **cabeza** *head* 40

cada *each* 14

el **café** *coffee* 25 *cafe* 178

la **cafetería** *cafeteria* 100

los **calcetines** *socks* 22

el **cálculo** *calculation* 139

el **calendario** *calendar* 106

cálido(a) *warm* 189

caliente *hot* 24

la **calle** *street* 178

la **cama** *bed* 12

la **cámara de fotos** *camera* 112

la **cámara de video** *camcorder* 112

cambiar *to change* 49

el **cambio** *change* 51

caminar *to walk* 66

el **camino** *way* 55

la **camisa** *shirt* 22

la **camiseta** *T-shirt* 22

el/la **campeón(a)** *champion* 130

el **cámping** *campsite* 168

el **campo** *countryside* 39 *field* 127

el **canal** *canal* 245

la **canasta** *basket* 125

la **cancha** *court (sports)* 125

la **canción** *song* 113

cansado(a) *tired* 4

el/la **cantante** *singer* 111

cantar *to sing* 104

la **cantidad** *quantity* 218

la **capital** *capital city* 224

la **cara** *face* 40

la **característica** *feature* 4

característico(a) *characteristic, typical* 78

caribeño(a) *Caribbean* 136

el **cariño** *love* 118

el **carnaval** *carnival* 135

la **carne** *meat* 24

la **carrera** *race* 39

la **carta** *menu* 24

el **cartel** *poster* 137

la **casa** *house* 12

el **casco** *helmet* 122

casi *almost* 134

casi nunca *almost never* 18

casi siempre *most of the time* 18

el **castillo** *castle* 77

las **cataratas** *waterfalls* 145

la **catedral** *cathedral* 57

la **categoría** *category* 247

católico(a) *Catholic* 33

la **causa** *cause* 210

la **caza** *hunting* 255

cazar *to hunt* 255

la **celebración** *celebration* 133

celebrar *to celebrate* 9

cenar *to have dinner* 31

central *central* 182

el **centro** *downtown* 21 *middle, center* 76

el **centro comercial** *shopping center, mall* 99

cepillarse *to brush (one's hair, teeth)* 48

el **cepillo** *hairbrush* 48

el **cepillo de dientes** *toothbrush* 48

la **cerámica** *ceramics, pottery* 227

cerca de *close to* 16

los **cereales** *cereals* 67

cerrado(a) *closed* 22

cerrar (e > ie) *to close* 20

el **césped** *lawn* 14

el **champú** *shampoo* 48

la **chaqueta** *jacket* 22

la **chica** *girl* 2

el/la **chicano(a)** *Chicano* 134

el **chico** *boy* 2

D

la **danza**   *dance* 136

dar   *to give* 64

el **dato**   *piece of information* 132

de   *of* 3   *than* 47   *from* 172

de ida y vuelta   *round trip* 148

de nuevo   *again* 192

de viaje   *on a trip* 152

debajo de   *under* 16

deber   *must* 238

débil   *weak* 54

decidir   *to decide* 25

decir   *to say, to tell* 42

declarar   *to declare* 181

decorar   *to decorate* 47

dedicarse a   *to do for a living* 92

el **dedo**   *finger, toe* 40

defender (e > ie)   *to defend* 97

la **deforestación**   *deforestation* 219

dejar   *to leave (smething)* 232

del   *of the* 5

delante de   *in front of* 16

el **delfín**   *dolphin* 237

delgado(a)   *thin* 4

delicioso(a)   *delicious* 164

los/las **demás**   *rest* 61

los **demostrativos**   *demonstratives* 30

dentro   *inside* 64

denunciar   *to denounce* 190

el **departamento**   *department* 164

el **deporte**   *sport* 122

el **depósito**   *deposit* 211

el **desafío**   *challenge* 32

el **desarrollo**   *development* 110

desayunar   *to have breakfast* 69

el **desayuno**   *breakfast* 28

descansar   *to rest* 50

el **descanso**   *rest* 47

descender (e > ie)   *to descend* 188

el/la **descendiente**   *descendant* 215

describir   *to describe* 2

descriptivo(a)   *descriptive* 135

descubrir   *to discover* 208

desde   *from* 43   *since* 57

desesperado(a)   *desperate* 80

el **desfile**   *parade* 133

el **desierto**   *desert* 216

el **desodorante**   *deodorant* 48

despacio   *slowly* 176

despertarse (e > ie)   *to wake up* 50

después   *later on* 53

después de   *after* 69

el **destino**   *destination* 168

destruir   *to destroy* 80

el/la **detective**   *detective* 38

detrás de   *behind* 16

el **día**   *day* 43

el **diablo**   *devil* 166

el **diario**   *diary* 221

diario(a)   *daily* 53

el **dibujo**   *drawing* 190

el **diente**   *tooth* 40

la **dieta**   *diet* 51

la **diferencia**   *difference* 220

diferente   *different* 49

difícil   *difficult* 41

el **dinero**   *money* 191

la **dirección**   *direction* 166

el/la **director(a)**   *director* 96   *principal* 128

dirigir   *to direct, to run* 97

el **disco**   *disc* 117

diseñar   *to design* 67

el **diseño**   *design* 47

disfrutar   *to enjoy* 76

la **distancia**   *distance* 152

distinto(a)   *different* 26

la **diversidad**   *diversity* 136

divertido(a)   *fun* 9

divertirse (e > ie)   *to enjoy oneself* 113

dividir   *to divide* 223

la **división**   *division* 224

doblar a la derecha/izquierda   *to turn to the right/left* 178

el/la **doctor(a)**   *doctor* 34

el **documental**   *documentary* 85

el **documento**   *document* 148

el **dólar**   *dollar* 23

doler (o > ue)   *to hurt* 58

el **dolor**   *ache, pain* 56

el **domingo**   *Sunday* 157

el **dominó**   *dominoes* 88

don   *Mr.* 5

¿Dónde?   *Where?* 12

dormir (o > ue)   *to sleep* 61

dormirse (o > ue)   *to fall asleep* 50

el **dormitorio**   *bedroom* 12

la **ducha**   *shower* 12

ducharse   *to take a shower* 48

dulce   *sweet* 24

el **dulce de leche**   *milk caramel typical of Argentina and other countries in the Rio de la Plata region* 187

durante   *for* 39   *during* 49

durar   *to last* 185

E

el **eclipse**   *eclipse* 208

la **ecología**   *ecology* 251

el **edificio**   *building* 12

el **ejemplo**   *example* 97

él   *he* 6

el, la   *the* 10

el año pasado   *last year* 170

el año que viene   *next year* 106

el mes pasado   *last month* 170

la **electricidad**   *electricity* 238

eléctrico(a)   *electric* 115

el **elefante**   *elephant* 254

elegante   *elegant* 183

el **elemento**   *element* 193

ella   *she* 6

ellas   *they (feminine)* 6

ellos   *they (males, males and females)* 6

emocionado(a)   *excited* 4

emocionante   *exciting* 37

empacar   *to pack* 237

la **empanada**   *pie* 111

empezar (e > ie)   *to begin, to start* 20

el/la **empleado(a)**   *employee* 96

el/la **empresario(a)**   *businessman, businesswoman* 95

en   *in* 16

en brazos   *in one's arms* 80

en cambio   *instead* 105

en directo   *live* 139

en el centro de   *in the middle of* 161

en general   *in general* 73

en realidad   *actually* 192

Encantado(a).   *Nice to meet you.* 2

encima de   *on, on top of* 16

encontrar (o > ue)   *to find* 46

encontrarse (o > ue)   *to feel* 60

encontrarse (o > ue) con   *to run into, to meet with* 173

el **encuentro**   *meeting, encounter* 74

la **encuesta**   *survey* 43

la **energía**   *energy* 61

enero   *January* 223

la **enfermedad**   *illness* 56

el/la **enfermero(a)**   *nurse* 56

enfermo(a)   *sick* 4

el/la **enfermo(a)**   *patient* 56

enloquecido(a)   *mad* 80

enojado(a)   *angry* 4

enorme *huge* 203
enriquecedor(a) *enlightening* 205
la ensalada *salad* 27
enseñar *to teach* 97
enseñar el pasaporte *to show one's passport* 160
entender (e > ie) *to understand* 20
entonces *then* 25
entrar *to enter* 31
entre *between* 73 *among* 103
entregar *to give* 193
el/la entrenador(a) *coach* 96
entretener *to entertain* 34
la entrevista *interview* 212
la época *age* 46
equilibrado(a) *well-balanced* 51
el equipaje *baggage* 160
el equipamiento *equipment* 138
el equipo *team* 122
equivaler *to be equivalent* 173
equivocado(a) *wrong* 192
el error *mistake* 167
la escalera *stairs* 12
el escalón *step* 222
el escenario *scenario* 78
escoger *to choose* 35
escolar *school* 220
escribir *to write* 3
escribir correos *to write e-mails* 112
escribir mensajes *to write instant messages* 104
escuchar *to listen* 3
el escudo *shield* 37
la escuela *school* 96
ese, esa *that (nearby)* 30
esos(as) *those (nearby)* 30
el espacio *space* 212
la espada *sword* 80
la espalda *back* 56
el español *Spanish (language)* 6
español(a) *Spanish* 73
el/la español(a) *Spaniard* 43
especial *special* 25
especialmente *specially* 79
la especialidad *specialty* 25
espectacular *spectacular* 189
el espectáculo *show* 43
el/la espectador(a) *spectator* 133
la esperanza *hope* 80
esperar *to wait for* 35
espontáneo(a) *spontaneous* 4
la esposa *wife* 202
el esposo *husband* 159

el esquema *diagram* 67
esquiar *to ski* 195
esta mañana *this morning* 106
esta noche *tonight, this evening* 106
esta tarde *this afternoon/ evening* 106
la estación *station* 152 *season* 217
el estadio *stadium, arena* 122
las estadísticas *statistics* 123
el estado *condition* 54 *state* 76
los Estados Unidos *United States* 9
el/la estadounidense *American (noun)* 137
la estantería *bookcase* 12
estar *to be* 6
estar en forma *to be in shape* 66
estar listo(a) *to be ready* 148
estar preparado(a) *to be ready* 148
la estatua *statue* 103
este, esta *this* 30
el este *east* 169
Este(a) es... *This is ...* 2
el estilo *style* 43
Estimado(a)... *Dear...* 49
esto *this (neutral)* 77
el estómago *stomach* 56
Estoy enfermo(a). *I am sick.* 36
la estrategia *strategy* 81
la estrella *star* 208
el/la estudiante *student* 2
los estudiantes *students (males, males and females)* 97
el estudio *study* 164
estudioso(a) *studious* 4
la estufa *stove* 12
la etapa *stage* 38
el/la europeo(a) *European* 188
el evento *event* 46
evitar *to avoid* 61
exactamente *exactly* 188
el examen *test* 5
la excursión *excursion, field trip* 48
la excusa *excuse* 69
la existencia *existence* 16
existir *to exist* 219
el éxito *success* 99
la expedición *expedition* 198
la experiencia *experience* 160
experto(a) *expert* 94
explorar *to explore* 208
la exposición *exhibition* 108
expresar *to express* 8
la expresión *expression* 16

extenderse (e > ie) *to spread out* 78
extenso(a) *vast* 77
la extinción *extinction* 237
extraordinario(a) *extraordinary* 108

F

la fábrica *factory* 96
la fachada *front, facade* 59
facturar el equipaje *to check the luggage* 160
las fajitas *fajitas* 134
la falda *skirt* 22
fallado(a) *failed* 53
falso(a) *false* 25
la familia *family* 2
familiar *family* 9
famoso(a) *famous* 31
el/la famoso(a) *celebrity* 93
el/la fan *fan* 44
fantástico(a) *fantastic* 117
la farmacia *pharmacy, drugstore* 56
la fauna *fauna* 233
favorito(a) *favorite* 105
la fecha *date* 136
femenino(a) *feminine* 10
el fenómeno *phenomenon* 219
feo(a) *ugly* 5
ferroviario(a) *railway* 134
festejar *to celebrate* 133
el festejo *festivity* 137
el festival *festival* 131
la ficha *domino* 101 *file card* 254
la fiebre *fever* 56
la fiesta *party* 9
la figura *figure* 207
fijarse *to notice* 43
el fin de semana *weekend* 15
el final *end* 45
finalmente *finally* 166
físico(a) *physical* 4
el flamenco *flamenco* 43
la flor *flower* 234
la flora *flora* 233
la florería *flower shop* 171
folclórico(a) *folk* 229
la forma *way* 61
formado(a) por *formed by* 167
formar parte de *to be part of* 215
el fósil *fossil* 219
la foto *photo, picture* 11

la **fotografía**   photo, picture 43
   photography 92
el/la **fotógrafo(a)**   photographer 91
la **fotonovela**   photonovel 38
el **francés**   French (language) 92
la **frecuencia**   frequency 18
   frente a   in front of 251
   frío(a)   cold 24
la **frontera**   border 224
la **fruta**   fruit 24
el **fuego**   fire 80
   fuerte   strong 38
   funcionar   to function, to work 15
   fundado(a)   founded 103
el **fútbol**   soccer 122
el **fútbol americano**   football 122
el **futuro**   future 106

G

las **gafas**   glasses 210
la **gala**   gala 111
la **galería**   gallery 95
   ganar   to win 37
el **garaje**   garage 12
la **garganta**   throat 56
   gastar   to waste 238
la **gastronomía**   gastronomy 132
el **gato**   cat 8
el **gaucho**   gaucho 144
el **gel**   gel 48
   general   general 221
la **gente**   people 17
la **geografía**   geography 216
   geográfico(a)   geographical 209
   geométrico(a)   geometric 47
el **germen**   germ 61
el **gerundio**   present participle 116
   gigantesco(a)   gigantic 246
el **gimnasio**   gym 67
   girar   to turn 208
el **glaciar**   glacier 188
el **gobierno**   government 67
el **golf**   golf 122
el **golpe**   knock 38
   gordo(a)   fat 4
el **gorro**   cap 22
   grabar   to tape, to record 112
   gracias   thank you 3
   gracias a   thanks to 99
   gracioso(a)   funny 4
el **grado**   degree 26
la **graduación**   graduation 113

la **gramática**   grammar 6
   gran, grande   big 13   great 77
   Gran Bretaña   Great Britain 173
   gratis   free (of charge) 47
la **gripe**   flu 61
el **grupo**   group 86
el **guante**   glove 122
   guapo   handsome 5
   guardar   to put … away 193
la **guerra**   war 80
el/la **guía**   guide 108
la **guía turística**   tourist guide 160
la **guitarra**   guitar 42
   gustar   to like 26
los **gustos**   likes 22

H

   haber   auxiliary verb 16
la **habitación**   room 47
   habitado(a)   inhabited 135
el/la **habitante**   inhabitant 188
el **hábitat**   habitat 254
el **hábito**   habit 51
   habitual   habitual 12
   hablar   to talk 3
   hablar por teléfono   to talk on the
   phone 14
   Hace frío.   It's cold. 197
   Hace sol.   It's sunny. 5
   hacer   to do, to make 30
   hacer deporte   to play sports 66
   hacer ejercicio   to exercise 66
   hacer turismo   to travel
   around 168
   hacia   towards 78
la **hamburguesa**   burger 98
   hasta   up to 151   to 172
   until 236
   Hasta pronto.   See you soon. 9
   hay   there is, there are 16
   hay que…   one has to … 28
el **helado**   ice cream 24
el **hemisferio**   hemisphere 217
la **herencia**   heritage 79
la **hermana**   sister 2
el **hermano**   brother 2
los **hermanos**   brothers, siblings 2
el **héroe**   hero 100
   hidratante   moisturizing 50
el **hielo**   ice 212
la **hierba**   grass 189
la **higiene**   hygiene 48
la **hija**   daughter 2

el **hijo**   son 2
los **hijos**   son and daughter, sons 2
   hispánico(a)   Hispanic 88
   hispano(a)   Hispanic 95
   hispanohablante   Spanish
   speaker 188
la **Historia**   history (subject) 101
la **historia**   story 45
   histórico(a)   historical 181
la **historieta gráfica**   comic
   strip 190
el **hockey**   hockey 237
la **hoja**   leaf 234
   Hola.   Hello. 2
el **hombre**   man 2
   honesto(a)   honest 99
el **honor**   honor 199
la **hora**   hour 65
el **horario**   schedule 23
el **horror**   horror 80
el **hospital**   hospital 56
el **hostal**   guest house 33
el **hotel**   hotel 168
   hoy   today 106
la **huella**   influence 133
el **huevo**   egg 24
   humano(a)   human 69
el **humor**   humor 190

I

la **idea**   idea 49
   ideal   ideal 109
la **identidad**   identity 134
   identificar   to identify 2
la **iglesia**   church 178
   igual   same 69   equal 173
   igual que   similar to 153
la **imagen**   image 215
el **imperativo**   imperative (tense),
   command (tense) 68
   importante   important 39
la **impresión**   impression 219
   impresionante   impressive 167
   inaugurar   to inaugurate 153
   incluir   to include 228
   increíble   incredible 110
los **indefinidos**   indefinites 218
la **independencia**   independence 136
   indicar   to indicate 192
   indígena   indigenous 31
la **industria**   industry 161
la **influencia**   influence 79
la **información**   information 94

informal *informal* 101

informativo(a) *informative* 164

el/la **ingeniero(a)** *engineer* 96

el **inglés** *English (language)* 92

el **inglés** *English (subject)* 163

el **ingrediente** *ingredient* 134

inmediatamente *at once* 153

el **inodoro** *toilet* 12

el **insecto** *insect* 234

las **instrucciones** *directions* 179

el **instrumento** *instrument* 115

inteligente *intelligent* 4

la **intención** *intention* 102

intenso(a) *intense* 78

intercambiar *to exchange* 105

interesante *interesting* 65

el **interior** *interior* 77

internacional *international* 39

interracial *interracial* 134

la **intervención** *intervention* 255

el/la **intruso(a)** *intruder* 13

la **investigación** *research* 79

el **invierno** *winter* 126

la **invitación** *invitation* 171

el/la **invitado(a)** *guest* 9

invitar *to invite* 9

ir *to go* 16

ir a... *to go to ...* 106

ir a pie *to go on foot* 152

ir al cine *to go to the movies* 112

ir bien *to do well (school)* 101

ir de compras *to go shopping* 22

ir de excursión *to go on an excursion* 152

ir de vacaciones *to go on vacation* 152

ir en... *to go by ...* 152

irregular *irregular* 20

irritado(a) *irritated* 43

la **isla** *island* 216

el/la **italiano(a)** *Italian* 174

el **itinerario** *itinerary* 161

J

el **jabón** *soap* 48

el **jai alai** *jai alai* 125

el **jamón** *ham* 5

el **jardín** *yard* 12   *garden* 47

el **jersey** *jersey* 39

el **jonrón** *home run* 120

joven *young* 4

el/la **joven** *young man/woman* 94

la **joya** *jewel* 227

el **juego** *game* 101

el **juego de mesa** *board game* 72

el **jueves** *Thursday* 170

el/la **juez(a)** *judge* 99

el/la **jugador(a)** *player* 122

jugar (u > ue) (a/al) *to play (sports and games)* 122

jugar (u > ue) a los videojuegos *to play videogames* 112

el **jugo** *juice* 24

julio *July* 189

junio *June* 241

junto *together* 72

junto a *next to* 129

juntos(as) *together* 9

la **juventud** *youth* 136

K

el **karaoke** *karaoke* 155

el **kilo** *kilogram* 192

el **kilómetro** *kilometer* 134

el **krill** *shrimp-like crustacean marine animal* 254

L

la, las *the* 10

la, las *her, it/them* 28

la próxima semana *next week* 106

la semana pasada *last week* 170

la semana que viene *next week* 106

el **laberinto** *maze* 245

el **lado** *side* 32

el **lago** *lake* 216

la **laguna** *lagoon* 211

el **lapislázuli** *semi-precious stone that has been valued since antiquity for its intense blue color* 227

largo(a) *long* 41

la **lata** *can, tin* 238

latino(a) *Latino* 89

latinoamericano(a) *Latin American* 108

el **lavabo** *sink* 12

el **lavaplatos** *dishwasher* 12

lavar *to wash* 18

lavarse *to get washed, wash (up)* 50

le, les *(to) him, her, you (formal)/ (to) them, you (plural)* 28

la **leche** *milk* 24

la **lectura** *reading* 80

leer *to read* 14

legal *legal* 139

las **legumbres** *legumes* 67

lejos *far away* 64

lejos de *far from* 16

la **lengua** *language* 78

levantarse *to get up* 48

la **libertad** *liberty* 103

la **libra** *pound* 239

libre *free* 147

el **libro** *book* 16

el **libro de texto** *textbook* 241

la **licencia** *license* 153

el/la **líder** *leader* 38

limeño(a) *from Lima* 31

el **limón** *lemon* 27

limpiar *to clean* 14

limpio(a) *clean* 15

lindo(a) *lovely* 192

la **lista** *list* 86

listo(a) *ready* 206

el **litro** *liter* 62

llamado(a) *called, named* 134

llamar *to phone* 147

la **llanura** *plain* 189

llenar *to fill* 248

lleno(a) *full* 61

la **llegada** *arrival* 34   *finish line* 163

llegar *to arrive* 59

llevar *to wear* 23   *to contain* 25   *to lead* 57   *to bring* 67

llorar *to cry* 80

llover (o > ue) *to rain* 174

la **lluvia** *rain* 225

lluvioso(a) *rainy* 217

lo, los *him, it/them* 28

Lo siento. *I am sorry.* 35

la **localidad** *town* 247

la **localización** *location* 178

lógico(a) *logic* 195

luego *later* 106

el **lugar** *place, location* 16

la **Luna** *Moon* 208

el **lunes** *Monday* 53

la **lupa** *magnifying glass* 245

la **luz** *light* 129

M

la **madre** *mother* 2

el/la **maestro(a)** *teacher* 96

el **maíz** *corn* 24

mal *badly* 36 *wrongly* 166

la **maleta** *suitcase* 160

mal, malo(a) *bad* 43

la **mamá** *mom, mommy* 21

el **mamífero** *mammal* 237

mandar *to order* 192

la **mano** *hand* 40

el **mantel** *tablecloth* 24

mantener *to keep* 51

el **manuscrito** *manuscript* 103

la **manzana** *apple* 71

mañana *tomorrow* 9

la **mañana** *morning* 23

mañana por la mañana *tomorrow morning* 106

mañana por la noche *tomorrow night* 106

mañana por la tarde *tomorrow afternoon/evening* 106

el **mapa** *map* 76

maquillarse *to make (oneself) up* 48

el/la **mar** *sea* 216

el **maracuyá** *passion fruit* 50

el **maratón** *marathon* 158

maravilloso(a) *marvelous* 174

el **marco** *setting* 193

marinero(a) *sailor* 77

marino(a) *marine* 237

Marte *Mars* 208

el **martes** *Tuesday* 53

marzo *March* 154

más *more* 15

el/la **más** *most* 41

más de *more than* 47

más... que *more ... than* 26

más tarde *later on* 133

la **mascota** *pet* 14

masculino(a) *masculine* 10

las **Matemáticas** *math* 5

matemático(a) *mathematical* 139

el **material** *material* 235

mayo *May* 95

mayor *old* 4

el/la **mayor** *biggest* 76 *adult* 107

me *(to) me* 28 *myself* 50

Me duele/duelen... *I have a ... ache* 56

Me llamo... *My name is ...* 2

Me siento bien. *I feel fine.* 36

Me siento mal. *I don't feel well.* 36

la **medianoche** *midnight* 151

el **medicamento** *medication, medicine* 66

la **Medicina** *medicine (science)* 57

el/la **médico(a)** *doctor* 56

el **medio** *middle* 80

el **medio ambiente** *environment* 234

el **mediodía** *noon* 73

los **medios de comunicación** *mass media* 133

los **medios de transporte** *means of transport* 194

medir (e > i) *to measure* 20

mediterráneo(a) *Mediterranean* 79

mejor *better* 69

el/la **mejor** *best* 9

menos *less* 27

menos... que *less ... than* 26

el **mensaje** *message* 227

el **mensaje electrónico** *text message* 44

la **menta** *mint* 49

mental *mental* 51

el **merengue** *merengue* 108

el **mes** *month* 133

la **mesa** *table* 12

el/la **mesero(a)** *server, waiter/waitress* 24

la **meseta** *plateau* 77

la **mesita de noche** *night stand* 12

la **meta** *finish lane* 165

el **metal** *metal* 234

el **metro** *meter* 151 *subway* 152

la **mezcla** *mixture* 134

la **mezquita** *mosque* 79

mi, mis *my* 8

el **microondas** *microwave* 12

el **miércoles** *Wednesday* 156

miles *thousands* 57

la **milla** *mile* 163

el **millón** *million* 123

el **mineral** *mineral* 50

el **minuto** *minute* 35

mirar *to look at* 38

mismo(a) *same* 164

el **mito** *myth* 191

el **moái** *monolithic human figures carved from rock on the Polynesian island of Easter Island, Chile* 203

la **mochila** *backpack* 46

la **moda** *fashion* 136

modernista *modernist* 79

moderno(a) *modern* 78

el **molino de viento** *windmill* 78

la **monarquía** *monarchy* 76

el **monasterio** *monastery* 33

la **moneda** *currency* 225

el **monje** *monk* 65

el **monstruo** *monster* 45

la **montaña** *mountain* 168

montar en bicicleta *to ride a bike* 104

el **monumento** *monument* 134

morado(a) *purple* 22

morder (o > ue) *to bite* 248

moreno(a) *brunet(te)* 4

morir (o > ue) *to die* 116

el **mostrador de información** *information desk* 160

mostrar (o > ue) *to show* 136

el **motivo** *motive* 211

mover (o > ue) *to move* 108

el **movimiento** *movement* 16

muchas veces *usually, normally, many times* 18

mucho *a lot, much* 26

mucho(a)(os)(as) *many, a lot of* 218

Mucho gusto. *It's a pleasure.* 2

los **muebles** *furniture* 14

las **muelas** *teeth (molars)* 54

la **muerte** *death* 80

el/la **muerto(a)** *dead* 80

la **mujer** *woman* 2

la **multiplicación** *multiplication* 248

el **mundo** *world* 57

el **mural** *mural* 134

el **muralismo** *muralism* 134

el **museo** *museum* 21

la **música** *music* 14

musical *musical* 111

el/la **músico(a)** *musician* 111

muy *very* 9

¡Muy bien! *Very well!* 92

N

nacer *to be born* 78

los **nachos** *nachos* 134

el **nacimiento** *birth* 249

la **nación** *nation* 136

nacional *national* 167

nada *nothing* 26

nadar *to swim* 104

la **naranja** *orange* 24

la **nariz** *nose* 40

la **narración** *narration* 193

la **natación** *swimming* 122

natural *natural* 41

la **naturaleza** *nature* 234

navegar   *to sail* 192

la   navegación   *navigation* 192

necesario(a)   *necessary* 97

necesitar   *to need* 15

negativo(a)   *negative* 176

el   negocio   *business* 95

negro(a)   *black* 22

neoyorquino(a)   *New Yorker* 108

nervioso(a)   *nervous* 15

nevar (e > ie)   *to snow* 5

ni   *nor* 43

los   nietos   *grandchildren, grandsons* 2

ningún, ninguno(a)   *no, (not) any* 218

la   niña   *girl* 2

el   niño   *boy* 2

los   niños   *boys, boys and girls* 10

el   nivel   *level* 151

No importa.   *It does not matter.* 148

No pasa nada.   *It does not matter.* 148

la   nobleza   *nobility* 227

la   noche   *night* 23

nocturno(a)   *night, nocturnal* 209

nombrar   *to name* 135

el   nombre   *noun* 10   *name* 30

el   noreste   *northeast* 169

normalmente   *usually, normally* 19

el   noroeste   *northwest* 55

el   norte   *north* 41

nos   *(to) us* 28   *ourselves* 50

nosotros(as)   *we* 6

la   nota   *grade* 139   *note* 173

la   noticia   *news* 113

la   novela   *novel* 78

la   novia   *girlfriend* 2

noviembre   *November* 159

el   novio   *boyfriend* 2

la   nube   *cloud* 144

nuestro(a)   *our* 8

nuevo(a)   *new* 17

el   número   *number* 123

nunca   *never* 18

la   nutria   *otter* 254

la   nutrición   *nutrition* 67

Ñ

el   ñandú   *rhea* 237

los   ñoquis   *Argentinian pasta similar to gnocchi* 191

O

el   oasis   *oasis* 107

obediente   *obedient* 192

el   objeto   *object* 43

las   obligaciones   *duties* 49

la   obra   *construction site* 96

la   obra de arte   *work of art* 102

obrero(a)   *working-class* 191

observar   *to observe* 213

el   océano   *ocean* 216

octubre   *October* 133

ocurrir   *to happen* 198

el   oeste   *west* 169

la   oferta   *offer* 210

la   oficina   *office* 96

la   oficina de turismo   *tourist office* 160

la   Oficina del Censo   *Census Bureau* 132

ofrecer   *to offer* 107

los   oídos   *ears* 56

oír   *to hear* 40

el   ojo   *eye* 40

oler   *to smell* 40

olvidar   *to forget* 147

la   oportunidad   *opportunity* 100

opuesto(a)   *opposite* 217

la   oración   *sentence* 84

la   orden   *order* 64

ordenar   *to tidy* 15

las   orejas   *ears* 40

la   organización   *organization* 103

organizado(a)   *organized* 52

organizar   *to organize* 97

orgulloso(a)   *proud* 219

el   origen   *origin* 95

original   *original* 69

originalmente   *originally* 55

la   orilla   *bank (river)* 248

la   orquesta   *orchestra* 190

os   *(to) you (informal, plural)* 28   *yourselves (informal)* 50

el   otoño   *fall* 111

otro(a)   *other* 32

la   oveja   *sheep* 207

P

la   paciencia   *patience* 98

el/la   paciente   *patient* 34

el   padre   *father* 2

los   padres   *parents* 2

la   paella   *traditional rice dish from Spain* 25

pagar   *to pay* 195

la   página   *web site* 67

el   país   *country* 224

el   paisaje   *landscape* 77

el   pájaro   *bird* 234

el   pájaro carpintero   *woodpecker* 237

la   palabra   *word* 38

el   palacio   *palace* 47

los   pantalones   *pants* 22

los   pantalones cortos   *shorts* 22

el   papá   *dad* 30

la   papa   *potato* 24

el   papel   *paper* 234

la   papelería   *stationery store* 223

el   paquete   *package* 193

para   *for* 15   *to* 25   *in order to* 25

el   parador   *state-run hotel* 55

parafrasear   *to paraphrase* 249

parecer   *to seem* 69   *to look like* 203

la   pared   *wall* 54

la   pareja   *pair* 35   *couple* 190   *partner* 207

parlamentario(a)   *parliamentary* 76

el   parque   *park* 35

la   parte   *part* 40

el/la   participante   *participant* 43

participar   *to participate* 39

la   partida   *match, game* 93

el   partido   *match, game* 122

el   partido político   *political party* 179

el   pasado   *past* 133

pasado(a)   *past* 170

el   pasaporte   *passport* 160

pasar   *to pass* 41   *to happen* 45   *to spend (time)* 107

pasar la aspiradora   *to vacuum* 14

pasarlo bien   *to have a good time* 118

el   pasatiempo   *pastime, hobby* 104

pasear   *to stroll* 14

el   paseo   *avenue* 77   *walk, stroll* 113

el   paso   *step* 86   *passage* 190

la   pasta de dientes   *toothpaste* 48

pedir (e > i)   *to ask for* 20

peinarse   *to comb (one's hair)* 48

el   peine   *comb* 48

la   película   *movie* 112

el   peligro   *danger* 223

peligroso(a) *dangerous* 199

el pelo *hair* 40

la pelota *ball* 122

pensar (e > ie) *to think* 20

pequeño(a) *small* 41

perder (e > ie) *to lose* 122

perdido(a) *lost* 37

Perdón. *Excuse me.* 35

perdonar *to forgive* 74

el/la peregrino(a) *pilgrim* 55

¡Perfecto! *Perfect!* 92

perfecto(a) *perfect* 174

el perfume *perfume* 40

el/la periodista *journalist* 99

el período *period* 51

el/la perito(a) *expert* 199

permanentemente *permanently* 211

el permiso *permission* 236

pero *but* 9

el perro *dog* 14

la persona *person* 2

el/la personaje *character* 147

personal *personal* 46

la personalidad *personality* 4

personalizar *to personalize* 44

la perspectiva *perspective* 43

pertenecer *to belong* 117

la pesca *fishing* 77

el pescado *fish* 24

pesimista *pessimistic* 176

el peso *Chilean currency* 225

el pez *fish (alive)* 234

el piano *piano* 104

picado(a) *chopped* 134

picante *hot (spicy)* 24

el pico *peak* 233

el pie *foot (part of the body)* 40
foot (unit of measurement) 209

la piedra *stone* 227

la pierna *leg* 40

la pimienta *pepper* 24

el/la pintor(a) *painter* 43

la pintura *painting* 69

la pirámide *pyramid* 67

la piscina *swimming pool* 122

la pista *clue* 215

la pizarra *chalkboard* 17

la pizza *pizza* 5

el plan *plan* 53

el planeta *planet* 208

la planta *plant* 234

plantar *to plant* 238

el plástico *plastic* 234

el plato *dish* 24 *course* 25

la playa *beach* 168

la plaza *square, plaza* 178

el plural *plural* 6

la población *population* 133

poblado(a) *populated* 188

el/la poblador(a) *settler* 246

poco *little, not much* 26

poco(a)(os)(as) *some, few* 218

poder (o > ue) *can, to be able to* 20

el poema *poem* 246

el/la policía *policeman, policewoman* 97

político(a) *political* 177

el pollo *chicken* 24

poner *to put* 30

poner atención *to pay attention* 99

poner buena cara *to put on a good face* 94

poner la mesa *to set the table* 29

poner notas *to grade* 139

popular *popular* 73

la popularidad *popularity* 123

por *by* 14 *for* 44 *around* 103 *because of* 210

por ejemplo *for example* 17

por favor *please* 25

¿por qué? *why?* 210

porque *because* 210

el portafolios *briefcase* 96

la posesión *possession, ownership* 8

la postal *postcard* 198

el póster *poster* 86

el postre *dessert* 24

practicar deportes *to play sports* 104

la preferencia *preference* 22

preferir (e > ie) *to prefer* 20

la pregunta *question* 21

preguntar *to ask* 147

premiado(a) *awarded* 111

el premio *award* 89 *prize* 246

prender *to turn on* 18

preocuparse *to worry* 54

preparar *to prepare* 28

los preparativos *preparations* 151

la presencia *presence* 132

la presentación *introduction* 2 *presentation* 143

presente *present* 132

presente *present tense* 6

el presente continuo *present progressive* 114

presidencial *presidential* 179

el/la presidente(a) *president* 179

prestado(a) *borrowed* 105

prestigioso(a) *prestigious* 111

el pretérito *preterite tense* 154

previo(a) *previous* 137

la primavera *spring* 209

primero *first of all* 15

primer, primero(a) *first* 30

el primer piso *first floor* 12

el/la primo(a) *cousin* 2

los primos *cousins (male, male and female)* 2

principal *main* 57

principalmente *mainly* 135

el principio *beginning* 43

probar (o > ue) *to try* 187

el problema *problem* 38

proceder *to come from* 134

la producción *production* 227

el producto *product* 47

la profesión *profession, occupation* 96

profesional *professional* 91

el/la profesor(a) *teacher* 2

los profesores *teachers (males, males and females)* 6

el programa *show (noun)* 43

el progreso *progress* 136

la prohibición *prohibition* 236

prohibir *to forbid* 255

promover (o > ue) *to promote* 103

los pronombres de objeto directo *direct object pronouns* 28

los pronombres de objeto indirecto *indirect object pronouns* 28

pronto *soon* 50

la propuesta *proposal* 136

el/la protagonista *main character* 78

proteger *to protect* 238

la provincia *province* 159

el/la próximo(a) *next* 106

el proyecto *project* 86

prudente *prudent* 141

la prueba *test* 53

publicar *to publish* 246

público(a) *public* 153

el pueblo *town* 224

el puente *bridge* 151

la puerta *door* 12

el puerto *mountain pass* 41 *harbor, port* 79

el **punto cardinal** *cardinal point* 169
la **pureza** *purity* 227

Q

¿**Qué?** *What?* 5
¡**Qué bien!** *Great!* 118
¡**Qué día!** *What a day!* 156
¡**Qué dolor!** *How painful!* 38
¡**Qué emoción!** *How exciting!* 227
¡**Qué horror!** *How awful!* 174
¡**Qué impresionante!** *How impressive!* 204
¡**Qué lástima!** *What a pity!* 187
¡**Qué pena!** *What a shame!* 164
¡**Qué suerte!** *How lucky!* 113
¿**Qué tal?** *How are you doing?* 3
Que te mejores. *Get well.* 36
¿**Qué te pasa?** *What's wrong?* 36
quedar *to fit* 39
quedarse *to stay* 164
querer (e > ie) *to want* 20   *to love* 156
Querido(a)… *Dear…* 101
el **queso** *cheese* 5
¿**Quién?** *Who?* 3
la **quinceañera** *fifteen year old girl's party* 9

R

la **radio** *radio* 112
la **raíz** *stem* 20
rapanui *native Polynesian inhabitants of Easter Island* 214
rápido *quickly* 64
rápido(a) *quick* 125
la **raqueta** *racket* 122
rara vez *rarely* 18
raro(a) *rare* 103
el **rasgo** *feature* 4
la **razón** *reason* 210
real *royal* 47
la **receta** *recipe* 15
el **reciclaje** *recycling* 234
reciclar *to recycle* 234
recomendar (e > ie) *to recommend* 67
reconocer *to recognize* 136
recordar (o > ue) *to remember* 20
recorrer *to cover* 57
el **recuerdo** *souvenir* 155
el **recurso** *resource* 235
la **red** *net* 122

reducir *to reduce* 235
el **refresco** *refreshment, soda* 24
el **refrigerador** *refrigerator* 12
regalar *to give a present* 165
el **regalo** *gift* 22
la **región** *region* 77
regresar *to come back* 173
regular *regular* 18
regularmente *regularly* 65
relajarse *to relax* 47
el **remedio** *remedy* 66
rentar *to rent* 153
el **repaso** *review* 82
repetir (e > i) *to repeat* 20
representar *to perform* 25   *to represent* 43
la **república** *republic* 188
la **reserva** *reserve* 161
reservar habitación *to reserve a room* 168
el **resfriado** *cold* 56
resolver (o > ue) *to solve* 206
respirar *to breathe* 185
responder *to reply* 49
responsable *responsible* 98
la **respuesta** *answer* 148
restar *to subtract* 225
el **restaurante** *restaurant* 25
el **retrato** *portrait* 43
la **reunión** *meeting* 139
reunirse *to meet, to gather* 95
la **revista** *magazine* 14
la **revolución** *revolution* 177
el **rey** *king* 33
rico(a) *rich* 233
el **río** *river* 216
la **riqueza** *richness* 136
el **ritmo** *rhythm* 108
la **roca** *rock* 206
rocoso(a) *rocky* 214
rodear *to surround* 215
rojo(a) *red* 22
romano(a) *Roman* 47
la **ropa** *clothing* 22
la **rosa de los vientos** *compass rose* 169
rosado(a) *pink* 22
rubio(a) *blond(e)* 4
la **ruta** *route* 166
la **rutina** *routine* 48

S

el **sábado** *Saturday* 141
los **sábados** *on Saturdays* 19

saber *to know how* 30
el **sabor** *flavor* 24
saborear *to taste* 40
sacar *to take out* 14
sacudir *to dust* 14
la **sal** *salt* 24
la **sala** *living room* 12   *lounge* 47
salado(a) *salty* 24
el **salar** *salt flat* 211
la **salida** *start* 163
salir *to leave* 30
el **salón** *living room* 202
el **Salón de la Fama** *Hall of Fame* 121
la **salsa** *salsa (dance)* 108   *sauce* 134
la **salud** *health* 57
saludable *healthy* 61
saludar *to greet* 165
salvar *to save* 235
el **sándwich** *sandwich* 26
sano(a) *healthy* 26
el/la **santo(a)** *saint* 135
el **satélite** *satellite* 208
se *himself, herself, itself, yourselves, themselves* 50
se puede/pueden *it is allowed* 236
seco(a) *dry* 216
el/la **secretario(a)** *secretary* 96
Secundaria *secondary (high school)* 94
la **sede** *seat, venue* 177
seguir (e > i) recto *to keep (walking/driving) straight* 178
según *according to* 67
el/la **segundo(a)** *second* 176
la **selva** *jungle* 189
la **semana** *week* 39
semiprecioso(a) *semiprecious* 227
sensacional *sensational* 156
sentarse (e > ie) *to sit* 31
los **sentidos** *senses* 38
sentirse (e > ie) *to feel* 60
el **señor** *Sir* 25
la **señora** *Madam* 31
septiembre *September* 44
ser *to be* 6
ser de *to be from* 99
serio(a) *serious* 4
la **servilleta** *napkin* 24
servir (e > i) *to serve* 116
si *if* 60
sí *yes* 13

tu, tus *your (informal)* 8
el **túnel** *tunnel* 151
el **turismo** *tourism* 77
el/la **turista** *tourist* 55
turístico(a) *touristic* 53

U

último(a) *last* 117
un, una *a, an* 10
Un momento. *Just a moment.* 31
unido(a) *united* 137
el **universo** *universe* 208
unos, unas *some* 10
usar *to use* 19
usted *you (singular, formal)* 6
ustedes *you (plural)* 6
útil *useful* 36
utilizar *to utilize* 137

V

las **vacaciones** *holidays, vacations* 109
Vale. *All right.* 120
válido(a) *valid* 158
el **valle** *valley* 206
el **valor** *value* 225
variado(a) *varied* 77
la **variedad** *variety* 233
el **vaso** *glass* 24
el/la **vecino(a)** *neighbor* 137

la **velocidad** *speed* 125
vender *to sell* 159
venir *to come* 17
la **ventana** *window* 28
ver *to watch* 14 *to see* 40
ver películas *to see movies* 112
el **verano** *summer* 103
el **verbo** *verb* 6
la **verdad** *truth* 98
¿Verdad? *Right?* 64
verde *green* 22
las **verduras** *vegetables* 24
el **vestido** *dress* 22
vestir (e > i) *to dress* 20
vestirse (e > i) *to get dressed* 48
la **vez** *time* 85
el **viaducto** *viaduct* 151
viajar *to travel* 104
el **viaje** *trip* 147
el/la **viajero(a)** *traveler* 153
la **vicuña** *vicuna* 237
la **vida** *life* 65
el **video** *video* 113
el **videojuego** *videogame* 112
el **vidrio** *glass* 234
el **viento** *wind* 210
el **viernes** *Friday* 164
el **viñedo** *vineyard* 77
violento(a) *violent* 236
la **visita** *visit* 55
el/la **visitante** *visitor* 73
visitar *to visit* 21
la **vitalidad** *vitality* 129

la **vitamina** *vitamin* 69
vivir *to live* 61
el **vocabulario** *vocabulary* 2
volar (o > ue) *to fly* 20
el **volcán** *volcano* 214
el **voleibol** *volleyball* 122
volver (o > ue) *to return* 20
vosotros(as) *you (plural, informal)* 6
la **votación** *voting* 37
el **vuelo** *flight* 158
la **vuelta al mundo** *around the world* 192
la **vuelta ciclista** *cycling race* 32
vuestro(a) *your (plural, informal)* 8

Y

y *and* 2
ya *already* 165
yo *I* 2
Yo soy... *I am ...* 2

Z

la **zapatería** *shoe store* 22
los **zapatos** *shoes* 22
el **zigzag** *zigzag* 151
la **zona** *area, region* 41 *zone* 47

Los números

uno	1	trece	13	veinticinco	25	cien	100
dos	2	catorce	14	veintiséis	26	ciento uno	101
tres	3	quince	15	veintisiete	27	ciento diez	110
cuatro	4	dieciséis	16	veintiocho	28	doscientos	200
cinco	5	diecisiete	17	veintinueve	29	trescientos	300
seis	6	dieciocho	18	treinta	30	cuatrocientos	400
siete	7	diecinueve	19	cuarenta	40	quinientos	500
ocho	8	veinte	20	cincuenta	50	seiscientos	600
nueve	9	veintiuno	21	sesenta	60	setecientos	700
diez	10	veintidós	22	setenta	70	ochocientos	800
once	11	veintitrés	23	ochenta	80	novecientos	900
doce	12	veinticuatro	24	noventa	90	mil	1000

Órdenes para hacer las actividades

Adivina	Guess	**Escucha**	Listen
Analiza	Analyze	**Explica**	Explain
Anuncia	Announce	**Habla**	Speak
Busca	Look for	**Haz**	Do
Clasifica	Classify	**Identifica**	Identify
Compara	Compare	**Investiga**	Research
Completa	Complete. Fill in the blank	**Lee**	Read
Conecta	Connect	**Ordena**	Put in order
Contesta	Answer	**Organiza**	Organize
Corrige	Correct	**Piensa**	Think
Crea	Create	**Prepara**	Prepare
Decide	Decide	**Presenta**	Present
Define	Define	**Relaciona**	Relate. Connect. Match.
Dibuja	Draw	**Representa**	Act out
Diseña	Design	**Responde**	Respond
Elige	Choose	**Selecciona**	Select
Escoge	Choose	**Une**	Match
Escribe	Write		

GLOSARIO INGLÉS-ESPAÑOL

A

a, an   *un, uno* 10
a lot   *mucho* 26
a lot of   *mucho(a)(os)(as)* 218
about   *sobre* 69
above   *sobre* 151
abundance   *la abundancia* 77
accent   *el acento* 99
accident   *el accidente* 38
accomodations   *el alojamiento* 168
according to   *según* 67
accordion   *el acordeón* 115
ache   *el dolor* 56
act   *el acto* 248
to   act   *actuar* 104
action   *la acción* 12
active   *activo(a)* 214
activity   *la actividad* 14
actor   *el actor* 113
actually   *en realidad* 192
ad   *el anuncio* 73
to   add   *sumar* 225
adjective   *el adjetivo* 6
adolescence   *la adolescencia* 51
adult   *el/la mayor* 107
adventure   *la aventura* 78
adverbs of frequency   *los adverbios de frecuencia* 18
adverbs of location   *los adverbios de lugar* 16
adverbs of quantity   *los adverbios de cantidad* 26
advice   *el consejo* 64
advisor   *el/la consejero(a)* 101
affirmative   *afirmativo(a)* 68
after   *después de* 69
afternoon   *la tarde* 23
again   *de nuevo* 192
age   *la época* 46
agenda   *la agenda* 97
agriculture   *la agricultura* 161
air   *el aire* 234
airport   *el aeropuerto* 152
all   *todo(a)* 218
All right.   *Vale.* 120
almost   *casi* 134
almost never   *casi nunca* 18
along   *a lo largo de* 113
already   *ya* 165
also   *también* 9
although   *aunque* 188
always   *siempre* 18
amazing   *sorprendente* 149
American   *el/la estadounidense* 137 *americano(a)* 159

among   *entre* 103
and   *y* 2
(the) Andes   *los Andes* 200
angry   *enojado(a)* 4
animal   *el animal* 234
anniversary   *el aniversario* 181
announcer   *el comentarista* 38
annually   *anualmente* 229
answer   *la respuesta* 148
any   *algún, alguno(a)(os)(as)* 218 *ningún, ninguno(a)* 218
apple   *la manzana* 71
approximately   *aproximadamente* 188
aquatic   *acuático(a)* 109
Arab   *árabe* 47
archipelago   *el archipiélago* 76
architecture   *la arquitectura* 65
Are you OK/ill?   *¿Te sientes bien/mal?* 36
area   *la zona* 41   *el área* 135
arena   *el estadio* 122
Argentinian   *argentino(a)* 153
arid   *árido(a)* 189
arm   *el brazo* 40
around   *por* 103   *alrededor de* 208
around the world   *la vuelta al mundo* 192
arrival   *la llegada* 34
to   arrive   *llegar* 59
art   *el arte* 103
article   *el artículo* 10
artist   *el/la artista* 103
artistic   *artístico(a)* 43
as ... as   *tan... como* 26
to   ask   *preguntar* 147
to   ask for   *pedir (e > i)* 20
astronaut   *el/la astronauta* 208
At ... (time)   *A la(s)...* 16
at once   *inmediatamente* 153
at the same time   *a la vez* 117
athlete   *el/la atleta* 77
athletic   *atlético(a)* 4
Atlantic   *atlántico(a)* 76
to   attend   *asistir* 100
to   attract   *atraer* 191
August   *agosto* 241
aunt   *la tía* 2
authentic   *auténtico(a)* 214
author   *el/la autor(a)* 190
avenue   *el paseo* 77 *la avenida* 79
to   avoid   *evitar* 61
award   *el premio* 89
awarded   *premiado(a)* 111

B

back   *la espalda* 56
backpack   *la mochila* 46
bad   *mal, malo(a)* 43
badly   *mal* 36
bag   *la bolsa* 160
baggage   *el equipaje* 160
ball   *el balón, la bola, la pelota* 122
ballpoint   *el bolígrafo* 17
banana   *la banana* 27
band   *la banda* 115
bank   *el banco* 178
bank (river)   *la orilla (river bank)* 248
baseball   *el béisbol* 122
basic   *básico(a)* 66
basket   *la canasta* 125
basketball   *el baloncesto* 122
bat   *el bate* 122
to   bathe   *bañar* 77
bathroom   *el baño* 12
bathtub   *la bañera* 12
to   be   *estar, ser* 6
to   be acquainted   *conocer* 30
to   be afraid   *tener miedo* 4
to   be born   *nacer* 78
to   be called   *llamarse* 2
to   be cold   *tener frío* 4
to   be equivalent   *equivaler* 173
to   be fit   *estar en forma* 64
to   be from   *ser de* 99
to   be hot   *tener calor* 4
to   be hungry   *tener hambre* 4
to   be in shape   *estar en forma* 66
to   be part of   *formar parte de* 215
to   be ready   *estar listo(a), estar preparado(a)* 148
to   be right   *tener razón* 83
to   be thirsty   *tener sed* 4
to   be sleepy   *tener sueño* 61
to   be ... years old   *tener... años* 8
beach   *la playa* 168
beach resort   *el balneario* 217
beautiful   *bello(a)* 79
beauty   *la belleza* 69
because   *porque* 210
because of   *por* 210   *a causa de* 241
bed   *la cama* 12
bedroom   *el dormitorio* 12
before   *antes (de)* 48
to   begin   *empezar (e > ie)* 20 *comenzar (e > ie)* 151

beginning   el principio 43
behind   detrás de 16
to believe   creer 110
to belong   pertenecer 117
best   el/la mejor 9
better   mejor 69
between   entre 73
big   gran, grande 13
biggest   el/la mayor 76
bilingual   bilingüe 97
bill   el billete 225
biography   la biografía 249
bird   el ave 211   el pájaro 234
birth   el nacimiento 249
birthday   el cumpleaños 9
birthplace   la cuna 78
to bite   morder (o > ue) 248
bitter   amargo(a) 24
black   negro(a) 22
block   la cuadra 192
blond(e)   rubio(a) 4
blouse   la blusa 22
blue   azul 22
board game   el juego de mesa 72
body   el cuerpo 40
book   el libro 16
bookcase   la estantería 12
border   la frontera 224
boring   aburrido(a) 69
borrowed   prestado(a) 105
bottle   la botella 24
bowling   el boliche 122
boy   el chico, el niño 2
boyfriend   el novio 2
breakfast   el desayuno 28
to breathe   respirar 185
bridge   el puente 151
to bring   traer 30   llevar 67
brother   el hermano 2
brunet(te)   moreno(a) 4
to brush   cepillarse 48
brutality   la brutalidad 80
to build   construir 181
building   el edificio 12
   la construcción 79
bull   el toro 80
bulletin   el boletín 220
burger   la hamburguesa 98
bus   el autobús 152
business   el negocio 95
businessman   el empresario 95
businesswoman   la empresaria 95
but   pero 9
to buy   comprar 17
by   por 14

C

cabin   la cabaña 253
cafe   el café 178
cafeteria   la cafetería 100
cake   la torta 24
calculation   el cálculo 139
calendar   el calendario 106
called   llamado(a) 134
calm   tranquilo(a) 148
camcorder   la cámara de video 112
camera   la cámara de fotos 112
campsite   el cámping 168
can (container)   la lata 238
canal   el canal 245
cap   el gorro 22
capital city   la capital 224
car   el coche 152
cardinal point   el punto
   cardinal 169
care   el cuidado 160
Caribbean   caribeño(a) 136
carnival   el carnaval 135
castle   el castillo 77
cat   el gato 8
category   la categoría 247
cathedral   la catedral 57
Catholic   católico(a) 33
cause   la causa 210
to celebrate   celebrar 9
   festejar 133
celebration   la celebración 133
celebrity   el/la famoso(a) 93
Census Bureau   la Oficina del
   Censo 132
central   central 182
century   el siglo 43
ceramics   la cerámica 227
cereals   los cereales 67
certain   cierto(a) 133
chair   la silla 12
chalk   la tiza 96
chalkboard   la pizarra 17
challenge   el desafío 32
champion   el/la campeón(a) 130
change   el cambio 51
to change   cambiar 49
character   el personaje 147
characteristic   característico(a) 78
to chat   conversar 95
cheap   barato(a) 153
to check the luggage   facturar
   el equipaje   160
cheese   el queso 5
Chicano   chicano(a) 134
chicken   el pollo 24

Chilean   chileno(a) 159
chili   el chile 134
chocolate   el chocolate 25
choir   el coro 65
to choose   escoger 179
chopped   picado(a) 134
chore   la tarea 15
Christian   el/la cristiano(a) 57
chronicle   la crónica 198
church   la iglesia 178
cinematography   el cine 114
city   la ciudad 168
civil   civil 80
civilization   la civilización 215
class   la clase 21
classmate   el/la compañero(a) 18
classroom   la clase 17
clean   limpio(a) 15
to clean   limpiar 14
clear   claro(a) 130
clearly   claro 99
client   el/la cliente(a) 97
climate   el clima 77
to climb   subir 151
to close   cerrar (e > ie) 20
close to   cerca de 16
closed   cerrado(a) 22
closet   el armario 12
clothing   la ropa 22
cloud   la nube 144
clue   la pista 215
coach   el/la entrenador(a) 96
coach class   la clase turista 158
coast   la costa 168
coastal   costero(a) 247
code   el código 223
coffee   el café 25
cold   frío(a) 24   el resfriado 56
collection   la colección 103
Colombian   colombiano(a) 69
to colonize   colonizar 133
color   el color 22
colorful   colorido(a) 136
comb   el peine 48
to comb one's hair   peinarse 48
to come   venir 17
to come from   proceder 134
comet   el cometa 208
comfortable   cómodo(a) 50
comic strip   la historieta
   gráfica 190
command (tense)   el imperativo
   68
communication   la comunicación
   44
community   la comunidad 97
company   la compañía 10

R29

comparison la comparación 26
compass rose la rosa de los vientos 169
to **compete** competir (e > i) 20
competition la competición 39
to **complete** completar 2
comprehension la comprensión 81
computer la computadora 8
concentration la concentración 133
concert el concierto 107
condition el estado 54
to **confess** confesar (e > ie) 44
conjunction la conjunción 210
connection la relación 40 la conexión 51
to **consider** considerar 177
construction la construcción 97
construction site la obra 96
to **contact** contactar 139
to **contain** llevar 25
container el contenedor 234
contest el concurso 229
continent el continente 216
to **continue** continuar 192
to **contradict** contradecir 192
to **contribute** contribuir 219
contribution la contribución 136
to **control** controlar 255
to **convert** convertir (e > ie) 77
to **cook** cocinar 213
corn el maíz 24
correct correcto(a) 166
correctly bien 167
to **cost** costar (o > ue) 20
cotton el algodón 23
cough la tos 56
to **count** contar (o > ue) 20
country el país 224
countryside el campo 39
couple la pareja 190
course (meal) el plato 25
court (sports) la cancha 125
cousin el/la primo(a) 2
to **cover (distance)** recorrer 57
covered cubierto(a) 189
to **create** crear 45
credit card la tarjeta de crédito 29
to **cross** cruzar 178
crossed atravesado(a) 189
crunchy crujiente 134
crustacean el crustáceo 254
to **cry** llorar 80
Cuban cubano(a) 95
cubism el cubismo 43
cubist cubista 43
cuisine la cocina 134

cultural cultural 76
culture la cultura 39
cup la taza 24
to **cure** curar 97
curiosity la curiosidad 108
curious curioso(a) 254
currency la moneda 225
custom la costumbre 73
customer el/la cliente(a) 25
to **cut** cortar 14
cybercafe el cibercafé 164
cycling ciclista 32
cycling race la vuelta ciclista 32
cyclist el/la ciclista 39

D

dad el papá 30
daily diario(a) 53 a diario 73
dance el baile 114 la danza 136
to **dance** bailar 104
danger el peligro 223
daring atrevido(a) 4
date la fecha 136
daughter la hija 2
day el día 43
dead el/la muerto(a) 80
Dear ... Estimado(a)... 49 Querido(a)... 101
death la muerte 80
to **decide** decidir 25
to **declare** declarar 181
to **decorate** decorar 47
to **defend** defender (e > ie) 97
deforestation la deforestación 219
degree el grado 26
delicious delicioso(a) 164
demonstratives los demostrativos 30
to **denounce** denunciar 190
deodorant el desodorante 48
department el departamento 164
deposit el depósito 211
to **descend** descender (e > ie) 188
descendant el/la descendiente 215
to **describe** describir 2
descriptive descriptivo(a) 135
desert el desierto 216
design el diseño 47
to **design** diseñar 67
desperate desesperado(a) 80
dessert el postre 24
destination el destino 168
to **destroy** destruir 80

detective el/la detective 38
development el desarrollo 110
devil el diablo 166
diagram el esquema 67
diary el diario 221
to **die** morir (o > ue) 116
diet la dieta 51
difference la diferencia 220
different distinto(a) 26 diferente 49
difficult difícil 41
to **direct** dirigir 97
direct object pronouns los pronombres de objeto directo 28
direction la dirección 166
directions las instrucciones 179
director el/la director(a) 96
dirty sucio(a) 85
disc el disco 141
to **discover** descubrir 208
dish el plato 24
dishwasher el lavaplatos 12
distance la distancia 152
diversity la diversidad 136
to **divide** dividir 223
division la división 224
to **do** hacer 30
to **do for a living** dedicarse a 92
to **do well in school** ir bien 101
doctor el/la doctor(a) 34 el/la médico(a) 56
doctor's office la consulta 61
document el documento 148
documentary el documental 85
dog el perro 14
dollar el dólar 23
dolphin el delfín 237
domino la ficha 101
dominoes el dominó 88
Don't worry. Tranquilo(a). 148
door la puerta 12
down abajo 80
downtown el centro 21
drawing el dibujo 190
dream el sueño 184
to **dream** soñar (o > ue) 213
dress el vestido 22
dresser la cómoda 12
drink la bebida 24
to **drink** beber 25 tomar 121
to **drive** conducir 153
drugstore la farmacia 56
dry árido(a) 189 seco 216
during durante 49
to **dust** sacudir 14
duties las obligaciones 49

political *político(a)* 177
political party *el partido político* 179
pollution *la contaminación* 237
popular *popular* 73
popularity *la popularidad* 123
populated *poblado(a)* 188
population *la población* 133
port *el puerto* 79
portrait *el retrato* 43
possession *la posesión* 8
possessive adjectives *los adjetivos posesivos* 8
poster *el póster* 86 *el cartel* 137
potato *la papa* 24
pottery *la cerámica* 227
pound *la libra* 239
to prefer *preferir (e > ie)* 20
preference *la preferencia* 22
preparations *los preparativos* 151
to prepare *preparar* 28
presence *la presencia* 132
present *presente* 132
present participle *el gerundio* 116
present progressive *el presente continuo* 114
present tense *el presente* 6
presentation *la presentación* 143
to preserve *conservar* 117
president *el presidente* 179
presidential *presidencial* 179
prestigious *prestigioso(a)* 111
preterite tense *el pretérito* 154
pretty *bonito(a)* 11
previous *previo(a)* 137
principal *el/la director(a)* 128
prize *el premio* 246
problem *el problema* 38
product *el producto* 47
production *la producción* 227
profession *la profesión* 96
professional *profesional* 91
progress *el progreso* 136
prohibition *la prohibición* 236
project *el proyecto* 86
to promote *promover (o >ue)* 103
properly *bien* 160
proposal *la propuesta* 136
to protect *proteger* 238
province *la provincia* 159
prudent *prudente* 141
public *público(a)* 153
to publish *publicar* 246
purity *la pureza* 227
purple *morado(a)* 22
to put *poner* 30
to put ... away *guardar* 193

to put on a good face *poner buena cara* 94
pyramid *la pirámide* 67

Q

quantity *la cantidad* 218
question *la pregunta* 21
quick *rápido(a)* 125
quickly *rápido* 64
quite *bastante* 26

R

race *la carrera* 39
racket (sports) *la raqueta* 122
radio *la radio* 112
railway *ferroviario(a)* 134
rain *la lluvia* 225
to rain *llover (o > ue)* 174
rainy *lluvioso(a)* 217
rare *raro(a)* 103
rarely *rara vez* 18
to reach *alcanzar* 185
to read *leer* 14
reading *la lectura* 80
ready *listo(a)* 206
reason *la razón* 210
recipe *la receta* 15
to recognize *reconocer* 136
to recommend *recomendar (e > ie)* 67
to record *grabar* 112
to recycle *reciclar* 234
recycling *el reciclaje* 234
red *rojo(a)* 22
to reduce *reducir* 235
refreshment *el refresco* 24
refrigerator *el refrigerador* 12
region *la zona* 41 *la región* 77
regular *regular* 18
regularly *regularmente* 65
to relax *relajarse* 47
relevant *relevante* 149
remedy *el remedio* 66
to remember *recordar (o > ue)* 20
to rent *rentar* 153
to repeat *repetir (e > i)* 20
to reply *responder* 49
to represent *representar* 43
republic *la república* 188
research *la investigación* 79
reserve *la reserva* 161
to reserve a room *reservar habitación* 168

resource *el recurso* 235
responsible *responsable* 98
rest *el descanso* 47 *los/las demás* 61
to rest *descansar* 50
restaurant *el restaurante* 25
to return *volver (o > ue)* 20
review *el repaso* 82
revolution *la revolución* 177
rhythm *el ritmo* 108
rice *el arroz* 24
rich *rico(a)* 233
richness *la riqueza* 136
riddle *la adivinanza* 45
to ride a bike *montar en bicicleta* 104
Right? *¿Verdad?* 64
ring *el anillo* 212
river *el río* 216
rock *la roca* 206
rocky *rocoso(a)* 214
Roman *romano(a)* 47
room *el cuarto* 44 *la habitación* 47
rough *aproximado(a)* 225
round trip *de ida y vuelta* 148
route *la ruta* 166
routine *la rutina* 48
royal *real* 47
rule *la regla* 236
to run *correr* 66 *dirigir* 97
to run into *encontrarse (o > ue) con* 173

S

sad *triste* 4
to sail *navegar* 192
sailor *marinero(a)* 77
saint *el/la santo(a)* 135
salad *la ensalada* 27
salsa (dance) *la salsa* 108
salt *la sal* 24
salt flat *el salar* 211
salty *salado(a)* 24
same *igual* 69 *mismo(a)* 164
sandwich *el sándwich* 26
satellite *el satélite* 208
Saturday *el sábado* 141
sauce *la salsa* 134
to say *decir* 42
scenario *el escenario* 78
scent *el aroma* 192
schedule *el horario* 23
school *la escuela* 96 *escolar* 220
science *las ciencias* 61 *la ciencia* 67
scientist *el/la científico(a)* 219

sea el/la mar 216

season la temporada 126
la estación 217

seat (government) la sede 177

second el/la segundo(a) 176

secondary (school) Secundaria 94

secretary el/la secretario(a) 96

to **see** ver 40

to **see movies** ver películas 112

See you soon. Hasta pronto. 9

to **seem** parecer 69

self-evaluation la autoevaluación 87

self-portrait el autorretrato 41

to **sell** vender 159

sensational sensacional 156

senses los sentidos 38

sentence la oración 84

September septiembre 44

serious serio(a) 4

to **serve** servir (e > i) 116

server el/la mesero(a) 24

to **set the table** poner la mesa 29

setting el marco 193

settler el/la poblador(a) 246

shampoo el champú 48

to **shave** afeitarse 48

shaving cream la crema de afeitar 48

she ella 6

sheep la oveja 207

shield el escudo 37

to **shine** brillar 208

ship el barco 152

shirt la camisa 22

shoe store la zapatería 22

shoes los zapatos 22

shopping las compras 155

shopping center el centro comercial 99

shore la costa 168

short bajo(a) 4   corto(a) 41

shorts los pantalones cortos 22

show el espectáculo 43
el programa 43

to **show** mostrar (o > ue) 136

to **show one's passport** enseñar el pasaporte 160

shower la ducha 12

shy tímido(a) 4

siblings los hermanos 2

sick enfermo(a) 4

side el lado 32

similar similar 46

similar to igual que 153

similarity la similitud 220

simple simple 248

since desde 57

Sincerely yours. Atentamente. 52

to **sing** cantar 104

singer el/la cantante 111

singular el singular 6

sink el lavabo 12

Sir el señor 25

sister la hermana 2

to **sit** sentarse (e > ie) 31

size el tamaño 254

to **ski** esquiar 195

skirt la falda 22

sky el cielo 208

to **sleep** dormir (o > ue) 61

slowly despacio 176

small pequeño(a) 41

to **smell** oler 40

smile la sonrisa 91

sneakers los tenis 22

to **snow** nevar (e > ie) 5

so tan 176

so that así que 192

soap el jabón 48

soccer el fútbol 122

social social 46

society la sociedad 88

socks los calcetines 22

soda el refresco 24

sofa el sofá 12

Solar System el sistema solar 208

to **solve** resolver (o > ue) 206

some unos, unas 10   algún, alguno(a)(os)(as) 218
poco(a)(os)(as) 218

something algo 54

sometimes a veces 18

son el hijo 2

son and daughter los hijos 2

song la canción 113

soon pronto 50

soup la sopa 24

sour agrio(a) 24

south el sur 47

southeast el sureste 169

southwest el suroeste 169

souvenir el recuerdo 155

space el espacio 212

Spaniard el/la español(a) 43

Spanish (language) el español 3

Spanish español(a) 73

Spanish speaker hispanohablante 188

special especial 25

specially especialmente 79

specialty la especialidad 59

spectacular espectacular 189

spectator el/la espectador(a) 133

speed la velocidad 125

to **spend (time)** pasar 107

spontaneous espontáneo(a) 4

spoon la cuchara 24

sport el deporte 122

sport competition la competición deportiva 138

to **spread out** extenderse (e > ie) 78

spring la primavera 209

square la plaza 178

stadium el estadio 122

stage la etapa 38

stairs las escaleras 12

star la estrella 208

start (race) la salida 163

to **start** empezar (e > ie) 20

state el estado 76

state-run hotel el parador 55

station la estación 152

stationery store la papelería 223

statistics las estadísticas 123

statue la estatua 103

to **stay** quedarse 164   alojarse 195

to **stay in shape** estar en forma 66

stem la raíz 20

step el paso 86   el escalón 222

stomach el estómago 56

stone la piedra 227

store la tienda 22

story la historia 45

stove la estufa 12

strategy la estrategia 81

street la calle 178

stroll el paseo 113

to **stroll** pasear 14

strong fuerte 38

student el/la estudiante 2

studious estudioso(a) 4

study el estudio 164

style el estilo 43

substance la sustancia 212

to **subtract** restar 225

subway el metro 152

success el éxito 99

sugar el azúcar 24

suggestion la sugerencia 72

suitcase la maleta 160

summer el verano 103

Sun el Sol 208

Sunday el domingo 157

supermarket el supermercado 24

to **surprise** sorprender 73

to **surround** rodear 215

survey la encuesta 43

sweater el suéter 28

to **sweep** barrer 14

sweet dulce 24

to **swim** *nadar* 104
swimming *la natación* 122
swimming pool *la piscina* 122
sword *la espada* 80
symbol *el símbolo* 80
symbolism *el simbolismo* 80
symptom *el síntoma* 56

T

table *la mesa* 12
tablecloth *el mantel* 24
tacos *los tacos* 134
to **take a bath** *bañarse* 48
to **take a means of transport** *tomar* 151
to **take a shower** *ducharse* 48
to **take advantage** *aprovechar* 100
to **take care of** *cuidar* 14
to **take care of oneself** *cuidarse* 66
to **take medicines** *tomar medicamentos* 66
to **take out** *sacar* 14
to **take pictures** *tomar fotos* 112
to **take place** *tener lugar* 223
to **take time** *tardar* 193
to **talk** *hablar* 3 *conversar* 95
to **talk on the phone** *hablar por teléfono* 14
tall *alto(a)* 4
to **tape** *grabar* 112
task *la tarea* 97
to **taste** *saborear* 40
taxi *el taxi* 152
tea *el té* 71
to **teach** *enseñar* 97
teacher *el/la profesor(a)* 2 *el/la maestro(a)* 96
team *el equipo* 122
teeth (molars) *las muelas* 58
telephone *el teléfono* 14
television *el televisor* 12 *la televisión* 14
to **tell** *decir* 42
temperature *la temperatura* 5
temple *el templo* 79
temporal *temporal* 106
tennis *el tenis* 122
tension *la tensión* 179
tent *la tienda de campaña* 213
terminal *la terminal* 153
territory *el territorio* 76
test *el examen* 5 *la prueba* 53
testimony *el testimonio* 133
Texan *tejano(a)* 115

text message *el mensaje electrónico* 44
textbook *el libro de texto* 241
than *de* 47
thank you *gracias* 3
thanks to *gracias a* 99
that *ese, esa* 30
that (far) *aquel, aquella* 30
that (far, neutral) *aquello* 206
the *el, la, los, las* 10
the day before yesterday *anteayer* 170
theater *el teatro* 21
their *su* 8
them *los, las* 28
(to) them *les* 28
theme *el tema* 143
themselves *se* 50
then *entonces* 25
there *ahí* 16
there (far) *allí* 16
there is/are *hay* 16
they *ellas, ellos* 6
thin *delgado(a)* 4
thing *la cosa* 10
to **think** *pensar (e > ie)* 20 *parecer* 69
third *el tercer, el/la tercero(a)* 176
this *este, esta* 30
this (neutral) *esto* 77
this afternoon *esta tarde* 106
this evening *esta tarde, esta noche* 106
this morning *esta mañana* 106
those (nearby) *esos(as)* 30
thousands *miles* 57
throat *la garganta* 56
to **throw away** *botar* 234
Thursday *el jueves* 170
ticket *el boleto* 108 *el billete* 160
to **tidy** *ordenar* 15
tied *atado(a)* 125
tile *el azulejo* 37
time *el tiempo* 46 *la vez* 85
timid *tímido(a)* 4
tin *la lata* 238
tired *cansado(a)* 4
title *el título* 249
to *a* 16 *para* 25 *hasta* 172
to the *al* 16
to the left of *a la izquierda de* 16
to the right of *a la derecha de* 16
today *hoy* 106
toe *el dedo* 40
together *junto* 72

tomorrow *mañana* 9
tomorrow afternoon/evening *mañana por la tarde* 106
tomorrow morning *mañana por la mañana* 106
tomorrow night *mañana por la noche* 106
tonight *esta noche* 106
tooth *el diente* 40 *la muela* 54
toothbrush *el cepillo de dientes* 48
toothpaste *la pasta de dientes* 48
total *total* 248
to **touch** *tocar* 40
tourism *el turismo* 77
tourist *el/la turista* 55
tourist guide *la guía turística* 160
tourist office *la oficina de turismo* 160
touristic *turístico(a)* 53
tournament *el torneo* 108
towards *hacia* 78
towel *la toalla* 48
town *el pueblo* 224 *la localidad* 247
track *el circuito* 213
tradition *la tradición* 9
train *el tren* 152
to **transform** *transformar* 136
transformation *la transformación* 71
transportation *el transporte* 152
travel agency *la agencia de viajes* 160
to **travel around** *hacer turismo* 168
traveler *el/la viajero(a)* 153
tree *el árbol* 234
trip *el viaje* 147
tropical *tropical* 216
true *cierto(a)* 5
truth *la verdad* 98
to **try** *probar (o > ue)* 187
T-shirt *la camiseta* 22
Tuesday *el martes* 53
to **turn** *girar* 208
to **turn off** *apagar* 43
to **turn on** *prender* 18
to **turn to the right/left** *doblar a la derecha/izquierda* 178
TV *la tele* 139
type *el tipo* 67
typical *típico(a)* 43 *característico(a)* 78

U

ugly *feo(a)* 5
uncle *el tío* 2

ÍNDICE GRAMATICAL

CRÉDITOS FOTOGRÁFICOS

Cubierta: Preysler/Atrezzo: Helen Chelton; Alfio Garozzo, Robert Harding/Michael Busselle/CuboImages/CORDON PRESS; Pat Canova, Luis Castañeda/A. G. E. FOTOSTOCK; **Contracuberta:** Vincent Villafañe/EFE; J. Lucas; Guy Christian, Robert Harding/Marco Simoni/CuboImages/CORDON PRESS: **I** Preysler/Atrezzo: Helen Chelton; **IV** Preysler/Atrezzo: Helen Chelton; ISTOCKPHOTO; S. Jiménez; **V** Preysler/Atrezzo: Helen Chelton; Gavin Hellier/Getty Images Sales Spain; F. Morera; **VI** ISTOCKPHOTO; Miguel Ángel Muñoz/A. G. E. FOTOSTOCK; **VII** ISTOCKPHOTO; **X** O. Torres; **XI** J. Lucas; GARCÍA PELAYO/Juancho; F. Ontañón; Horizon, Laurent Guerinaud, Kord.com/A. G. E. FOTOSTOCK; SEIS x SEIS; Preysler/Atrezzo: Helen Chelton; O. Torres; **XII** Hayden Roger Celestin/EPA/EFE; **XIII** Horizon, Laurent Guerinaud, Kord.com/A. G. E. FOTOSTOCK; SEIS x SEIS; Philippe Renault/CORDON PRESS; Preysler/Atrezzo: Helen Chelton; Hayden Roger Celestin/EPA; Patrick Frilet/SIPA-PRESS/EFE; **XIV** Mary Kate Denny/Getty Images Sales Spain; **XV** Horizon, Laurent Guerinaud, Johnny Stockshooter, Kord.com/A. G. E. FOTOSTOCK; SEIS x SEIS; Preysler/Atrezzo: Helen Chelton; J. Lucas; Edgar Dominguez/EFE; J. Ramallo; **XVI** Tips/Luis Castaneda, John Warburton-Lee/FOTONONSTOP; **XVII** Tips/Luis Castaneda, Walter Bibikow/FOTONONSTOP; Horizon, Laurent Guerinaud, Kord.com/A. G. E. FOTOSTOCK; SEIS x SEIS; Patricio Cabezas Vieyra; Preysler/Atrezzo: Helen Chelton; **000** Preysler/Atrezzo: Helen Chelton; **002** AbleStock.com/HighRes Press Stock, COVER; J. Jaime; Prats i Camps; **003** Andersen Ross/A. G. E. FOTOSTOCK, J. Jaime; **004** AbleStock.com/HighRes Press Stock; A. Toril; ISTOCKPHOTO; J. Jaime; J. M.ª Escudero; STOCKBYTE/SERIDEC PHOTOIMAGENES CD; **005** AbleStock.com/HighRes Press Stock; Prats i Camps; **007** AbleStock.com/HighRes Press Stock; Glowimages/Getty Images Sales Spain; Image Source Limited/SERIDEC PHOTOIMAGENES CD; AbleStock/Jupiterimages; ISTOCKPHOTO; Prats i Camps; Preysler/Atrezzo: Helen Chelton; S. Enríquez; S. Padura; **008** ISTOCKPHOTO; **009** ISTOCKPHOTO; **011** AbleStock.com/HighRes Press Stock; A. G. E. FOTOSTOCK; COMSTOCK; Photos.com Plus/Getty Images Sales Spain; **012** Prats i Camps; Preysler/Atrezzo: Helen Chelton; **013** AbleStock.com/HighRes Press Stock; ISTOCKPHOTO; Prats i Camps; **014** AbleStock.com/HighRes Press Stock; Ryan McVay/Getty Images Sales Spain; COMSTOCK; ISTOCKPHOTO; J. M.ª Escudero; PHOTOALTO/SERIDEC PHOTOIMAGENES CD; Prats i Camps; Preysler/Atrezzo: Helen Chelton; S. Enríquez; **015** F. Orte; ISTOCKPHOTO; J. Jaime; S. Enríquez; **017** J. Jaime; Prats i Camps; **018** J. M.ª Escudero; **019** Preysler/Atrezzo: Helen Chelton; **021** ISTOCKPHOTO; J. Jaime; Preysler/Atrezzo: Helen Chelton; **022** KAIBIDE DE CARLOS FOTÓGRAFOS; A. Toril; COMSTOCK; FOTONONSTOP; ISTOCKPHOTO; J. Jaime; MATTON-BILD; Prats i Camps; Preysler/Atrezzo: Helen Chelton; **023** ISTOCKPHOTO; Preysler/Atrezzo: Helen Chelton; **024** GARCÍA-PELAYO/Juancho; Christian Schwier, David Innes, Dirk Pieters/A. G. E. FOTOSTOCK; A. Toril; C. Díez Polanco; C. Roca; HighRes Press Stock; ISTOCKPHOTO; J. Jaime; J. Lucas; MATTON-BILD; Preysler/Atrezzo: Helen Chelton; S. Enríquez; **025** AbleStock.com/HighRes Press Stock; Preysler/Atrezzo: Helen Chelton; J. Jaime; MATTON-BILD; PHOTODISC, STOCKBYTE/SERIDEC PHOTOIMAGENES CD; S. Enríquez/Cafetería Alverán, Boadilla del Monte; **027** MATTON-BILD; Dirk Pieters, K. Arras/A. G. E. FOTOSTOCK; COMSTOCK; HighRes Press Stock; J. Jaime; Preysler/Atrezzo: Helen Chelton; **028** COMSTOCK; ISTOCKPHOTO; MATTON-BILD; Preysler/Atrezzo: Helen Chelton; **029** AbleStock.com/HighRes Press Stock; ISTOCKPHOTO; J. Jaime; SERIDEC PHOTOIMAGENES CD; **030** Prats i Camps; **032** Manuel Bruque/EFE; J. Lucas; **033** R. Matina/A. G. E. FOTOSTOCK; S. Padura; **034** GARCÍA-PELAYO/Juancho; Prats i Camps; **035** ISTOCKPHOTO; Preysler/Atrezzo: Helen Chelton; S. Enríquez; **036** AbleStock.com/HighRes Press Stock; Moodboard/CORBIS/CORDON PRESS; ISTOCKPHOTO; Preysler/Atrezzo: Helen Chelton; **037** EFE; ISTOCKPHOTO; Preysler/Atrezzo: Helen Chelton; S. Padura; T. Arias; **038** Imago sportfotodienst/Sirotti, REUTERS/Víctor Fraile/CORDON PRESS; Preysler/Atrezzo: Helen Chelton; **039** Hugo Philpott/EPA/EFE; Sirotti/Imago/CORDON PRESS; A. G. E. FOTOSTOCK; T. Albir/EFE; David Taylor/AGENCE D.P.P.I./FERY-PRESS; JOHN FOXX IMAGES/SERIDEC PHOTOIMAGENES CD; **040** AbleStock.com/HighRes Press Stock; Heather Weston, Robert Harding World Imagery/Sergio Pitamitz, Tetra Images, Image Source/David Ryle, www.sylent-press.de/CORBIS/CORDON PRESS; PHOTOALTO/SERIDEC PHOTOIMAGENES CD; ISTOCKPHOTO; M.ª A. Ferrándiz; S. Enríquez; **041** Tim De Waele/CORBIS/CORDON PRESS; Preysler/Atrezzo: Helen Chelton; **043** Patrick Morin/SIPA-PRESS/SIPA ICONO/EFE; Preysler/Atrezzo: Helen Chelton; **045** Prats i Camps; Preysler/Atrezzo: Helen Chelton; **046** Adam Woolfitt/A. G. E. FOTOSTOCK, Preysler/Atrezzo: Helen Chelton; **047** ISTOCKPHOTO; Melba Agency; Prats i Camps; **048** ISTOCKPHOTO; J. Jaime; PHOTOALTO/SERIDEC PHOTOIMAGENES CD; Prats i Camps; **049** ISTOCKPHOTO; **050** A. Prieto/Agencia Estudio San Simón; **051** STOCKPHOTO; Preysler/Atrezzo: Helen Chelton; **052** J. Lucas; Prats i Camps; **053** C. Pérez; J. Jaime; P. Esgueva; Preysler/Atrezzo: Helen Chelton; **054** A. Toimil; Preysler/Atrezzo: Helen Chelton; **055** Nik Wheeler/CORBIS/CORDON PRESS; Ken Cavanagh/A. G. E. FOTOSTOCK; C. Pérez; ISTOCKPHOTO; PHOTODISC/SERIDEC PHOTOIMAGENES CD; **056** Cham/SIPA-PRESS/EFE; Pixtal, ARCO/Rudolf/A. G. E. FOTOSTOCK; Blend Images/J. L. Pelaez, Inc./CORBIS/CORDON PRESS; ISTOCKPHOTO; J. Jaime; KAIBIDE DE CARLOS FOTÓGRAFOS; Prats i Camps; S. Enríquez; **057** J. Jaime; **058** Preysler/Atrezzo: Helen Chelton; **059** A. Toimil; ISTOCKPHOTO; **060** Roberto Schmidt/AFP/Getty Images Sales Spain; Pixtal/A. G. E. FOTOSTOCK; ISTOCKPHOTO; **061** S. Enríquez; **062** SERIDEC PHOTOIMAGENES CD; **063** A. Toimil; Preysler/Atrezzo: Helen Chelton; T. Arias; **064** Preysler/Atrezzo: Helen Chelton; S. Padura; **065** AbleStock.com/HighRes Press Stock; José Ramón San Sebastián/EFE; Preysler/Atrezzo: Helen Chelton; SERIDEC PHOTOIMAGENES CD; **066** Jupiterimages/Getty Images Sales Spain; Pixtal/A. G. E. FOTOSTOCK; ISTOCKPHOTO; J. Escandell.com; S. Enríquez; SERIDEC PHOTOIMAGENES CD; **067** HighRes Press Stock; My Pyramid.gov/United States Department of Agriculture (USDA) AbleStock.com; **068** AbleStock.com/HighRes Press Stock; C. Pérez; ISTOCKPHOTO; MATTON-BILD; **069** akg-images/ALBUM; J. Martin/MUSEUM ICONOGRAFÍA; **070** AbleStock.com/HighRes Press Stock; Kate Kunz/CORBIS/CORDON PRESS; A. G. E. FOTOSTOCK; ISTOCKPHOTO; P. Esgueva; Preysler/Atrezzo: Helen Chelton; SERIDEC PHOTOIMAGENES CD; **071** Prats i Camps; Preysler/Atrezzo: Helen Chelton; S. Padura; SERIDEC PHOTOIMAGENES CD; **072** Prats i Camps; S. Enríquez; **073** COMSTOCK; D. López; ISTOCKPHOTO; Prats i Camps; Preysler/Atrezzo: Helen Chelton; **074** Panoramic Images/Getty Images Sales Spain; A. Toimil; F. Ontañón; Preysler/Atrezzo: Helen Chelton; **075** F. Ontañón; Preysler/Atrezzo: Helen Chelton; **076** ISTOCKPHOTO; **077** Javier Larrea/A. G. E. FOTOSTOCK; J. C. Muñoz; J. Navarro; **078** J. L. G. Grande; O. Torres; S. Enríquez; **079** GARCÍA-PELAYO/Juancho; S. Vannini/SYGMA/CONTIFOTO; O. Boé; **080** ORONOZ/MUSEO NACIONAL CENTRO DE ARTE REINA SOFÍA; Dalmas/SIPA-PRESS/EFE; **081** ORONOZ/MUSEO NACIONAL CENTRO DE ARTE REINA SOFÍA; **083** ISTOCKPHOTO; Preysler/Atrezzo: Helen Chelton; **085** J. Martin/MUSEUM ICONOGRAFÍA; Preysler/Atrezzo: Helen Chelton; **086** Prats i Camps; **087** MATTON-BILD; **088** Alamy Images/ACI AGENCIA DE FOTOGRAFÍA; J. M.ª Escudero; **089** Joseph Sohm/Corbis/Visions of America/CORDON PRESS; **090** ISTOCKPHOTO; S. Enríquez; **091** ISTOCKPHOTO; Preysler/Atrezzo: Helen Chelton; SEIS x SEIS; **092** Preysler/Atrezzo: Helen Chelton; S. Enríquez; **093** ISTOCKPHOTO; AbleStock.com/HighRes Press Stock; Tophan/CORDON PRESS; ISTOCKPHOTO; Preysler/Atrezzo: Helen Chelton; **094** Dennis MacDonald/A. G. E. FOTOSTOCK; J. Jaime; Preysler/Atrezzo: Helen Chelton; SEIS x SEIS; **095** Prats i Camps; SEIS x SEIS; **096** AbleStock.com/HighRes Press Stock; A. G. E. FOTOSTOCK; COVER; ISTOCKPHOTO; J. Jaime; MARGEN FOTOGRAFÍA; S. Enríquez; SERIDEC PHOTOIMAGENES CD; STOCK PHOTOS; **097** Preysler/Atrezzo: Helen Chelton; S. Enríquez; SERIDEC PHOTOIMAGENES CD; **098** COMSTOCK; ISTOCKPHOTO; SERIDEC PHOTOIMAGENES CD; STOCK PHOTOS; **099** Wirelmage/Dave Rossman/Getty Images Sales Spain; FOTONONSTOP; Preysler/Atrezzo: Helen Chelton; **100** J. Jaime; MATTON-BILD; S. Enríquez; **101** Preysler/Atrezzo: Helen Chelton; **102** Preysler/Atrezzo: Helen Chelton; Miguel Rajmil/EFE; Topham/CORDON PRESS; **103** DigitalVision/SERIDEC PHOTOIMAGENES CD; T. Abad/A. G. E. FOTOSTOCK; **104** AbleStock.com/HighRes Press Stock; Luis Castilla/EFE; ISTOCKPHOTO; J. Jaime; PHOTODIS/SERIDEC PHOTOIMAGENES CD; Prats i Camps; **105** C. Díez Polanco; HighRes Press Stock; M. Barcenilla; **107** AbleStock.com/HighRes Press Stock; J. Jaime; M. Barcenilla; MATTON-BILD; Preysler/Atrezzo: Helen Chelton; S. Enríquez; **108** S. Enríquez; **109** Miguel Rajmil/EFE; ISTOCKPHOTO; Preysler/Atrezzo: Helen Chelton **110** P. Anca/REAL MUSICAL, MADRID; Ted Soqui/CORBIS/CORDON PRESS; Robert Mora/Getty Images Sales Spain; ISTOCKPHOTO; PHILIPS; Preysler/Atrezzo: Helen Chelton; **111** AbleStock.com/HighRes Press Stock; COMSTOCK; CORDON PRESS; ISTOCKPHOTO; **112** Saitek; Canon; CREATIVE LABS; EFE; ISTOCKPHOTO; Prats i Camps; Preysler/Atrezzo: Helen Chelton; S. Enríquez; **113** Pat Canova/A. G. E. FOTOSTOCK; Canon; CREATIVE LABS; ISTOCKPHOTO; Kodak EasyShare; LG ELECTRONICS; Nokia Corporation; **114** GARCÍA-PELAYO/Juancho; **115** Steve Snowden/Getty Images Sales Spain; **117** SERIDEC PHOTOIMAGENES CD; ISTOCKPHOTO; Preysler/Atrezzo: Helen Chelton; **118** AbleStock.com/HighRes Press Stock; A. Prieto/Agencia Estudio San Simón; JVC; LG ELECTRONICS; VERBATIM; **119** AbleStock.com/HighRes Press Stock; Michael Buckner/Getty Images Sales Spain; A. G. E. FOTOSTOCK; ISTOCKPHOTO; Prats i Camps; Preysler/Atrezzo: Helen Chelton; **120** Ilubi Images/A. G. E. FOTOSTOCK; Danny Moloshok/REUTERS/CORDON PRESS; ISTOCKPHOTO; Preysler/Atrezzo: Helen Chelton; **121** Heinz Kluetmeier/Sports Illustrated/Getty Images Sales Spain; ISTOCKPHOTO; **122** AbleStock.com/HighRes Press Stock; Nik Wheeler/CORBIS/CORDON PRESS; J. M.ª Escudero/Instituto Municipal de Deportes de Madrid; A. Toril; ISTOCKPHOTO; J. Jaime; MATTON-BILD; Melba Agency; PHOTODISC/SERIDEC PHOTOIMAGENES CD; Prats i Camps; Preysler/Atrezzo: Helen Chelton; **123** DIGITALVISION/SERIDEC PHOTOIMAGENES CD; Preysler/Atrezzo: Helen Chelton; **124** Preysler/Atrezzo: Helen Chelton; **125** AbleStock.com/HighRes Press Stock; ISTOCKPHOTO; PHOTODISC/SERIDEC PHOTOIMAGENES CD; S. Yaniz; **126** AbleStock.com/HighRes Press Stock; HighRes Press Stock;